The Gospel Feast:

Proclaiming the Gospel Through the Lord's Supper

(καταγγέλλετε and 1 Corinthians 11:26)

Martin L. Hawley

ThM

Woodstock, GA: Wild Olive Press

May 2015

The Gospel Feast: Proclaiming the Gospel Through the Lord's Supper
(καταγγέλλετε and 1 Corinthians 11:26)

Woodstock, GA: Wild Olive Press, May 2015

wildolivepublishing@gmail.com

ISBN-13: 978-0-9962092-0-5
ISBN-10: 0996209204

Cover and book design by Shari R Hawley, Wild Olive Press, Woodstock, GA.
Author's portrait photograph by Nathan Fowler Photography, Atlanta, GA.

DEDICATION

This work is dedicated to my brothers and sisters in Christ at Hope Presbyterian Church, Marietta, Georgia, and to my fathers and brothers in the faith of the Northwest Georgia Presbytery of the Presbyterian Church in America, who are this generation's embodiment of Acts 2:42 – 47:

> ἦσαν δὲ προσκαρτεροῦντες τῇ διδαχῇ τῶν ἀποστόλων καὶ τῇ κοινωνίᾳ, τῇ κλάσει τοῦ ἄρτου καὶ ταῖς προσευχαῖς. Ἐγίνετο δὲ πάσῃ ψυχῇ φόβος, πολλά τε τέρατα καὶ σημεῖα διὰ τῶν ἀποστόλων ἐγίνετο. πάντες δὲ οἱ πιστεύοντες ἦσαν ἐπὶ τὸ αὐτὸ καὶ εἶχον ἅπαντα κοινά, καὶ τὰ κτήματα καὶ τὰς ὑπάρξεις ἐπίπρασκον καὶ διεμέριζον αὐτὰ πᾶσιν καθότι ἄν τις χρείαν εἶχεν· καθ' ἡμέραν τε προσκαρτεροῦντες ὁμοθυμαδὸν ἐν τῷ ἱερῷ, κλῶντές τε κατ' οἶκον ἄρτον, μετελάμβανον τροφῆς ἐν ἀγαλλιάσει καὶ ἀφελότητι καρδίας, αἰνοῦντες τὸν θεὸν καὶ ἔχοντες χάριν πρὸς ὅλον τὸν λαόν. ὁ δὲ κύριος προσετίθει τοὺς σῳζομένους καθ' ἡμέραν ἐπὶ τὸ αὐτό.
>
> *And they devoted themselves to the apostles' teaching and the fellowship, to the breaking of bread and the prayers. And awe came upon every soul, and many wonders and signs were being done through the apostles. And all who believed were together and had all things in common. And they were selling their possessions and belongings and distributing the proceeds to all, as any had need. And day by day, attending the temple together and breaking bread in their homes, they received their food with glad and generous hearts, praising God and having favor with all the people. And the Lord added to their number day by day those who were being saved.*

PREFACE

The Gospel Feast is a volume written with an urgent purpose in mind. That purpose is to empower and encourage men of God serving in the ministry of the gospel of Jesus Christ to rediscover the Lord's Supper as an important means of proclaiming Christ crucified and risen from the dead. If pastors, teachers, and other people of God embrace this biblical purpose for the Supper in this generation, they will then restore the Sacrament to its rightful place in the worship and life of Christ's church. The author has been involved in regular pastoral ministry for more than ten years and has found that alongside the faithful preaching of God's Word, the Sacrament of the Supper is a powerful means to visually teach the gospel offer of salvation for all who repent, receive Jesus by the Holy Spirit, and acknowledge his atoning death in their place.

Beginning with the last Passover meal shared between Jesus Christ and his disciples on the night when he was betrayed, our Lord declared himself to be the fulfillment of the Passover hope. He also commanded that we should take and eat of the bread and drink of the cup as a means of remembering his substitutionary sacrifice – offering his sinless body and pouring out his cleansing blood for everyone who believes in his name. Thus, the body of Christ, his church, was commanded to celebrate Communion as a key element of gospel worship.

The Apostle Paul, in 1 Corinthians 11:26, provides a further elaboration on Jesus' intentions for regular participation in the Lord's Supper when he writes, *For as often as you eat this bread and drink the cup, you proclaim the Lord's death until he comes*. Thus, our times of Supper celebration are in fact not only Communion (fellowship with the Lord and with one another), or Eucharist (offering of thanksgivings unto God in Christ), but also *Gospel Feast* – Lord's Supper as proclamation of the good news of Jesus Christ. May everyone who reads this book rediscover the Supper as a *Gospel-proclaiming Feast.*

TABLE OF CONTENTS

CHAPTERS	PAGE
DEDICATION	iii
PREFACE	iv
INTRODUCTION	1
I: GOSPEL PROCLAMATION THROUGH THE LORD'S SUPPER: EXEGETING καταγγέλλετε IN 1 CORINTHIANS 11:26	5
II: PROCLAMATION IN DECLINE: THE LORD'S SUPPER AND PROCLAMATION IN THE EARLY CHURCH	39
III: PROCLAMATION FORGOTTEN: THE LORD'S SUPPER AS EUCHARIST IN THE POST-NICENE CHURCH TO THE REFORMATION	53
IV: PROCLAMATION REDISCOVERED: THE LORD'S SUPPER AS PROCLAMATION DURING THE REFORMATION	69
V: PROCLAMATION SEPARATED: THE LORD'S SUPPER IN PROTESTANT CHURCH PRACTICE SINCE THE REFORMATION	87
VI: PROCLAMATION RESTORED: GOSPEL PROCLAMATION THROUGH THE LORD'S SUPPER TODAY – A GOSPEL-CENTERED WAY FORWARD	125
VII: PROCLAMATION IMPLEMENTED: THE PRACTICE OF LORD'S SUPPER GOSPEL PROCLAMATION IN TODAY'S CHURCHES	133
APPENDIX I	141
APPENDIX II	229
BIBLIOGRAPHY	233
INDEXES	241

The First Lord's Supper

Now as they were eating, Jesus took bread, and after blessing it broke it and gave it to the disciples, and said, "Take, eat; this is my body." And he took a cup, and when he had given thanks he gave it to them, saying, "Drink of it, all of you, for this is my blood of the covenant, which is poured out for many for the forgiveness of sins. I tell you I will not drink again of this fruit of the vine until that day when I drink it new with you in my Father's kingdom."

(Matthew 26:26 – 29)

INTRODUCTION

> *I cannot close my eyes to the fact that to most people in the tradition to which I belong the sacrament means less now. Is that true of all Protestant churches? Have they all lost something of its meaning and power? Or may we venture to hope that after a period of loss we are recapturing some of it now?*
>
> (Donald M. Baillie, Late Professor, Systematic Theology, University of St. Andrews)[1]

Any given Lord's Day across the globe, thousands of ministers of God's Word, engaging myriad thousands of professing Christians in worship, recite the words of institution and distribute among their congregants the bread and the cup of the Lord's Supper. Whether spoken in Mandarin Chinese, Farsi, English, Swahili, Afrikaans, or ten thousand other languages and dialects, many of these pastors remind their communicants of the importance of the celebration of the Eucharist using the words of the Apostle Paul to a faction-afflicted, Greek-speaking congregation found in 1 Corinthians 11:23 – 26:

> For I received from the Lord what I also delivered to you, that the Lord Jesus on the night when he was betrayed took bread, and when he had given thanks, he broke it, and said, "This is my body which is for you. Do this in remembrance of me." In the same way also he took the cup, after supper, saying, "This cup is the new covenant in my blood. Do this, as often as you drink it, in remembrance of me." For as often as you eat this bread and drink the cup, you proclaim the Lord's death until he comes.

These leaders among the Christian faithful, whether traditional, modern, or postmodern, bring to their administration of the Sacrament presuppositions and assumptions that sharply impact how they teach, explain, and exhort communicants using the 1 Corinthians 11 text. For many if not most Protestant ministers, the significance of the Lord's Supper and its usefulness to their congregants is in serving as a means to induce remembrance, remembrance specifically through the words of

---

[1] D. M. Baillie, *The Theology of the Sacraments* (London: Faber and Faber, 1957), p. 92.

the Apostle Paul's epistle and through the bread and the cup, of the atoning body and blood of the Lord Jesus Christ.

For those serving as priests within the Roman Catholic, Eastern Orthodox, or Anglican and African Anglican traditions, the Eucharist is far more imperative and at the same time mysterious, in their view really and truly reenacting in each celebration the atoning sacrifice of the Lamb of God. There are also the ancient, interwoven threads of thanksgiving and transubstantiation, as well as resacrifice, underlying their Mass.

While distancing themselves from both Roman and Orthodox understandings of the Supper as a vivial resacrifice of Christ, Lutheran ministers maintain the significance of Christ's real physical presence during the observance of Communion, teaching that "while the bread and wine remain bread and wine, yet Christ, through a real physical union with the elements, is really corporally present 'in, with, under' the bread and wine."[2]

Within the Reformed tradition ministers bring to the celebration of this covenantal meal an enthusiasm for its use as one of the means of grace. This is underlined diligently and passionately by many pastors, while at the same time affirming as the Apostle Paul wrote to the Corinthians, that this is indeed a meal rich with significant remembrance. As is customary in other areas of theology and ecclesiology, Reformed scholars – Continental, Scot, and North American – have searched the Scriptures concerning the Lord's Supper and have published treatises and whole volumes on the subject in the span of more than four hundred years.

However, no matter which treatise or tome you diligently search, and no matter the denominational tradition or the presuppositions held by the variety of ministers celebrating Communion around the globe on any particular Sunday, it is quite rare to find any of them teaching, explaining, or exhorting communicants about the Lord's Supper as Paul describes it in 1 Corinthians 11:26 – a "proclaim[ing] [of] the Lord's death until he comes."

---

[2] Robert L. Reymond, *A New Systematic Theology of the Christian Faith* (Nashville: Thomas Nelson, 1998), p. 960.

How is it that since Paul addressed his letter to the congregation in Corinth in the first century, with so many generations of theologians, churchmen, and pastors at work, that so little weight has been given to the significance of the Lord's Supper as a means of *proclaiming* the gospel? Has the church in all its multi-colored local manifestations and differentiated denominations deprived itself of a crucial biblical principle which could transform the celebration and the impact of the Lord's Supper? And, if the church has deprived itself of a crucial principle, or at least a sharper understanding of that principle, what is it and how can it be recaptured and applied to the worship of the church today? These are the imperative questions this book seeks to answer.

Pick up any standard commentary available today concerning 1 Corinthians, turn to the chapter or subsection dealing with the latter portions of chapter 11 and you will find extensive exegesis, analysis, and scholarly references related to the nature of the Lord's presence in the Supper, the importance of Communion as remembrance, perhaps as a means of thanksgiving, and certainly its use as a means of grace. Yet little ink is expended in detailing the importance of 1 Corinthians 11:26 and what Paul means when he writes, "For as often as you eat this bread and drink the cup, you *proclaim* the Lord's death until he comes." Perhaps this is the case because the question remains to be settled. Much scholarly speculation is raised concerning this question, yet scant exegetical work is published. "Are the words of interpretation spoken separately over the two signs of bread and wine meant to serve as proclamation of death? Is the anamnesis, the explicit reference to the death, resurrection, and glorification itself the proclamation?"[3]

Verse 26 in 1 Corinthians 11 is the crux of Paul's argument in this pericope, for it is his own summary of the Supper's importance when it is celebrated, using here the word καταγγέλλετε to describe its impact. Verse 26 differs from verses 23 – 25 in that it introduces material unrepeated in the Synoptic Gospels and yet predates Matthew,

---

[3] Mary D. Collins, "Eucharistic Proclamation of God's Presence," *Worship*, vol. 41, no. 9 (1967): p. 539.

Mark and Luke,[4] leading to the conclusion that these words are his pastoral application of the importance of the Supper to the situation in Corinth.

Any effort to discover what Paul means when he equates the taking of Communion as proclamation of the Lord's death must begin with careful exegesis of 1 Corinthians 11:26, the pericope, the wider life context of the believers in Corinth, and the typical way in which Paul and others of the New Testament era employed the term καταγγέλλετε.

It is also important to understand how the Church through the ages between the first century and today has understood this text. Was the importance of the Lord's Supper as gospel proclamation understood or embraced in prior generations? And just as importantly, how did the various understandings in different times and places impact regular Eucharist practice within the life of congregations?

Finally, exegetical analysis of the text and an understanding of the historical interpretive threads must bring us to the Church today and its celebration of the Lord's Supper. If Paul truly is teaching that partaking of the Lord's Supper is another means of proclaiming the gospel of Jesus Christ, how must that impact ministerial teaching, explaining, and exhorting, and what should that look like in congregational practice? Thus the present work seeks not only to answer academic, interpretive questions, but also to provide practical application of this biblical teaching to congregational celebrations of the Lord's Supper. In doing so, it is hoped that Christ's Church in the 21st century may once again celebrate Communion as Christ's Gospel Feast.

---

[4] For discussion of this point see F. W. Grosheide, *Commentary on the First Epistle to the Corinthians. The New International Commentary on the New Testament* (Grand Rapids: Wm. B. Eerdmans Publishing Company, 1953, ninth printing, 1979), p. 272.

I

GOSPEL PROCLAMATION THROUGH THE LORD'S SUPPER: EXEGETING καταγγέλλετε IN 1 CORINTHIANS 11:26

> *In the Lord's Supper, the apostle Paul tells us, we 'proclaim the Lord's death till he comes' – that is, as long as the world lasts, and in prospect of Jesus' coming again at the end of the age. We proclaim the death that gave us life. We proclaim the Saviour who rose from the grave, having conquered sin and death, in order to give everlasting life to all who would believe in him. The great question here is, of course, 'What does it mean to proclaim Christ's death in this way?'*
>
> (Gordon J. Keddie, minister, Grace Presbyterian Church, State College, Pennsylvania)[5]

The Apostle Paul recognized that he was facing a thorny problem among the believers in Corinth, based upon the reports he was getting about their factional relationships and factional worship. Everybody was choosing sides and foregoing the unity of the body of Christ. Paul begins his letter straight away, immediately after the customary greetings, addressing this dangerous situation in 1 Corinthians 1:10 – 17:

> I appeal to you, brothers, by the name of our Lord Jesus Christ, that all of you agree, and that there be no divisions among you, but that you be united in the same mind and the same judgment. For it has been reported to me by Chloe's people that there is quarreling among you, my brothers. What I mean is that each one of you says, "I follow Paul," or "I follow Apollos," or "I follow Cephas," or "I follow Christ." Is Christ divided? Was Paul crucified for you? Or were you baptized in the name of Paul? I thank God that I baptized none of you except Crispus and Gaius, so that no one may say that you were baptized in my name. (I did baptize also the household of Stephanas. Beyond that, I do not know whether I baptized anyone else.) For Christ did not send me to baptize but to preach the gospel, and not with words of eloquent wisdom, lest the cross of Christ be emptied of its power.

Just as it happens in congregations today, so it was happening in Corinth nearly two thousand years ago. Broken into factions, each of which gathered under the banner of this or that leader, the divisions were bound to interrupt healthy church body life and

[5] Gordon J. Keddie, *The Lord's Supper Is a Celebration of Grace: What the Bible Teaches About Communion* (Darlington, UK: Evangelical Press, 2000), p. 47.

bring disunity into the ministries of the church, the public testimony of the church, and particularly the gatherings of the Corinthian believers for corporate worship.

Specific reports were coming to the Apostle about how much these divisions and the Corinthians' failure to love one another were disrupting the Lord's Supper. This was deeply grievous to Paul, especially as he recalled the words of the Lord Jesus concerning the Sacrament of Communion and what the Apostle himself understood it was given to the Church to proclaim – "the death of the Lord Jesus until he comes."

And so, in the second half of chapter 11 of his 1 Corinthians epistle, Paul pastorally chides the believers in the Greek city for their abuse of the Lord's Supper, an act of devotion and worship of Jesus which should unite them, rather than underscore their divisions. "Christians ate these common meals to express their fellowship with one another and also with direct reference to Jesus,"[6] not simply to satisfy physical hunger or their desire for alcoholic beverages. In fact his introduction of verses 17 – 22 to the entire topic of the Lord's Supper's significance begins with an abrupt and strongly worded admonition. So concerned was the Apostle that he began addressing their misuse of the Supper before describing its proper practice and import:

> But in the following instructions I do not commend you, because when you come together it is not for the better but for the worse. For, in the first place, when you come together as a church, I hear that there are divisions among you. And I believe it in part, for there must be factions among you in order that those who are genuine among you may be recognized. When you come together, it is not the Lord's supper that you eat. For in eating, each one goes ahead with his own meal. One goes hungry, another gets drunk. What! Do you not have houses to eat and drink in? Or do you despise the church of God and humiliate those who have nothing? What shall I say to you? Shall I commend you in this? No, I will not.

It is within the context of a factionalized church body that any effort to define what Paul is saying about the Lord's Supper must be framed. The church in Corinth represents a specific scenario in the life of a body of believers. 1 Corinthians (and thus 1 Corinthians 11:17 – 34) must be interpreted first and foremost as an

---

[6] Larry W. Hurtado, *Lord Jesus Christ: Devotion to Jesus in Earliest Christianity* (Grand Rapids: William B. Eerdmans Publishing Company, 2003), p. 145. Hurtado also discusses 1 Corinthians 11:23 – 26 as having a been a tradition of Jesus' words which predated Paul's letter to the Corinthians, passed to him by his "predecessors in the Christian faith."

impassioned pastoral letter, tailored with great specificity for the presenting congregational issues. Among these urgent matters is the great gospel-denying way in which the Corinthians celebrated Communion.

It is while bearing this strife-ridden socio-historical context in mind that the exegetical linguistic process begins in 1 Corinthians 11:26. Of supreme importance in understanding Paul on the Supper in this verse is establishing the meaning of the word καταγγέλλετε, the second person, plural, present active indicative form of καταγγέλλω. According to Grosheide, if the words Paul writes in verse 26 are his own and not a repetition of non-synoptic words of Jesus, the "indicative is the more probable (as opposed to the imperative). He notes that the use of "γὰρ also points to an indicative."[7] The term, typically rendered in English as *you proclaim* or *show forth*, occurs with reference to the significance of believers in Corinth participating in the symbolic actions of the Supper – eating the bread and drinking the cup. In the Greek text, the word order of the second phrase emphasizes the Lord's death as the content of what is being *proclaimed*:

> ὁσάκις γὰρ ἐὰν ἐσθίητε τὸν ἄρτον τοῦτον καὶ τὸ ποτήριον πίνητε, τὸν θάνατον τοῦ κυρίου **καταγγέλλετε**, ἄχρι οὗ ἔλθῃ.

The first question is whether or not "proclaim" is a valid rendering of the Greek term καταγγέλλετε (καταγγέλλω) as Paul uses it in 1 Corinthians 11:26. This is a source of some disagreement among New Testament scholars, not so much in terms of the use of the English word *proclaim* for καταγγέλλετε, but rather as to how proclamation is connected with the Lord's Supper in Paul's exhortation which is forcefully pressed home in the text. Indeed, comparing the contextual usage of this term to its other occurrences in Pauline and other New Testament literature seems to indicate that understanding the term as equivalent in English to *proclaim* in 1 Corinthians 11:26 is a valid position to take. And yet this is only the first step in arriving at a satisfactory understanding of how the Corinthians' participation in the Lord's Supper is in fact gospel proclamation. Troels Engberg-Pedersen of the University of Copenhagen rightly summarizes the key question to be answered:

[7] F. W. Grosheide, *Commentary on the First Epistle to the Corinthians*, p. 273.

> There are. . . important issues in this verse. (a) proclaim: Is Paul saying that when the Corinthians eat "this" bread and drink the cup ("this" cup, no matter which text one prefers), they are *eo ipso* proclaiming the Lord's death? Or is he referring to some kind of *verbal* proclamation that may have accompanied the eating and drinking? . . . There is an additional problem, however, stemming from the fact that καταγγέλλειν ("proclaim") is most often used of making a verbal proclamation toward *outsiders* (cf., e.g., Rom 1:8), which cannot be what Paul is directly thinking of here. But that precisely gives added point to his use of the term: when the Corinthians eat and drink from the consecrated bread and cup, they are *doing* something *within* the group which *equals proclaiming* the Lord's death toward *outsiders*. They are not just having a pleasant in-group meal together.[8]

Engsberg-Pedersen may be on the right track in describing the actions of verse 26 as producing proclamation through the eating and drinking within the congregation. Thus in doing so they are projecting Christ's death in view of those who are not yet part of the Christian community in Corinth. This is also the interpretation of Maurice Barnett, who notes that, "*katangello* is specific of some proclamation of message that is given *from one to another*. When we eat and drink the Lord's Supper we do the proclaiming by the authority of the Lord."[9]

It remains to be seen through textual analysis what the most likely referent for *proclamation* might be 1 Corinthians 11:26. The chart immediately following illustrates the other usages of this term by the Apostle Paul (or his anamnesis) and in the Lukan material of Acts. Such comparisons do not in and of themselves prove with absolute certainty one way of the other what Paul intends in 1 Corinthians 11:26, but they do shed light on the prevailing meaning of the term καταγγέλλω in the mid-first century New Testament literature attribute to Paul and his immediate circle. (Note that the typical range of meaning conveyed by the English translation is that of a message transmitted through verbal communication.)

---

[8] T. Engberg-Pedersen, "Proclaiming the Lord's Death: 1 Corinthians 11:17 – 34 and the Forms of Paul's Theological Argument," in *Pauline Theology. Vol II: 1 and 2 Corinthians* (Minneapolis: Fortress Press, 1993), p. 115. Engberg-Pedersen argues that Paul is saying that when the Corinthians eat this bread and drink the cup they are *eo ipso* proclaiming the Lord's death.

[9] Maurice Barnett, "Arrangement for the Lord's Supper (1)," in *The Gospel Anchor* (June 1986), p. 298.

Table 1

Pauline/Lukan Table of Occurrences of καταγγέλλω

Date	Author	Text	Key Word(s)	Contextual Usage
AD 53 – 55	Paul	*1 Corinthians 2:1*	καταγγέλλων	"proclaiming"
AD 53 – 55	Paul	*1 Corinthians 9:14*	καταγγέλλουσιν	"who proclaim"
AD 53 – 55	Paul	*1 Corinthians 11:26*	καταγγέλλετε	"you proclaim"
AD 61	Paul	*Philippians 1:17*	καταγγέλλουσιν	"[the former] proclaim"
AD 61	Paul	*Philippians 1:18*	καταγγελλεται	"[Christ] is proclaimed"
AD 61	Paul	*Colossians 1:18*	καταγγέλλομεν	"we proclaim"
AD 61	Paul	*Colossians 1:28*	καταγγέλλομεν	"we proclaim"
Pre-AD 70	Luke	*Acts 4:2*	καταγγέλλειν	"proclaiming"
Pre-AD 70	Luke	*Acts 13:5*	κατήγγελλον	"they proclaimed"
Pre-AD 70	Luke	*Acts 13:38*	καταγγέλλεται	"is proclaimed"
Pre-AD 70	Luke	*Acts 15:36*	κατηγγείλαμεν	"we proclaimed"
Pre-AD 70	Luke	*Acts 16:17*	καταγγέλλουσιν	"who proclaim"
Pre-AD 70	Luke	*Acts 16:21*	καταγγέλλουσιν	"set forth," "advocate," "announce," or "proclaim"
Pre-AD 70	Luke	*Acts 17:3*	καταγγέλλω	"I proclaim"
Pre-AD 70	Luke	*Acts 17:13*	κατηγγέλη	"was proclaimed"
Pre-AD 70	Luke	*Acts 17:23*	καταγγέλλω	"I announce," or "I proclaim"
Pre-AD 70	Luke	*Acts 26:23*	καταγγέλλειν	"he would proclaim"

While the precise Koine term καταγγέλλετε occurs only in 1 Corinthians 11:26 in the text of the Greek New Testament, many other forms of καταγγέλλω are used by Paul and those in his circle. As the above chart demonstrates, there are some variations in the preferred English equivalent terms in texts like Acts 16:21 or Acts 17:23, each of the occurrences of the term καταγγέλλω are rendered in most translations as *proclaim*, in the sense that in these situations there is a definite proclamation of a message, usually the gospel. An alternative term used by Paul and by Luke in related contexts is the word κηρύσσω, typically rendered either as *preach* or *proclaim*.

Yet Louw and Nida draw a distinction between καταγγέλλω and the term κηρύσσω. While there is great semantic overlap, καταγγέλλω falls within the range of "to announce, with focus upon the extent to which the announcement or proclamation extends – to proclaim throughout, to announce, to speak out about."[10] The term κηρύσσω on the other hand, while also carrying with it the sense of public announcement, is more precise in content, confined according to Louw and Nida to the public announcement of "religious truths and principles with urging acceptance and compliance *to preach*."[11]

Therefore, on the basis of the analysis of comparative uses of the term καταγγέλλω within the Pauline corpus and within the connected Lukan literature, the reasonable conclusion is that Paul intends the Corinthians to understand that their celebration of the Lord's Supper in some way *proclaims* the Lord Jesus' death, until he returns in glory. The Apostle deliberately chose to use a word in this verse, while making what to him was a key theological and pastorally practical point, that he ordinarily uses with reference to the oral, public declaration of the gospel. Thus in Paul's understanding, the Supper employs the visual symbols of the bread and the cup and the actions of eating and drinking by those who acknowledge Jesus as Lord in communicating the gospel message. And yet Paul in this context did not select the more precise term from within his vocabulary, κηρύσσω, which he often chooses to convey the preaching of gospel content.

[10] Louw & Nida, *Greek –English Lexicon of the New Testament Based Upon Semantic Domains*, v. 1; S, 33.256 (New York: United Bible Societies, 1989), p. 411.
[11] Louw & Nida, *Greek –English Lexicon of the New Testament*, v. 1; O, 33:204, p. 417.

While there can be little serious debate concerning the semantic range of the word καταγγέλλετε (proclaim) as Paul typically uses it, and scant evidence of a unique deviation in his meaning when he uses it in 1 Corinthians 11:26, there remains the real interpretive difficulty of how in some way the Lord's Supper accomplishes a proclamation of the Lord's death. What place does a term almost entirely used to describe verbal declaration have within a text concerning the Sacrament of the Lord's Supper? This is the crux of the interpretive challenge in 1 Corinthians 11:23 – 26. Perhaps an overview of some of the competing scholarly responses to that question will be helpful.

In his socio-historical investigation, *Paul and the Lord's Supper*, Panayotis Coutsoumpos argues that both the Corinthians' participation in the meal in sharing the elements, as well as the Lord's words of institution result in the Supper accomplishing gospel proclamation:

> … the passage indicates that the Supper of the Lord involves a body of believers who participate in the meal as his followers and who receive the cup as an indication of conscious participation in the benefits of the new covenant with the Lord. Paul recalls the exact words of the institution to make the emphasis that as often as they eat the meal and drink the cup, it is the Lord's remembrance. …
>
> The celebration (in the Primitive Church) was a thanksgiving meal which looked forward to the return of Christ. This partaking of the bread and wine is for Paul a proclaiming of the death and resurrection of the Lord "until he comes." Paul further assumes, in agreement with the early Christian Church's idea, that eating and drinking in the Eucharist Meal in fellowship with Christ is the anticipation of the table fellowship with the Lord at the Messianic banquet. It is along this line that Paul calls the celebration a drinking of the cup of the Lord and an eating at the table of the Lord (1 Cor. 10:21). …
> . . .Thus, this eschatological motif and proclamation is what Paul has in mind, when the bread is broken and the cup is shared. . . .
>
> . . .Paul uses the verb καταγγέλλετε and it could be indicative or imperative. Since Paul uses the word γὰρ, it is more likely to be indicative. Is Paul trying to say that the Eucharistic action is a proclamation of the death of Jesus, or does he mean that the proclamation is an explicit idea in it? Because there is not such thing as a liturgical rite without proclamation we have to consider the latter.[12]

[12] Panayotis Coutsoumpos, *Paul and the Lord's Supper: A Socio-Historical Investigation, Studies in Biblical Literature, vol. 84* (New York: Peter Lang Publishing, 2005), pp. 123 – 124. Coutsoumpos continues in this portion of his work to draw the connections between

Schniewind, writing in Kittel's *Theological Dictionary of the New Testament*, quickly dismisses any hint of the possibility that the bread or the cup, the participation, or the actions themselves are the referent of Paul's καταγγέλλετε in 1 Corinthians 11:26. As he puts it, "τὸν θάνατον τοῦ Κυρίου καταγγέλλετε (indicative) does not refer to the Lord's Supper as an action. This would be in keeping neither with the meaning of καταγγέλλειν nor with the Passover and mysteries."[13] But has Schniewind arrived at his conclusion from study of the immediate text and the socio-historical problem Paul is addressing, or has he stilted his interpretive grid in favor of his understanding of the more typical contexts he has seen outside of 1 Corinthians 11? Is it not entirely possible that the Apostle Paul employed καταγγέλλετε in 1 Corinthians 11 in a somewhat unique way, tailored to address the specific pastoral problem among the Corinthians? It would certainly seem to be a more proper reading of the immediate context. And, as to Schniewind's dismissal of καταγγέλλετε as referring to the symbols and acts of the Supper because of some discontinuity with the Passover, it must be remembered that the Passover observance depended upon the use of the symbols of the unleavened bread, the lamb, and the cup of blessing, which were given context through the recitation of the biblical Passover deliverance narrative.

It has been demonstrated by some scholars that the equivalent to the Hebrew לִבִנְךָ (*shall tell*) in Exodus 13:8 introducing the Passover instruction is none other than Paul's καταγγέλλετε in 1 Corinthians 11:26.[14] The pattern of instruction Paul uses concerning the Lord's Supper to the Corinthians does in some respects image the Passover instruction. And perhaps this should not be surprising considering that the original context of the first Lord's Supper involved a Passover celebration. The Lord Jesus instructed his disciples to prepare the Passover feast (Luke 22:18), as well as sending them to locate the large, upper room (Mark 14:15) which had been furnished

---

proclamation and parousia.

[13] *Theological Dictionary of the New Testament*, vol. 1 ed. Gerhard Kittel, trans. Geoffrey W. Bromily, English edition (Grand Rapids: Eerdmans, 1967), pp. 71 – 72.

[14] Norman Hook, *The Eucharist in the New Testament* (London: The Epworth Press, 1964), p.129. Hook refers in this matter to Buchanan Gray and his work *Sacrifice in the Old Testament* (1925), p. 395.

for such a purpose. In the midst of the Last Supper, Jesus commented that, *I have earnestly desired to eat this Passover with you before I suffer* (Luke 22:15).

Both Passover and Supper bring about remembrance of God's saving acts through the use of symbolic physical elements, received by the participants, and contextualized by verbal recitation. All these aspects united together constitute biblical sacramental observance:

Passover Institution of Exodus 13	Lord's Supper Institution of 1 Corinthians 11
[6] Seven days you shall eat unleavened bread, and on the seventh day there shall be a feast to the LORD. ***A(**[7]Unleavened bread shall be eaten for seven days); no leavened bread shall be seen with you, and no leaven shall be seen with you in all your territory. [8] ***B** (**You shall tell**) your son on that day, 'It is because of what the LORD did for me when I came out of Egypt.' [9] ***C (And it shall be to you as a sign on your hand and as a memorial between your eyes**,) that the law of the LORD may be in your mouth. For with a strong hand the LORD has brought you out of Egypt. [10] ***D** You shall therefore keep this statute at its appointed time from year to year.	[23]For I received from the Lord what I also delivered to you, that the Lord Jesus on the night when he was ***A** (betrayed took bread), [24]and when he had given thanks, he broke it, and said, "This is my body which is for you. ***C (Do this in remembrance of me.")** [25]In the same way also he took the cup, after supper, saying, "This cup is the new covenant in my blood. Do this, ***D** as often as you drink it, ***C (in remembrance of me**.") [26] ***D** For as often as you eat this bread and drink the cup, ***B** (**you proclaim**) the Lord's death until he comes. **Key:** **A** Symbolic Element (bread) **B Command to Tell/Proclaim** **C For a Memorial/Remembrance** **D.** Ongoing Sacral Observance

Anthony Thiselton also connects Paul's pastoral theology on the proclamation of the Lord's Supper with the Passover observance and the idea of proclamation through participation. In his commentary, *The First Epistle to the Corinthians*, Thiselton writes:

> The verb καταγγέλλετε regularly means in the NT *to announce or to* **proclaim** *the gospel* (1 Cor. 9:14), *to preach the word of God* (Acts 13:5), or *to preach Christ* (Acts 4:2; Phil 1:17, 18). It also carries overtones of *speaking* or *preaching publicly*, *to publish* or *to promulgate*, or to perform *a declarative-speech act* openly. Hence Paul now further likens what the assembled congregation does in the actions of eating and drinking the bread and wine that makes believers contemporary with the cross *to the recital of*

> *the Passover Haggadah as gospel proclamation*. However, this is not simply a publishing of the objective event of the cross. It includes this (**the bread is broken** and **the cup** ... *in the same way*...). Yet like those who recite the Haggadah of the Passover on the understanding that *"in every generation a man must so regard himself as he came forth himself out of Egypt"* (*m. Pesahim* 10:5), it *also* witnesses to *the participant's self-involving appropriation of the cross both for redemption and lifestyle* as those who *share Christ's death* in order to *share Christ's life*.[15]

Another representative of the idea that Paul's teaching of the Supper involved actions and elements, as well as verbal expression, is N. T. Wright. Although Wright is more interested in the kingdom dimensions of the Supper, he sees in Paul's 1 Corinthians 11:23 – 26 presentation of the Lord's Supper a continuation of Old Testament prophetic symbolism and Passover observance from which the Supper originated:

> Jesus' actions with the bread and the cup . . . must be seen in the same way as the symbolic actions of certain prophets in the Hebrew scriptures. Jeremiah smashes a pot; Ezekiel makes a model of Jerusalem under siege. The actions carry prophetic power, effecting the events (mostly acts of judgment) which are then to occur. They are at once explained in terms of those events, or rather YHWH's operating through them. In the same way, Jesus' central actions during the meal seem to have been designed to reinforce the point of the whole meal: the kingdom-agenda to which he had been obedient throughout his ministry was now at last reaching its ultimate destination. Passover looked back to the exodus, and on to the coming of the kingdom. Jesus intended this meal to symbolize the new exodus, the arrival of the kingdom through his own fate. The meal, focused on Jesus' actions with the bread and the cup, told the Passover story, and Jesus' own story, and wove these two into one. [16]

Yet Bauer, in his *Greek-English Lexicon of the New Testament and other Early Christian Literature*, regards Paul in 1 Corinthians 11:26 as writing of the Supper as proclamation, "by celebrating the sacrament rather than with words."[17] Bauer places the weight of Paul's referent for καταγγέλλετε upon the elements, the actions, and the

---

[15] Anthony C. Thiselton, *The First Epistle to the Corinthians* (The New International Greek Testament Commentary) (Grand Rapids: William B. Eerdmans, 2000), pp. 886 – 887. Emphases is the author's.
[16] N. T. Wright, *Jesus and the Victory of God*. (Minneapolis: Fortress Press, 1996), pp. 558 – 559.
[17] *A Greek-English Lexicon of the New Testament and other Christian Literature (BDAG)*, 3rd ed. ed. & trans. Frederick William Danker, English edition (Chicago: University of Chicago Press, 2000), p 515.

participatory aspects of the Supper. While many scholars have been quick to dismiss this interpretation, on closer examination it seems to more faithfully fit the text as well as the context at hand. This is the case particularly if the position is not as 'absolute' as Bauer's, in that the *importance* of the contextualizing words of institution are not dismissed – let alone excluded from the celebration.

This is similar to the position taken by Engberg-Pedersen in his exegesis with 1 Corinthians 11:26. He identifies three key factors that lead him to conclude that Paul's meaning when he writes of the Supper's impact as "proclamation," concerns primarily the elements, the actions, and the participation during the periodic celebrations:

> For (i) throughout the passage Paul aims, as we shall see, to focus his addressees' attention on the very act of eating and drinking that constitutes participation in the Eucharist. (ii) Nor is there any indication elsewhere that each individual (and the individual too is in focus throughout the passage) would do any verbal proclaiming as part of participating in the Eucharist. (iii) Finally, *if* there is any verbal proclamation involved in celebrating the Eucharist, v 26 itself suggests that it will be the one implied in (*ὸν ἄρτον*) *τοῦτον*, thus referring us back to the sayings of vv 24 – 25. [18]

Beverly Roberts Gaventa has probably done the most exhaustive work on this question of interpreting Paul's καταγγέλλετε in 1 Corinthians 11:26. She notes with reference to equating *proclamation* in verse 26 with the Hebrew word *higgid* (*narrate, tell*) that this is a largely unproven connection.[19] Yet it is this connection, that is most used to support the interpretation of καταγγέλλετε as limited in Paul's usage to *verbal* proclamation only. Citing several other examples of the way καταγγέλλετε is used outside the Pauline Corpus, Gaventa observes:

---

[18] T. Engberg-Pedersen, "Proclaiming the Lord's Death: 1 Corinthians 11:17 – 34 and the Forms of Paul's Theological Argument," in *Society of Biblical Literature Seminar Papers 30* (1991), p. 603.

[19] Beverly Roberts Gaventa, " 'You Proclaim the Lord's Death': 1 Corinthians 11:26 and Paul's Understanding of Worship," in *Review and Expositor 80* (1983), p. 381. Gaventa writes that scholars who make this claim usually refer to articles by G. H. Box and Douglas Jones written several decades ago. Neither, author, however, offered evidence for a connection between the two verbs.

> *Kataggellein* appears elsewhere in ways that may refer to proclamation by deeds rather than by speech. . . These examples, although they are admittedly exceptions to the normal usage of *kataggellein,* should make us wary of the notion that *kataggellein* in 1 Corinthians 11:26 must imply a sermon that accompanies the Lord's Supper. It may be that Paul means that the Supper itself constitutes a proclamation. That understanding of this verse is entirely consistent with remarks Paul makes elsewhere concerning the proclamation character of action and faith.[20]

Both interpretive sides in this debate as to Paul's referent for καταγγέλλετε, or *proclamation*, admit that something having to do with the Lord's Supper's celebration proclaims the Lord's death – proclaims the gospel of Jesus Christ. It seems, however, that most on each side stand at the extreme position (Thiselton and a few others excepted). They maintain on the one hand that Paul is saying in verse 26 that whenever the Corinthians observe the Lord's Supper, they include a verbal proclamation of the gospel, or on the other hand that Paul is saying the symbols of bread and cup, the actions, and the participation is all that is intended. But is it not just as reasonable that Paul's καταγγέλλετε refers to the entirety of the Supper – words, elements, actions, and participation – as proclaiming his death? Must we choose the one extreme or the other? Is Vincent Taylor correct in his interpretation, which represents one of these two extremes?

> The statement of I Corinthians xi. 26, 'For as often as you eat this bread, and drink the cup, ye proclaim (καταγγέλλετε) the Lord's death till he come', probably refers to the recital of the words of Jesus regarding His death at each celebration of the Supper, and is thus an indication of the close connexion between the rite and the Passion in the mind of the early Church. As J. Denney has truly said, 'the sacraments, but especially the sacrament of the Supper, are the stronghold of the New Testament doctrine concerning the death of Christ'.[21]

Few scholars and exegetes would deny either of Taylor's statements about the close connection between the Lord's Supper and the Passion of Jesus Christ in the early Church's theology and practice. Paul makes this evident in his own pastoral arguments throughout the passage. But is this proclamatory work accomplished by observing the Supper confined simply to the recitation of words of institution, or even of some lengthier verbal proclamation? Joachim Jeremias, like Taylor, was insistent

---

[20] Gaventa, " 'You Proclaim the Lord's Death': 1 Corinthians 11:26 and Paul's Understanding of Worship," p. 382.

[21] Vincent Taylor, *The Atonement in New Testament Teaching* (London: The Epworth Press, 1940; reprint 1954), p. 23.

that Paul's meaning in using καταγγέλλετε was a verbal form of proclamation – "the form of a recitation of the words of interpretation followed by an exposition."[22] Yet rather than excluding the symbolic elements of the bread and cup, the actions of breaking and blessing, or the sincere participation of those who celebrate the Supper from the contextual words as proclamation, it seems that a position closer to Anthony Thiselton's is a more balanced understanding of what Paul means here in 1 Corinthians 11:26.

Along the same lines as Thiselton, Malcolm Maclean sees the Lord's Supper celebration as gospel proclamation through the elements, actions, participation, and the contextualizing words of institution – composing together a kind of *prophetic symbolism*:

> The meal is also a proclamation that says something to those looking on. . . .
> It was this combination of ritual (taking the bread and wine) and Word (reading the accounts) that Paul referred to by 'proclaim', . . .
> . . .This combination of word and action suggests that the Lord's Supper is an act of *prophetic symbolism*. . . .
> . . .The unbelievers in Corinth would have asked why there were divisions at the Lord's Table, an indication that the believers were not functioning in a truly prophetic capacity. Prophetic symbolism is a reminder that the teaching contained in God's Word must be lived out in the lives of his people.[23]

Perhaps further study of the grammar connected with Paul's use of καταγγέλλετε will provide some clarity. Beginning with the immediate context of verse 26 we find that the verb forms used all three times are of what is often classified as the customary present. As Daniel Wallace notes, the verbal present tense forms here in 1 Corinthians 11:26 involve repeated action.[24] Thus the reader's attention is brought into focus

---

[22] Joachim Jeremias, *The Eucharistic Words of Jesus* (Philadelphia: Fortress Press, 1977, 2nd ed. 1981), pp. 106 – 107; 253. Jeremias correlates Paul's use of καταγγέλλετε (proclamation) with the Hebrew verb higgid, describing the recitation of the Exodus creedo. Thus the verbal contextual framework is separated from the symbolic elements, actions, and participation.
[23] Malcolm Maclean, *The Lord's Supper* (Ross-shire, Scotland: Christian Focus Publications, 2009), pp. 35 – 36.
[24] Daniel B. Wallace, *Greek Grammar Beyond the Basics: An Exegetical Syntax of the New Testament* (Grand Rapids: Zondervan, 1996), p. 522.

around these three repeated actions. The first two actions, eating and drinking, are paired together as the repeated symbolic actions of the Lord's Supper. Then these repeated symbolic actions propel the reader into the next phrase, which begins with "the Lord's death" and into the third action that results – proclaiming. Thus in the Greek, as in the English, this progression is apparent, albeit with added emphasis on "the Lord's death."

> ὁσάκις γὰρ ἐὰν **ἐσθίητε** τὸν ἄρτον τοῦτον καὶ τὸ ποτήριον **πίνητε**,
> τὸν θάνατον τοῦ κυρίου **καταγγέλλετε**, ἄχρι οὗ ἔλθῃ.

Clearly Paul in this single verse is connecting the first two recurring actions as the normative symbolic elements composing the Lord's Supper, which together result in the third action, "proclaim(ing) the Lord's death until he comes." There is nothing in the immediate context of this verse to indicate another referent for καταγγέλλετε than the prior, paired verbs describing the receiving of the bread and the cup of Communion. Thus the symbolic elements, the actions of the Supper, and sincere participation (eating, drinking) are in focus.

If this exegesis is sustained going forward, it in no way precludes the words of institution or the narration of Christ's atoning death as being integral to observing a biblical Lord's Supper. Jesus' words of institution remain essential. Yet word, visual elements, actions (breaking, blessing), and participation by faith are all necessary to biblical Communion celebration. But Paul's style of expression here, and his use of καταγγέλλετε in verse 26, do elevate the importance of the symbols, the actions, and the participation of the celebrants in communicating the gospel as well.

It is interesting to note at this stage in the exegesis that Gordon D. Fee notes many of the same grammatical and rhetorical points as have just been described. Yet nevertheless he arrives at the conclusion that Paul can only be referencing *verbal* proclamation in verse 26. In his magisterial commentary on 1 Corinthians, when describing 11:26, Fee writes:

> The reason for repeating those words (words of institution) is now being given. The bread and the cup of this meal together signify the death of the Lord; "For," he now explains, "as often as we do this, in his remembrance," we are to be reminded through proclamation of the salvation that was effected for us through that death.

> That this is Paul's intent is evident from several converging data: (1) the explanatory "for," (2) the word order, which puts the emphasis on his death, (3) the fact that he picks up the precise language of the final repetition command ("as often as you. . ."), (4) which in turn picks up the "eating of this bread" so as to include both parts of the meal in the explanation, and (5) the emphasis that both the bread and the cup proclaim Christ's death.[25]

Fee rightly goes on to declare that "the focus of Paul's concern is on this meal as a means of proclaiming Christ's death." Yet he argues that the verb καταγγέλλετε "probably does not mean that the meal in itself is proclamation," but that during the meal there is a verbal proclamation of Christ's death."[26] This conclusion is hard to accept, when in the next few sentences of explanation Fee attaches the words of institution – the bread and the cup sayings – with the elements and with the necessity of participating together as an undivided new people, free of the old distinctions. In other words, one cannot disconnect the words of institution from the elements, the actions, and the participation which the words of the Lord contextualize.

Charles Hodge sees in Paul's exhortation in verse 26 an emphasis upon the Supper as a perpetual commemoration, a proclamation of Jesus' death until the consummation. In his own commentary upon Paul's interpretive statement concerning the Supper, he writes:

> What Paul had received from the Lord is recorded in the preceding verses. Here and in what follows we have his own inferences from the account which the Lord had given him. The first of these inferences is, that the Lord's supper is, and was designed to be, a proclamation of the death of Christ to continue until his second advent. Those who come to it, therefore, should come, not to satisfy hunger, nor for the gratification of social feelings, but for the definite purpose of bearing their testimony to the great fact of redemption, and to contribute their portion of influence to the preservation and propagation of the knowledge of that fact. *For* indicates the connection with what proceeds. 'It is a commemoration of his death, *for* it is in its very nature a proclamation of that great fact.' . . . As the Passover was a perpetual commemoration of the deliverance out of Egypt, and a prediction of the coming and death of the Lamb of God, who was to bear away the sins of the world; so the Lord's supper is at once the commemoration of the death of Christ and a pledge of his coming the second time without sin unto salvation.[27]

---

[25] Gordon D. Fee, *The First Epistle to the Corinthians*, The New International Commentary on the New Testament (Grand Rapids: William B. Eerdmans, 1987), pp. 556 – 557.
[26] Ibid., 557.
[27] Charles Hodge, *Commentary on the First Epistle to the Corinthians* (Grand Rapids: Wm. B. Eermans Publishing Company, 1950), pp. 229 – 230.

Further indications that Paul intends for his readers to connect proclamation of the gospel with the symbols, the actions, and celebrant participation – as well as the words of institution – may be found at the beginning of this verse, as Paul transitions from his recitation of the words he received from the Lord (verses 23 – 25) into his summary of the Supper in verse 26. And it definitely appears that in verse 26 the Apostle, continuing in the second person plural, added some words to the tradition he received from the Lord "in order to explain certain things more clearly."[28] This is Paul's pastoral summary on the importance of the Supper observance, not part of the Lord's tradition he had received and passed along to the Corinthians. As J. M. Van Cangh notes in his *Le Texte Primitif De La Cene*, "Every time you eat this bread and drink this cup. . . (found in 1 Cor 11:26) is clearly a secondary addition, influenced by liturgical practice."[29] Charles Hodge and many others also maintain that this verse, "and in what follows we have his own inferences for the account which the Lord had given him."[30] In other words, the manner in which Paul begins verse 26 indicates that this is new explanatory material for addressing the problems of Lord's Supper observance in Corinth.

The Apostle moves from received teaching he is passing along to the troubled church, to his own pastoral theological statement on the impact of Communion, when he writes, ὁσάκις (as often as. . .) γὰρ (for) ἐὰν (when,whenever)[31], rendered as "For as

---

[28] F. W. Grosheide, *Commentary on the First Epistle to the Corinthians. The New International Commentary on the New Testament* (Grand Rapids: Wm. B. Eerdmans Publishing Company, 1953, ninth printing, 1979), p. 272. Grosheide continues: Further comparison shows that in none of the gospels is there anything corresponding to 1 Cor. 11:26. It is probable,therefore, that at least the words at the beginning of vs. 26 are words of Paul, the more so because those words seem to be an elaboration of the preceding thoughts.

[29] , J. M. Van Cangh, "Le Texte Primitif De La Cène," in *The Corinthian Correspondence*, R. Bieringer, ed. (Leuven, Belgium: Leuven University Press, 1996) p. 630. *Chaque fois que vous mangerez ce pain et que vous boirez cette coupe. . .(propre a 1 Co 11,26) est manifestement un ajout secondaire influence par la pratique liturgique.*

[30] Hodge, *Commentary on the First Epistle to the Corinthians*, p. 229.

[31] *A Greek-English Lexicon of the New Testament and other Christian Literature (BDAG)*, p. 267. Bauer indicates that ἐὰν may be used not only as a 'marker of condition,' but also as a 'marker of the prospect of an action in a point of time coordinated with another point of time.'

often as. . ."[32] That is, every time the Corinthian body gathers together intending to observe the Supper, what is supposed to happen is proclamation. Again, Paul's choice of words drives the reader's attention to the twin verbs of repeated action, emphasizing the receiving of the bread and cup, while also connecting those actions to the result – the third repeated action verb καταγγέλλετε – *proclaiming.*

And what is proclaimed whenever the Corinthian Christians gather together and eat the bread and drink the cup? The atoning death of the Lord Jesus Christ, which is the heart of the gospel! Paul arranged the phrases in the second half of verse 26 in order to bring this point into predominance. Whenever on the occasions the Corinthians engage in celebrating the Lord's Supper, whenever they eat the bread and drink the cup, it is "the Lord's death (they) proclaim until he comes." In fact perhaps modern English translations would do more justice to Paul's intentions and rhetorical flow if verse 26 captured the same order. Instead of, for example, the English Standard Version's:

> For as often as **you eat** this *bread* and **drink** the *cup*, **you proclaim** the Lord's death until he comes."[33]

> Paul should be rendered in English as:

> For as often as (or *whenever*) **you eat** this *bread* and **drink** *the cup*, (*it is*) ***the Lord's death*** **you proclaim**, until he comes.

If Paul intended for the Corinthian officers, the readers, and the hearers of his admonition on the Supper to understand his use of καταγγέλλετε (proclamation) as a 'separate' action, equivalent to the previous pair (eating, drinking), then why write his explanation such that it flows as though the pair of actions together *result* in the third action? Why separate the first two visual, symbolic, and participatory actions from the action of proclamation using Paul's phrase concerning *the Lord's death*? Word

---

32 Thiselton, *The First Epistle to the Corinthians*, pp. 886. Thiselton prefers "as many times as," noting that "as often as" carries the disadvantage of perhaps seeming to introduce unintended nuances of frequency or regularity.

33 Most current, popularly accepted English language versions employ this wording (i.e. *American Standard Version, English Standard Version, Holman Christian Standard Bible, New American Standard Bible, New International Version, New King James Version,* and the *Revised Standard Version*). Even the old King James Version employed the same rendering, inverting the order of Paul's language: *ye do shew the Lord's death till he come.*

order and phrase structure in this passage seem to indicate that in the Corinthians regular doing of A + B, C is the result, where A is eating the bread, B is drinking the cup, and C is proclaiming the Lord's death. To celebrate the Lord's Supper as the Lord has instructed is in effect to proclaim the Lord's death – to proclaim the gospel. As F. W. Grosheide writes in his commentary on this verse:

> *Ye proclaim* refers to the same thing *as in remembrance of Me*. Holy Communion shall be served in remembrance of Him, according to His own commandment. This can be done because every Communion proclaims His death. By speaking of proclaiming Jesus' death Paul implies that the Lord's Supper is not just a meal in commemoration of the Lord but also a meal of confession. He that comes to the Lord's table declares that he not only believes that Christ died to pay for the sins of His people, but that he also believes that Christ lives and that His death has significance for all times. This is implied in the use of the word "*Lord*" in *the Lord's death*, for it points to the glorified Lord in heaven.[34]

In exhorting the Corinthians to celebrate the Supper, *as often as*, in other words, as a repeated action of regular devotion to Jesus and remembrance of his death into the future, Paul provides for only one future contingency[35] which will bring about an end to their sacramental observances. They are to *eat this bread and drink the cup* in proclamation of the Lord's death, *until he comes* (ἄχρι οὗ ἔλθῃ).[36] Thus for Paul, the Supper includes an eschatological dimension in its proclamation of the gospel, as well as accomplishing a remembrance of the prior atonement event.[37] Leonhard Goppelt writes of this repeated action with a single *expiration* factor, " 'The Lord's death is proclaimed,' i.e. becomes effective in a current sense, 'until he comes' by means of the whole sacrament and not merely by means of the words spoken during it."[38]

---

[34] Grosheide, *Commentary on the First Epistle to the Corinthians*, p. 273.

[35] Daniel B. Wallace, *Greek Grammar Beyond the Basics*, p. 479. Wallace identifies Paul's subjunctive usage of ἔλθῃ here as part of an indefinite temporal clause. This is defined as using the subjunctive after a *temporal adverb* meaning *until* (e.g., ἕως, ἄχρι, μέχρι), . . . It indicates a future contingency from the perspective of the time of the main verb.

[36] F. Blass and A. Debrunner, *A Greek Grammar of the New Testament and Other Early Christian Literature*, Robert W. Funk trans., ed. (Chicago: University of Chicago Press, 1961, 5th ed. 1973), pp. 192 – 193. 383 (2): Where the subjunctive appears ἄν is at times omitted with ἕως and probably always with ἕως οὗ (ὅτου), ἄχρις (οὗ), μέχρις (οὗ).

[37] Reymond, *A New Systematic Theology of the Christian Faith*, p. 965. While the Supper (καταγγέλλετε) proclaims Christ's sacrificial death for the church, 1 Corinthians 11:26 "also gives to the Supper an eschatological orientation."

[38] Leonhard Goppelt, *Apostolic and Post-Apostolic Times*, translated by Robert A. Guelich (Grand Rapids: Baker Book House, 1977, 2nd ed. 1980), p. 220.

As we move from the immediate context of verse 26 into the near context of the pericope of verses 23 – 26, which contain Paul's full presentation of the Supper, the importance of the visual, material elements of the bread and the cup, and the construct of *participation* (eating and drinking) interpreted in verse 26 are confirmed, along with the use of Jesus' words of institution.

This is evident in Paul's recitation of Jesus' words, the explanatory language necessary in order to contextualize the bread, the cup, and the participation of the celebrants who receive them:

> For I received from the Lord what I also delivered to you, that the Lord Jesus on the night when he was betrayed took bread, and when he had given thanks, he broke it, and said, "This is my body which is for you. Do this in remembrance of me." In the same way also he took the cup, after supper, saying, "This cup is the new covenant in my blood. Do this, as often as you drink it, in remembrance of me."

The order of expressions and phrases of the English here maintain the flow of the Greek for verses 23 – 25. First, Paul emphasizes that the words of institution he declared to the Corinthians came to him from the Lord. He, as God's minister, had not taught them sacramental doctrine which he had developed, but rather had faithfully repeated the liturgical language just as it was conveyed to him.

After reciting the source and reminding the believers in Corinth of his involvement in teaching them concerning the Supper, Paul recites the earliest surviving form for the Sacrament. This form emphasizes three things about Communion for those who read it, or hear it as celebrants; the sacrificial death of Jesus, the symbolic nature of the bread and the cup, and that through participation (*this do. . .*) remembrance of Jesus' atonement is accomplished.

These three aspects of the Communion celebration are heightened through a repetitious structure in the twin phrases Jesus uses as preserved by the Apostle:

> The bread: Τοῦτό μού ἐστιν τὸ σῶμα τὸ ὑπὲρ ὑμῶν· **τοῦτο ποιεῖτε εἰς τὴν ἐμὴν ἀνάμνησιν**.

> The cup: Τοῦτο τὸ ποτήριον ἡ καινὴ διαθήκη ἐστὶν ἐν τῷ ἐμῷ αἵματι· **τοῦτο ποιεῖτε, ὁσάκις ἐὰν πίνητε, εἰς τὴν ἐμὴν ἀνάμνησιν**.

In each phrase, a physical element, first the bread (equated with Jesus' body) and then the cup (equated with Jesus' blood of the new covenant) are infused with rich symbolic significance, as visually representing the atoning death of Christ. While the thoughts expressed of sacramental correspondence between the elements mentioned and Jesus' person frame the first phrase of each pair, it is the second phrase in each pair which are identical, with the exception of the insertion in the second of the pair of the phrase ὁσάκις ἐὰν πίνητε (*as often as you drink it*). Written, or spoken in this way, the emphasis falls upon the elements, their symbolic correspondence with Jesus' body and blood, and the regular participation by celebrants – in remembrance of Christ.

Remembrance (ἀνάμνησιν) is underscored by Paul through its repetition and its placement here in both phrases. This remembrance accomplished through the Supper observance is part of what Paul is referring to when he later writes of the proclamation of the Lord's death (verse 26). Remembrance in this sacral sense flows from participation, as Arthur Patzia notes:

> By participating "in remembrance of me" the believer looks *back* to the cross and reflects on the broken body and shed blood of the Lord. This dimension is meant to "recall" the passion of the Lord in such a way that he becomes present to the believer. It is a sacred moment to thank God for the redemptive work of Christ.[39]

And what of this phrase inserted in the second sentence of the pair (verse 25), ὁσάκις ἐὰν πίνητε (as *often as you drink it*)? While this phrase does break the repetitive flow in verse 25 when compared to verse 24, it also is picked up by the Apostle Paul for the connecting link between the tradition he received from the Lord into his theological summation concerning the Supper's impact in verse 26. Paul alters the phrase slightly in order to maintain the same order for the distribution of the elements as Jesus originally prescribed it, ὁσάκις (γὰρ) ἐὰν ἐσθίητε (*for as often as you eat*).

From a rhetorical structural analysis, the phrase "as often as," seems to function as a bridge between the words of institution given by Christ into the interpretive, pastoral,

---

[39] Arthur G. Patzia, *The Emergence of the Church: Context, Growth, Leadership & Worship* (Downers Grove, IL: InterVarsity Press, 2001), p. 229.

and theological statement Paul then makes to underscore its importance to the Corinthians. The chart below provides some diagramming of the flow of thought in verses 23 – 26:

A. Paul reminds the Corinthians (vs. 23a) he taught them what he had received from the Lord.	23 Ἐγὼ γὰρ παρέλαβον ἀπὸ τοῦ κυρίου, ὃ καὶ παρέδωκα ὑμῖν,
B. Paul repeats for the Corinthians the sacramental words of institution he received from the Lord, phrases which emphasize the ongoing use of the elements of the bread and the cup, their symbolic correspondence with Christ's body and blood, and the concepts of ἀνάμνησιν (*remembrance*) and εὐχαριστήσας (*thanksgiving*). There is also the concept of the καινὴ διαθήκη (*new covenant*) meal.	ὅτι ὁ κύριος Ἰησοῦς ἐν τῇ νυκτὶ ᾗ παρεδίδετο ἔλαβεν ἄρτον 24 καὶ εὐχαριστήσας ἔκλασεν καὶ εἶπεν· Τοῦτό μού ἐστιν τὸ σῶμα τὸ ὑπὲρ ὑμῶν· τοῦτο ποιεῖτε εἰς τὴν ἐμὴν ἀνάμνησιν. 25 ὡσαύτως καὶ τὸ ποτήριον μετὰ τὸ δειπνῆσαι, λέγων· Τοῦτο τὸ ποτήριον ἡ καινὴ διαθήκη ἐστὶν ἐν τῷ ἐμῷ αἵματι· τοῦτο ποιεῖτε, **ὁσάκις ἐὰν πίνητε**, εἰς τὴν ἐμὴν ἀνάμνησιν.
A. Paul uses Jesus' phrase as a link between the sacramental tradition he received from Christ (vss. 23b – 25) and his pastoral, interpretive exhortation on the Supper (vs. 26).	26 **ὁσάκις γὰρ ἐὰν ἐσθίητε** τὸν ἄρτον τοῦτον καὶ τὸ ποτήριον πίνητε, τὸν θάνατον τοῦ κυρίου καταγγέλλετε, ἄχρι οὗ ἔλθῃ.

More exegetical clues as to Paul's meaning when he uses καταγγέλλετε in verse 26 are available in the wider context of the Apostle's entire Lord's Supper admonition and exhortation throughout the second half of chapter 11, in verses 17 – 34a. The section begins with a strong admonition to the Corinthians about their defective Lord's Supper celebrations. And Paul's emphasis in verses 17 – 22 is upon outward congregational behavior during their fellowship meals – behavior which publicly reflects their factionalist divisions and also indicates serious issues of the heart among their members:

> But in the following instructions I do not commend you, because when you come together it is not for the better but for the worse. For, in the first place, when you come together as a church, I hear that there are divisions among you. And I believe it in part, for there must be factions among you in order that those who are genuine among you may be recognized. When you come together, it is not the Lord's supper that you eat. For in eating, each one goes ahead with his own meal. One goes hungry, another gets drunk. What!

> Do you not have houses to eat and drink in? Or do you despise the church of God and humiliate those who have nothing? What shall I say to you? Shall I commend you in this? No, I will not.

Paul, driven to great disappointment and concern as an apostle and a pastor for the Corinthians, wastes no time in responding to the reports he has received about their Lord Supper celebrations. He does not begin by reminding them of the things he had taught them concerning Communion. He does not begin with the Eucharistic words of Jesus, nor his own sacramental theology. He begins as any passionate shepherd concerned for a local church might begin – sharply defining the presenting problem. As the Corinthians gather together for their agape meals, which include a celebration of the Lord's Supper, their behavior toward one another shows contempt for the church of God – the body of Christ – and their contempt for their fellow Christians who adhere to a different faction or perhaps hail from a lower economic strata of Corinthian society. In fact, the way the assembled church observed the Supper "defeated the very proclamation of the Lord, whose death was 'for us' and 'for the other' as one Body (12:12). It explicitly contradicted and undermined the very purpose of the Lord's Supper (οὐκ εἰς τὸ κρεῖσσον ἀλλὰ εἰς τὸ ἧσσον συνέρχεσθε,v. 17).[40]

The language Paul uses here draws attention to these divisions (σχίσματα), calling them αἱρέσεις (*factions*), "a term which draws attention to the leaders of the cliques, who were perhaps guilty of some deliberate interference with the Eucharistic teaching which he had previously (verse 23) imparted to the Corinthian church."[41] According to Paul, the Corinthians' gatherings around the table for a meal in no way approximated proper Lord's Supper observance.

It is evident from the text that this gathering of the Corinthians was an agape or fellowship meal because Paul describes, "each one go(ing) ahead with his own meal," and remarks that, "another gets drunk," indicating an abundance of food and drink.

---

[40] Thiselton, *The First Epistle to the Corinthians*, p. 850. Continuing on page 851, Thiselton sees the focus of proclaiming the Lord's death, as a parallel to the central point in 1:18 – 25. Just as the splits of chapters 1 – 4 undermine the heart of the gospel, so also the practices which surround the sharing of the meal (in Corinth) which (in Paul's view) points above all to the "for others" of the Lord's death undermine the very heart of why the worshipping community celebrates the Lord's Supper at all.

[41] A. J. B. Higgins, *The Lord's Supper in the New Testament* (London: SCM Press LTD, 1952, reprint 1956), p. 71.

The meal typically included a celebration of the Lord's Supper, a tradition that originated with the first gatherings of believers in Jerusalem as reported in the book of Acts. The Apostle Paul is grieved and exasperated that when the Corinthians gather for their agape meal and participate in the Lord's Supper (κυριακὸν δεῖπνον) they actually show contempt (*despise*) toward the church of God (τῆς ἐκκλησίας τοῦ θεοῦ), calling attention to the divisions among them, and denying the unity of the family of God in Christ.

How utterly horrified this shepherd of the Corinthian flock must have been when he realized how very much they had distorted the meaning and misused the Supper tradition he had passed along to them! Had they forgotten everything Paul had labored so hard to teach them? David Horrell recounts the framework of Paul's original pastoral instructions to the Corinthians:

> Paul did not simply instruct the Corinthian believers to get together regularly for a meal. They were to understand their meal as an imitation of the meal of Jesus with his disciples 'on the night in which he was betrayed' (11:23). In particular the meal was to include the sharing of bread and wine, understood as a sharing (κοινωνία) in the body and blood of Christ (11:23 – 25; 10:16). The fundamental rationale for the gathering was a 'memorial' of Jesus. It proclaimed his death 'until he comes (11:26). They heard Jesus' command as addressed to them: 'do this in memory of me' (11:24). Again, central elements of the Christian story – the self-giving death of Christ – are recalled, enacted, and embodied in this ritual celebration.[42]

This group of Christians had not only failed to properly carry out Paul's instruction, not only forgotten his exhortations about the Supper and table fellowship. They had also participated in the breakdown of biblical unity, a breakdown which negates the genuineness of their Communion celebration. Thus Paul is compelled in the following section (verses 23 – 26) to remind his readers about the original context in which the Lord Jesus inaugurated the Supper, the proper words and elements, the importance of regular participation, and the importance of the sacrament as another means of proclaiming the gospel (*the Lord's death until he comes*).

---

[42] David G. Horell, *The Social Ethos of the Corinthian Correspondence: Interests and Ideology from 1 Corinthians to 1 Clement* (Edinburgh: T & T Clark, 1996), p. 87.

Analysis of the third section within this Lord's Supper pericope, verses 27 – 34, lends further weight to the interpretation that Paul is using καταγγέλλετε in verse 26 with reference to the symbolic elements and the idea of participation, as well as the words of institution. In verses 27 – 29 Paul returns, albeit more broadly in scope, to the pastoral concern he previously raised in verses 17 – 22:

> Whoever, therefore, eats the bread or drinks the cup of the Lord in an unworthy manner will be guilty concerning the body and blood of the Lord. Let a person examine himself, then, and so eat of the bread and drink of the cup. For anyone who eats and drinks without discerning the body eats and drinks judgment on himself.

Now some interpreters have emphasized that what Paul is addressing in this portion of the pericope is a failure on the part of many of the Corinthians to discern Christ's presence – either physically or spiritually in the Sacrament. While there is an element of this concern represented in verse 27, it is quite clear that when the Apostle speaks of eating or drinking "in an unworthy manner," he is again taking aim at the presenting problem in Corinth that is denying the gospel during their Communion – the lack of biblical love for their fellow believers who make up the body of Christ in their community. Fee makes an insightful statement about this when he observes:

> If from this section we do not discover the answer to everything that piques our curiosity, we are indeed given more than enough to "examine" us as to our obedience at the Lord's Table. One wonders whether our making the text deal with self-examination has not served to deflect the greater concern of the text, that we give more attention at the Lord's Supper to our relationships with one another in the body of Christ.[43]

The question is further answered when verses 33 – 34 are studied in light of verses 17 – 22 and verses 27 – 29. Paul emphasizes the importance of "waiting for one another," and that, "if anyone is hungry, let them eat at home." The pastoral issue throughout the pericope remains focused upon the failure of the Corinthians to proclaim the death of Christ when they eat the bread and drink the cup, because of their factions and their disregard for one another.

The rhetorical flow within this pericope may be diagrammed in this way:

---

[43] Fee, *The First Epistle to the Corinthians*, p. 569.

Rhetorical Structure Notations (A – B – A)	Text of the Three Lord's Supper Sections
A. The Apostle Paul begins this section concerning the Lord's Supper by pastorally addressing the source of the problem as he understands it from reports he has received. When the Corinthians assemble (ἐκκλησίᾳ) together, there are factions (σχίσματα) among them. These divisions become apparent when there is a lack of love shown during the agape meals, which include the Lord's Supper (κυριακὸν δεῖπνον). Thus in effect, Paul says the Corinthians do not really celebrate the Lord's Supper. (*The immediate context/pericope*)	17 Τοῦτο δὲ παραγγέλλων οὐκ ἐπαινῶ ὅτι οὐκ εἰς τὸ κρεῖσσον ἀλλὰ εἰς τὸ ἧσσον συνέρχεσθε. 18 πρῶτον μὲν γὰρ συνερχομένων ὑμῶν ἐν ἐκκλησίᾳ ἀκούω σχίσματα ἐν ὑμῖν ὑπάρχειν, καὶ μέρος τι πιστεύω. 19 δεῖ γὰρ καὶ αἱρέσεις ἐν ὑμῖν εἶναι, ἵνα καὶ οἱ δόκιμοι φανεροὶ γένωνται ἐν ὑμῖν. 20 συνερχομένων οὖν ὑμῶν ἐπὶ τὸ αὐτὸ οὐκ ἔστιν κυριακὸν δεῖπνον φαγεῖν, 21 ἕκαστος γὰρ τὸ ἴδιον δεῖπνον προλαμβάνει ἐν τῷ φαγεῖν, καὶ ὃς μὲν πεινᾷ, ὃς δὲ μεθύει. 22 μὴ γὰρ οἰκίας οὐκ ἔχετε εἰς τὸ ἐσθίειν καὶ πίνειν; ἢ τῆς ἐκκλησίας τοῦ θεοῦ καταφρονεῖτε, καὶ καταισχύνετε τοὺς μὴ ἔχοντας; τί εἴπω ὑμῖν; ἐπαινέσω ὑμᾶς; ἐν τούτῳ οὐκ ἐπαινῶ.
B. Paul then moves to corrective application in verses 23 – 26. It is important for the Corinthians to remember that what Paul had passed along to them he had received from the Lord. He reminds his readers that the Lord's Supper was instituted on the night that the Lord was betrayed. **And, after describing the actions of the Supper – eating the bread and drinking of the cup – the Apostle emphasizes that "as often as you eat the bread and drink the cup, the death of the Lord you proclaim (καταγγέλλετε), until he comes."**	**23 Ἐγὼ γὰρ παρέλαβον ἀπὸ τοῦ κυρίου, ὃ καὶ παρέδωκα ὑμῖν, ὅτι ὁ κύριος Ἰησοῦς ἐν τῇ νυκτὶ ᾗ παρεδίδετο ἔλαβεν ἄρτον 24 καὶ εὐχαριστήσας ἔκλασεν καὶ εἶπεν· Τοῦτό μού ἐστιν τὸ σῶμα τὸ ὑπὲρ ὑμῶν· τοῦτο ποιεῖτε εἰς τὴν ἐμὴν ἀνάμνησιν. 25 ὡσαύτως καὶ τὸ ποτήριον μετὰ τὸ δειπνῆσαι, λέγων· Τοῦτο τὸ ποτήριον ἡ καινὴ διαθήκη ἐστὶν ἐν τῷ ἐμῷ αἵματι· τοῦτο ποιεῖτε, ὁσάκις ἐὰν πίνητε, εἰς τὴν ἐμὴν ἀνάμνησιν. 26 ὁσάκις γὰρ ἐὰν ἐσθίητε τὸν ἄρτον τοῦτον καὶ τὸ ποτήριον πίνητε, τὸν θάνατον τοῦ κυρίου καταγγέλλετε, ἄχρι οὗ ἔλθῃ.**
A. Beginning with verse 27, Paul returns to the presenting problem having to do with a lack of brotherly love and awareness when gathered together for fellowship and the Supper. He concludes with a stern word of warning concerning the consequences of failing to discern the body, and exhorts the Corinthians to wait for one another when they come together for the agape meal and	27 Ὥστε ὃς ἂν ἐσθίῃ τὸν ἄρτον ἢ πίνῃ τὸ ποτήριον τοῦ κυρίου ἀναξίως, ἔνοχος ἔσται τοῦ σώματος καὶ τοῦ αἵματος τοῦ κυρίου. 28 δοκιμαζέτω δὲ ἄνθρωπος ἑαυτόν, καὶ οὕτως ἐκ τοῦ ἄρτου ἐσθιέτω καὶ ἐκ τοῦ ποτηρίου πινέτω· 29 ὁ γὰρ ἐσθίων καὶ πίνων κρίμα ἑαυτῷ ἐσθίει καὶ πίνει μὴ διακρίνων τὸ σῶμα. 30 διὰ τοῦτο ἐν ὑμῖν πολλοὶ ἀσθενεῖς καὶ ἄρρωστοι καὶ κοιμῶνται ἱκανοί. 31 εἰ δὲ ἑαυτοὺς διεκρίνομεν, οὐκ ἂν ἐκρινόμεθα· 32 κρινόμενοι δὲ ὑπὸ κυρίου

the Sacrament.	παιδευόμεθα, ἵνα μὴ σὺν τῷ κόσμῳ κατακριθῶμεν. 33 Ὥστε, ἀδελφοί μου, συνερχόμενοι εἰς τὸ φαγεῖν ἀλλήλους ἐκδέχεσθε. 34 εἴ τις πεινᾷ, ἐν οἴκῳ ἐσθιέτω, ἵνα μὴ εἰς κρίμα συνέρχησθε. Τὰ δὲ λοιπὰ ὡς ἂν ἔλθω διατάξομαι.

What Paul has accomplished in 1 Corinthians 11:17 – 34 is a three-part pastoral triage and treatment for the Lord's Supper abuses taking place in Corinth. He begins (A) by identifying the problem. He continues in verses 23 – 26 (B) by presenting the proper way of taking the Supper – with the crucial interpretive conclusion that whenever the Sacrament is celebrated properly the gospel is proclaimed. And then Paul concludes the section by returning to the Corinthian errors in verses 27 – 34 (A), sharpening his rebuke with a warning of judgment and exhorting them to wait for one another in table fellowship.

It should be pointed out that other schemas have been proposed for the rhetorical structure of this chapter 11 pericope. James M. Hamilton Jr., writing in, *The Lord's Supper: Remembering and Proclaiming Christ Until He Comes*, proposes a chiastic structure subdivided into four, rather than three parts:

> Whether or not Paul intended a chiastic structure to 1 Cor 11:17 – 34, the text seems to fall out that way. The first section, 11:17 – 22, describes the Corinthians' problematic behavior, and the last section 11:33 – 34 provides the specific remedy to that abuse. Similarly, the two middle sections correspond to one another, with the recitation of the institution of the Lord's Supper in 11:23 – 26 matched by genera; instructions on taking the Supper in 11:27 – 32.[44]

And the final words of Paul in this pericope (verse 34) may also indicate the first written hint of a shift, from celebrating Communion within the regular agape fellowship meals, toward incorporating ongoing Lord's Supper observance within the framework of the Lord's Day worship service:

[44] James M. Hamilton, "The Lord's Supper in Paul: An Identity-Forming Proclamation of the Gospel," in *The Lord's Supper: Remembering and Proclaiming Christ Until He Comes*, edited by Thomas R. Schreiner and Matthew R. Crawford (Nashville: B & H Publishing, 2010), p. 92.

> if anyone is hungry, let him eat at home—so that when you come together it will not be for judgment. About the other things I will give directions when I come.

Certainly one way for the body of believers in Corinth to reduce the temptation to mistreat one another during the Lord's Supper would be to remove the celebration from within a highly-charged socially stratified meal setting and unite its proclaiming purpose with the proclamation of the gospel through preaching in the weekly worship setting. In doing this, audible proclamation of Jesus' atoning death would be united with the symbolic, visual, and tactile proclamation through the Sacrament. This is argued by A. J. B. Higgins in his, *The Lord's Supper in the New Testament*:

> It is very probable, . . . , that what Paul did waa to lay a renewed emphasis on the remembrance of the death of Christ which was already present, but which at Corinth was in danger of being forgotten – not to mention brotherly generosity and good manners. In seeking to correct these abuses by counseling the hungry to eat at home first, Paul took the initial step in the separation or the specifically Eucharistic celebration from the meal of which it formed part; and this celebration, consisting of 'this bread' and 'the cup of the Lord' (1 Cor. 11.27), was to 'proclaim the Lord's death until he comes'.[45]

In review, starting with the usual semantic range of καταγγέλλετε as rendered in English as "proclaim," and examining the grammatical structure as well as the rhetorical thought flow of the pericope of 1 Corinthians 11:17 – 34, there are a multitude of exegetical 'clues' as to the primary referents involved in the Lord's Supper functioning as gospel proclamation. It is evident that Paul intends the Corinthians to understand that whenever they gather together and celebrate the Lord's Supper, eating the bread and drinking the cup, under the rubric of Jesus' words of institution, they are in fact *proclaiming the Lord's death until he comes*. The use of the elements of the Table, as Jesus instructed, received with proper discernment of the unity of the body of Christ, represented by the brothers and sisters present for the meal, proclaims the gospel.

Moving further away from 1 Corinthians 11, verse 26, and outside the presenting larger segment of verses 17 – 34, there are indications elsewhere in the epistle concerning Paul's understanding of the importance of the Supper. In chapter 10 of 1 Corinthians, the Apostle warns the church in Corinth not to be double-minded,

---

[45] Higgins, *The Lord's Supper in the New Testament*, p. 63.

seeking to serve both God and the pagan gods so prominent in their culture. To make his pastoral point on this issue, Paul contrasts the celebration of the Lord's Supper with that of pagan rituals. He begins in verses 14 – 17:

> Therefore, my beloved, flee from idolatry. I speak as to sensible people; judge for yourselves what I say. 16 The cup of blessing that we bless, is it not a participation in the blood of Christ? The bread that we break, is it not a participation in the body of Christ? Because there is one bread, we who are many are one body, for we all partake of the one bread.

Notice that Paul here emphasizes the participation of the local members of the body of Christ in the Lord's Supper. As they receive the cup, by faith they are participating in the blood of Christ and as they receive the broken bread they are participating in the body of Christ. Paul uses the Greek term κοινωνία in these verses, which the ESV renders as "participation." Closer study of this term indicates that the meaning typically involves "close association or fellowship,"[46] as Paul uses the word earlier at the beginning of this pastoral letter in 1:9:

> πιστὸς ὁ θεὸς δι' οὗ ἐκλήθητε εἰς **κοινωνίαν** τοῦ υἱοῦ αὐτοῦ Ἰησοῦ Χριστοῦ τοῦ κυρίου ἡμῶν.
>
> God is faithful, by whom you were called into the fellowship of his Son, Jesus Christ our Lord.

Yet the term may be used by Paul in a slightly different way as well. Sometimes the Apostle uses the word κοινωνία with the meaning "to share," as in sharing "one's possessions with the implication of some kind of joint participation and mutual interest."[47] Whether Paul is using κοινωνία in connection with engaging in the celebration of Communion in the sense of relational fellowship, or that of sharing in joint participation in the Eucharist tradition, the conclusion that must be drawn is that in Paul's pastoral theology the Lord's Supper visually proclaims the atoning death of Christ and the unity or fellowship of those who believe in him as they participate in the bread and the cup. "And the Lord's Supper (in its original setting), after the proper Pauline warnings had been issued, seems to have been celebrated in a very simple way, usually in connection with the eating together of the common meal (the

---

[46] Louw & Nida, *Greek –English Lexicon of the New Testament*, v. 1; A, 34:5, pp. 446 – 447.
[47] Louw & Nida, p. 569. Reference is made to Paul's use of κοινωνία in 2 Corinthians 8:4 and Galatians 6:6.

Agape feast) and unaccompanied by the tinkling of bells, the swinging of censors of incense, and priestly and lay genuflection before the elements."[48]

In conclusion, the Apostle Paul brought the concerns of a pastor to bear upon the congregation in Corinth, Greece in the mid-first century. There were severe divisions within the body of believers, who aligned themselves into various factions under the guise of charismatic leaders. These divisions undermined the unity of the body of Christ and gave the lie to their testimony of the transforming truth of the gospel. Factionalism in Corinth infected every aspect of the church's life – relationships, ministries, and especially worship. Paul understood the grave danger upon receiving reports from eyewitnesses to these distressing trends.

By the time Paul reaches the portion of his 1 Corinthians pastoral letter known as chapter 11, the Apostle is commending, condemning, and exhorting the believers with respect to worship. The second half of this chapter begins with a severe admonition about how the divisiveness within the church undermined their celebrations of the Lord's Supper. For Paul it was impossible to properly participate in the Lord's Supper while refusing to acknowledge and to live-out the unity of the body which stemmed from the gospel. Thus, it was also impossible for a divided congregation to proclaim the death of Christ through their celebration of the Lord's Supper. Any attempt to participate in the Supper without discerning the body of Christ – without gospel-reconciled relationships among the brothers and sisters – would in fact invite the judgment of God for having despised his church.

Paul's summary of the importance of the Lord's Supper in verse 26 of chapter 11 emphasizes the celebration of Communion as "proclamation" (καταγγέλλετε) of the gospel, which for Paul is shorthanded as "the death of the Lord" (τὸν θάνατον τοῦ κυρίου). Yet included in this gospel proclamation, along with remembrance of Christ's past atonement are current presence, and eschatological expectation.[49]

---

[48] Robert L. Reymond, *Paul Missionary Theologian* (Ross-shire, UK: Christian Focus, 2000), p. 525.

[49] Guillermo J. Garlatti, "La eucaristia como memoria y proclamacion de la muerte del Senor (Aspectos de la celebracion de la cena del Senor segun San Pablo)," in *Revista Bíblica 47* no. 1 – 2 (1985), abstract. ". . . proclamation of the Lord's death is connected simultaneously with the historical event of the past, with the present Church, and with the eschatological manifestation of the New Covenant. And that through faith. This is how it carries out the

This is the aspect of the already and not yet displayed in the Supper. "Paul in effect . . .makes the Lord's Supper the cord which binds the already-not yet tension together and keeps it from falling apart."[50]

Based upon Paul's pairing of the actions and elements of eating the bread (ἐσθίητε τὸν ἄρτον) and drinking the cup (ποτήριον πίνητε) (verse 26), immediately following his reminder to the Corinthians of Jesus' words of institution (verses 23 – 25), the *proclamation* the Apostle speaks of as taking place *as often as* (ὁσάκις γὰρ ἐὰν) the Corinthians celebrate the Lord's Supper includes the use of the symbolic elements and the actions involved in participating in the Supper, as well as the necessary contextualizing words of institution.

For Paul, writing as a pastor as well as an apostle, deeply concerned for the believing community in Corinth, it was grievous that when this church regularly gathered for their agape meal and celebrated the Lord's Supper, their factions, divisions, and lack of gospel-centered love for one another were in fact proclaimed, rather than the death of Christ. As James Dunn notes:

> ...the Lord's Supper does this both by re(-)presenting the death of Christ and by proclaiming that death in and through shared celebration. And what it enshrines not least is the "for you" character of that death, the "new covenant" graciously given. It is above all, this "for you" character which lay at the heart of their shared meal which should have prevented the selfish abuse that so marred the Corinthians' coming together to eat.[51]

---

proclamation of the death of the Lord (v.26). And so, in Pauline theology, the proclamation of the gospel by word, whose content is the death and resurrection, reaches its maximum expression in the celebration of the meal." . . . *en tanto que proclamacion de la muerte del Senor, se conecta simultaneamente con el acontecimiento historico del pasado, con el presente eclesial y con la manifestacion escatologica de la Nueva Alianza. Y ello a traves de la fe. Es asi como se lleva a cabo la proclamacion de la muerte del Senor (v.26). Y de esta manera, para la teologia paulina, la proclamacion del evangelio por la palabra, cuyo contenido es la muerte y resurreccion del Senor, llega a su expresion maxima en la celebracion de la cena.*

[50] James D. G. Dunn, *The Theology of Paul the Apostle* (Grand Rapids: William B. Eerdmans, 1998), p. 622.

[51] Dunn, *The Theology of Paul the Apostle*, p. 622.

It was the very death of Christ Jesus, offered as an atoning sacrifice, that was the basis for the Lord's Supper. And Christ's death with all its unifying power within a believing assembly should be proclaimed as well – proclaimed through biblical unity within the body – as the brothers and sisters receive the bread and the cup. As Anthony Thiselton so forcefully puts it:

> It is no accident that καταγγέλλετε means **you are proclaiming** or *you are preaching*. By **eating this bread** and **drinking the cup** the whole assembly stands in a witness box and pulpit to proclaim their "part" (cf. in 10:16, κοινωνία objective sharing with a stake; and μετέχειν in 10:17, being an involved participant. . .).[52]

This is of such paramount importance to the Apostle in addressing the disunity of the Corinthians' Communion celebration that he introduces the Lord's Supper pericope with a firm admonishment of their usual divisive behavior (verses 17 – 22) and concludes the pericope with a fierce warning of judgment and exhortation to change, returning in effect to the same pastoral issue (verses 27 – 34). Carefully placed between these two admonitions are the key elements for the proper and powerful use of the Supper (verses 23 – 26). And within Paul's concluding summary of the importance of the Supper (verse 26), proclamation of the death of Christ through eating the bread and drinking the cup are given the greatest of importance.

Based upon the exegesis of 1 Corinthians 11:26 and the surrounding verses of Paul's Lord's Supper pericope, including the grammatical usage and rhetorical flow, and taking into account the importance of the specific historical and cultural milieu involving the church in Corinth, it is quite clear that the Apostle understands the entirety of the Sacrament – words, elements, actions, and genuine participation – not simply a *separately understood* verbal narrative – as powerfully proclaiming the gospel of Jesus Christ. As Gaventa writes, "Not only is it possible lexicographically that Paul understands the Supper itself as an act of proclamation, but the context and Paul's comments elsewhere make this the more compelling interpretation."[53] And this act of proclamation through the celebration of the Supper engages all those who partake by faith, just as Berkouwer notes:

---

[52] Thiselton, *The First Epistle to the Corinthians*, p. 887. Emphasis is the author's.
[53] Gaventa, " 'You Proclaim the Lord's Death': 1 Corinthians 11:26 and Paul's Understanding of Worship," p. 383.

> (Paul) refers in any case to the celebration of the Lord's Supper as announcement, as a proclaiming act wherein the community in faith gives expression to the glorious and decisive significance of the death of Christ.[54]

Just as the Passover celebrations of Israel prefigured the Lord's Supper in proclaiming God's deliverance of his people, so the Supper proclaims God's deliverance of his people once for all through the death of Jesus Christ. Just as the Passover feast was a powerful weaving together of words, elements, actions, and genuine participation, so its New Testament replacement unites audible, contextualizing words of institution, the elements of the bread and the cup, the actions of breaking and blessing, and the importance of genuine participation. This is roughly the same point made by I. Howard Marshall in his work, *Last Supper and Lord's Supper*:

> To eat and drink at the Supper is to proclaim the death of the Lord. The Supper is a memorial of Jesus in that each time it takes place it transforms the participants into preachers. The word use (*katagello*) is one that is particularly associated with the proclamation of the gospel, and hence the Supper is an occasion and a means of preaching the good news. And the content of the saving message is the death of Jesus which is clearly in mind in the framework of the words of institution, 'on the night when he was betrayed', and in the interpretive sayings themselves. The significance of the Supper is that the bread and the cup point to the death of Jesus as a means of salvation, and thus proclaim to all who witness the Supper that Jesus died for them. This of course does not mean that it was simply the actions of distributing the elements and eating and drinking them that constituted the proclamation. The interpretive sayings constituted an essential part of the actions, so that, to use later terminology, the Word is a constitutive part of the Sacrament.[55]

Rediscovering and applying this biblically derived understanding of the Lord's Supper must affect the way ministers and congregations celebrate Communion. Particularly for Protestant Christians, comprehending and embracing the Lord's Supper as proclamation of the gospel of Jesus Christ will profoundly deepen appreciation for the Sacrament. And this will also heighten the importance of its frequent (preferably weekly) use as an additional means of proclamation, after pulpit

---

[54] G. C. Berkouwer, *The Sacraments* (Grand Rapids: William B. Eerdmans, 1969), p. 193.

[55] I. Howard Marshall, *Last Supper and Lord's Supper* (Grand Rapids: William B. Eerdmans, 1981, reprint 1982), p. 113.

preaching, for declaring the death of the Lord. Central to this biblical understanding is that all of the constitutive elements of the Supper – words of institution, symbolic elements of bread and cup, breaking and blessing, and faithful participation – unite sacramentally as proclamation of the Lord's death until he comes:

> Like the dramatic actions of the Hebrew prophets, it (the Lord's Supper) illustrates, and emphasizes, and impresses on the memory a special proof of God's care for His people. It is Christ's last and supreme parable; a parable not merely told but acted by Himself. He sets forth His own death, and shows that those who would profit by it must make it their own by faith and love. As Chrysostom says, 'We do not then offer a different sacrifice, as the high priest formerly did, but always the same: or rather, *we celebrate a memorial* of a sacrifice.'[56]

[56] A. Plummer, "Lord's Supper," in *A Dictionary of the Bible*, vol. III, James Hastings, ed (Edinburgh: T & T Clark, 1900, 11th impression, 1950), p. 149.

Likewise, too, through the person of Solomon the Holy Spirit forecasts a type of the sacrifice of our Lord which is to come, referring to a victim offered in sacrifice, to bread and wine, and even to an altar and the apostles. Wisdom, he says, has built her own home, supporting it with seven pillars. She has slaughtered her own sacrificial victims; she has mixed her own wine and she has prepared her own table. And she has sent forth her own servants, with loud proclamation inviting men to partake of her cup, saying, Whoever is simple-minded, she says, let him come to visit me. And to those who lack understanding she has said: Come and eat of my bread, and drink the wine which I have mixed for you." Solomon declares that the wine has been mixed, that is to say he prophetically foretells that the cup of the Lord is mixed with water and wine Hence, it becomes evident that in the passion of our Lord that was accomplished what had already been predicted.

(Cyprian of Carthage, *Epistle 63.5 to Caecilius, on the sacrament of the cup of the Lord.*)[57]

---

[57] Cyprian of Carthage, *The Letters of St. Cyprian of Carthage*, vol. 3, G. W. Clarke, ed. (Mahwah, NJ: Paulist Press, 1986), p. 100.

II

PROCLAMATION IN DECLINE: THE LORD'S SUPPER AND PROCLAMATION IN THE EARLY CHURCH

You gave food and drink to men for enjoyment, that they might give thanks to you. But to us you freely gave spiritual food and drink and life eternal through your Servant.

(*Didache*, ca AD 80 – 140)[58]

Exegetical work in 1 Corinthians 11:17 – 34 indicates that Paul preached and taught the Lord's Supper as a means of proclaiming the gospel of Jesus Christ's atoning death and its transforming power in the lives of those who believe. Offered in the earliest days of the church's development as part of the agape meals, the contextualizing words of institution, the symbolic elements of the bread and the cup, the actions of breaking and blessing, and the sincere participation of those who were gathered, made a powerful statement audibly, visually, and tactilely, in proclaiming the gospel.

Before applying this aspect of the mid-first century church's understanding of the Lord's Supper to present day Communion celebrations, an overview of the church's understanding and use of the Supper in the centuries between Paul's time and today will also be helpful. What trends in the church's teaching on the Sacrament and its methods for observing the Supper may be discerned? And did Paul's emphasis on the Sacrament as *proclamation of the gospel* remain an emphasis for the church in later generations?

There is, in the earliest stages of transition from Apostolic to post-Apostolic times, an important piece of correspondence preserved between the church in Rome and the church in Corinth. This work, known as *1 Clement*, provides the first post-biblical insight into the development of both the theology and the practice of the church.

---

[58] David W. Bercot, *A Dictionary of Early Christian Beliefs* (Peabody, MA: Hendrickson Publishers, Inc., 1998), p. 251.

As the work has been variously dated between AD 69 (based upon internal language, descriptions, and present tense concerning the Temple services in Jerusalem) and AD 95, *1 Clement* provides a bridge between the decades represented by the New Testament texts and the early to mid-second century.

However, although *1 Clement*, like the Pauline epistles, addresses many of the same issues of disruptive body life associated with church leadership, as well as reminding the Corinthians to look to Christ and his atoning sacrifice, there are no direct references to the Lord's Supper or the manner in which it was celebrated or understood. The closest *1 Clement* comes to using language associated with the Supper is its use of the words *eucharistein* (*to give thanks*) in two places: 38:2 and 4. While some Catholic and Orthodox scholars see much sacrificial language in *1 Clement* and construct a Clementine sacramental theology from their reconstructions, it is a tenuous theory at best.[59]

While *1 Clement* does not provide much help in seeking to understand how the Lord's Supper was practiced and understood in the post-Apostolic era, there are two other arguably very early documentary resources. These are the collection of letters authored by Ignatius of Antioch (ca AD 105 – 110) and also the *Didache* (variously dated to between ca AD 80 – 140). Moving ahead into the later second century, an assessment of the works of Justin Martyr (ca AD 150 – 160), Irenaeus (ca AD 180), and Clement of Alexandria (ca AD 195) provide information concerning the Supper with which the development of its theology and observance may be recovered.

Ignatius was bishop of Antioch in the first decade of the second century. Martyred during the violent persecution that was instituted under Trajan in approximately AD 110, his letters to various churches as he made his way to his execution in Rome have survived. These letters contain descriptions and instructions related to celebrating the Lord's Supper.

---

[59] Willy Rordorf, et al., *The Eucharist of the Early Christians*, translated by Matthew J. O'Connell (Collegeville, MN: The Liturgical Press, 1978), p. 25. George Blond, in his contribution to this work, argues that even if Clement does not use the terms that later became technical designations for the Eucharist, the reality is present in the letter as far as the sacrificial aspect is concerned.

In two of Ignatius' letters, to the churches in Smyrna and Philadelphia, the common concern expressed with reference to the Lord's Supper is that it be only considered a valid celebration if the appointed bishop for the area presided:

> Let that be deemed a proper Eucharist which is administered either by the bishop or by one to whom he has entrusted it. . .Apart from the bishop, it is not lawful to baptize or to celebrate an agape. (*To the Smyrnaeans* 6 – 8)[60]

Aside from what is obviously a much more *institutionalized* or ecclesiastical understanding of the Supper, what else can be gleaned from Ignatius' letters? In his the letter to the church in Smyrna, there are phrases used with reference to the Eucharist that seem to indicate a theological movement already in place within parts of the early church for nascent transubstantiation:

> They abstain from the Eucharist and from prayer, because they do not confess the Eucharist to be the flesh of our Savior Jesus Christ, which suffered for our sins, and which the Father, in his goodness, raised up again. Those, therefore, who speak against this gift of God, incur death in the midst of their disputes. Yet it would be better for them to treat it with respect, that they also might rise again. (*To the Smyrnaeans* 6 – 8)[61]

Around the same time as Ignatius' martyrdom, a Roman provincial governor, named Pliny the Younger, carried out an investigation of this illegal religion that Trajan sought to stamp out. In the course of his investigation, Pliny composed a letter to his emperor describing his findings about Christianity. Of interest to this Lord's Supper investigation is that Pliny reported the testimony of some who had formerly been Christians and who recanted under threat of torture. These findings included descriptions of early Christian practice:

> They affirmed, however, that the whole of their guilt, or error, was that they were in the habit of meeting on a certain fixed day before it was light, when they sang in alternate verses a hymn to Christ, as to a god, and bound themselves by a solemn oath. . .Afterward it was their custom to disperse,

---

[60] Mike Aquilina, *The Mass of the Early Christians* (Huntington, IN: Our Sunday Visitor Publishing Division, 2007), p. 78.
[61] Ibid., p. 77.

> and then reassemble to partake of food – but food of an ordinary and innocent kind.[62]

Thus far there is little information in these early texts with which to construct an understanding of how the post-Apostolic church understood the Lord's Supper as proclamation. Clearly, there was more institutional structure in place and a theology of some change in the elements of the bread and the cup was already taking shape. But there is little to go on with respect to how 1 Corinthians 11:26 was applied to church teaching and practice.

The *Didache*, compiled sometime between AD 80 – 140, also offers little assistance in regard to the Lord's Supper as a means of proclaiming the gospel. It speaks of the bread and the cup as "spiritual food and drink . . . through Jesus your child."[63] Yet the sacramental meal described later in *Didache* 14.1 – 3 compares the Supper to a sacrifice. How this is to be interpreted is unclear:

> 1. Having assembled together on the Lord's day of the Lord, break bread and give thanks, having first confessed your faults, so that your sacrifice may be pure.
>
> 2. Let no one having a dispute with his neighbour assemble with you until they are reconciled, that your sacrifice may not be defiled.
>
> 3. For this is what was spoken by the Lord, 'In every place and time offer me a pure sacrifice; for I am a great king, says the Lord, and my name is wonderful among the nations.[64]

While it is possible that section 14 of the *Didache* is a later addition, when conjoined with the Ignatian texts, it certainly appears that accretions to Paul's Corinthian Lord's Supper theology and practice were already growing in the early second century. No longer is the concept of gospel proclamation at the forefront of Communion. Instead, the church has begun to travel down the pathway toward resacrifice and the transformation of the elements from ordinary bread and wine into Christ's body and blood.

---

[62] Ibid., p. 84.
[63] Paul Bradshaw, *Eucharistic Origins* (London: SPCK Publishing, 2004), pp. 25 – 26.
[64] Ibid., p. 25.

These theological trends are well-established by the time Justin Martyr addresses his *First Apology* to the Emperor Antoninus Pius between AD 150 – 160. Justin describes in two places (65.1 – 66.4 and 67.1 – 8) in his *Apology* the Christian orders of worship from his time. Here again, nothing is preserved describing the meal as proclamation of the death of Christ. Rather, the focus again is upon a change in the elements during the celebration, with the increasing emphasis on the Supper as *thanksgiving*:

> 66.1 And this food is called by us 'thanksgiving', of which it is permitted for no one to partake unless he believes our teaching to be true, and has been washed with the washing for forgiveness of sins and regeneration, and so lives as Christ handed down.
>
> 2. For not as common bead or common drink do we receive these things; but just as our Saviour Jesus Christ, being incarnate through (the) word of God, took both flesh and blood for our salvation, so too we have been taught that the food over which thanks have been given through (a) word of prayer which is from him, from which our blood and flesh are fed by transformation, is both the flesh and blood of that incarnate Jesus.[65]

Justin's *Dialogue with Trypho* furthers the impression of the development of a theology of the Lord's Supper very early in the life of the church, which is sacrificial and transubstantial, rather than proclamatory:

> 41.3 In this passage God already speaks of the sacrifices which we, the nations offer him in every place, namely, the bread of the eucharist and the cup of the eucharist. He adds that we glorify his name, while you defile it. …
>
> 117.1 All the sacrifices offered through his [Jesus'] name, as Jesus Christ ordered, that is, the sacrifices which Christians may offer in every place in the world where their eucharist over bread and cup – these God tells us in advance are pleasing to him. [66]

Irenaeus, writing near the close of the second century (ca AD 180), provides even more examples of the growth of the theology of the changing of the elements, as well as of the sacrificial, and the thanksgiving emphases. Where has the proper influence of 1 Corinthians 11:26 and Paul's, "for as often as you eat this bread and drink this

---

[65] Bradshaw, *Eucharistic Origins*, pp. 61 – 62.

[66] Rordorf, et al, *The Eucharist of the Early Christians*, pp. 77 – 78. Maurice Jourjon tellingly observes that in his view, "Justin provides, first of all, a description of the eucharist that shows how, despite variations according to the country and period of history, the eucharist of today is faithful to what it was in the second century."

cup, you proclaim the Lord's death until he comes" eluded the second century church? Examples from Irenaeus' own works demonstrate that gospel proclamation through the celebration of the Supper was increasingly taking the theological backseat to the mysteries of the changing of the bread and the wine into the actualized body and blood of Christ. Irenaeus' apologetic work, *Against Heresies*, contains multiple references to the then current theology of the Supper:

> . . . the bread and the wine are wisely put to man's use, and when they receive the word of God they become the Eucharist, that is, the body and blood of Christ.
>
> Here we see the marvelous continuity of God's plan: creation serves our bodily life; it receives its supreme consecration in becoming the body and blood of Christ and thus the food that renders man incorruptible.
>
> The cup which comes from his creation he declared to be his blood that mingles with ours, and the bread which comes from his creation he asserted is his body which gives growth to our bodies.[67]

Is the apparent loss of importance, or lack of emphasis, in the second century church on gospel proclamation through the Eucharist explainable simply in the changing of social and demographic circumstances? As the church grew in size and importance and wrestled with waves of persecutions, did this turn the focus of Communion from conscientiously outward to inward? That is the theory advanced by Eugene LaVerdiere:

> The relationship between the Eucharist and the Church also helps account for the diversity in Eucharistic understanding and practice. At the very beginning, when the Church was basically a movement dedicated to Christ's mission, and as it developed into missionary communities, the Eucharist was bound to be an evangelical, missionary event, proclaiming the death of the Lord until he comes" (1 Cor 11:26). . . . Later, when Church communities developed needs of their own, the Eucharistic assembly addressed those needs ministerially. . . . When the Church understood itself as a communion of communities, transcending every local community, the Eucharist was understood as a celebration of the whole Church symbolically gathered for one large banquet. . . . With Justin, the Eucharist became part of a way of life, one to be examined, reflected upon, and defended in the public forum.[68]

---

[67] Rordorf, et al, *The Eucharist of the Early Christians*, pp. 91 – 92.

[68] Eugene LaVerdiere, *The Eucharist in the New Testament and the Early Church* (Collegeville, MN: Liturgical Press, 1996), pp. 188 – 189.

LaVerdiere's hypothesis makes a great deal of sense, based upon the development of the church during its first one hundred years, and given the marked shift in sacramental theology and practice demonstrated in the source documents between the Apostle Paul's times and those of Justin or Irenaeus. And yet, if this was indeed the way gospel proclamation dimmed in Lord's Supper celebrations by the mid-to-late second century, that does not mean it was biblically proper. In light of Paul's own pastoral instruction to the Corinthians, they were to celebrate Communion such that the Lord's death was proclaimed – *until he comes*. This directive from the Apostle does not seem to be conditional relative to any circumstance, other than the return of Jesus at his Parousia!

Clement of Alexandria represents the transition from second to third century. Thus it should not be surprising to find the continued trajectory of practice away from Supper proclamation and toward the sacramental theology of sacrifice and conversion of the elements into the true physical body and blood of Christ. In Clement's, *The Teacher* (ca AD 195) 1:6, he relates:

> The Word is all to the child, both father and mother and tutor and nurse. "Eat my flesh," he says, "and drink my blood" (Jn 6:32, 33, 36). Such is the suitable food that the Lord serves, and he offers his flesh and pours forth his blood, and nothing is wanting for the children's growth. O amazing mystery![69]

And again in *The Teacher* 2:2, Clement writes of drinking the Lord's immortality:

> To drink the blood of Jesus is to become partaker of the Lord's immortality. . . . As wine is blended with water, so is the Spirit with man. . . . And the mixture of both – of the water and of the Word – is called the Eucharist, renowned and glorious grace. Those who by faith partake of it are sanctified both in body and soul.[70]

It would be overreaching to ascribe to the pre-Nicene church at this stage a fully developed theology and praxis involving transubstantiation, or a full statement of the Eucharist as resacrifice of Christ. However, the trend in theological direction from the days of Ignatius to the time of Clement of Alexandria favored these two primary emphases, while the Pauline 1 Corinthians theology of Lord's Supper as proclamation of the gospel virtually disappears from the available literature. Of course, as there are

---

[69] Aquilina, *The Mass of the Early Christians*, p. 143.
[70] Bercot, *A Dictionary of Early Christian Beliefs*, p. 252.

many works from the second century now lost to modern scrutiny, this conclusion derives from a fraction of what undoubtedly circulated within the church during those times.

Tertullian, also writing at the turn of centuries from second to third, "speaks in similar realistic terms of the Eucharistic elements as do the earlier writers, declaring that the bread is the Lord's body (e.g., *De or.* 19; *De idol.* 7) and that human flesh feeds on the body and blood of Christ in order that the soul may be fattened on God (*De res. Carn.* 8:3)."[71] In his *Against Marcion* (*Adv. Marcion*, lib. i. cap. 23), the apologist uses the "term 'Eucharistia' and also 'gratiarum actio,' or 'giving of thanks,' as its Latin equivalent."[72] Tertullian also developed and promulgated the idea of *figura*, whereby the bread and wine of the Last Supper are *prophetic prefigurations* of the body and blood of Christ. While it does not seem that Tertullian then applied his figurative theology of the Last Supper to the Lord's Supper in ongoing practice, it may nevertheless have influenced others to make that conceptual leap. Also, Tertullian identified the Supper with sacrifice in various places in his works. While the quotation below may assume the setting of prayer, rather than Eucharistic setting, Tertullian's view of the Supper and at least the element of the bread are evident:

> Similarly also on station days, many do not think that they should attend the sacrificial prayers, because the station would be undone by receiving the Lord's body. Does then the Eucharist destroy a service devoted to God or bind it more to God? Surely your station will be more solemn if you have also stood at God's altar? If the Lord's body is received and reserved, each point is secured, both the participation in the sacrifice and the discharge of the duty. (*De or.* 19)[73]

Further removing the concept of the Supper as proclamation from the practice of the early church was the growing institutionalization of the handling of Communion as a rite of such mystery and sanctity that not only should non-believers be dismissed from the assembly when its place in the liturgy occurred, but that catechumens and those under discipline were as well. Under these increasingly standardized measures, how indeed could the Eucharist function as a proclamation of the gospel – at least as proclamation to persons outside the inner circle of church membership?

---

[71] Bradshaw, *Eucharistic Origins*, p. 94.

[72] F. E. Warren, *The Liturgy and Ritual of the Anti-Nicene Church* (New York: E. & J. B. Young and Co., 1897), p. 112.

[73] Bradshaw, *Eucharistic Origins*, p. 100.

Stuart G. Hall describes this measure:

> The ordinary catechumen would hear these readings and expositions Sunday by Sunday at the church meeting or *synaxis*. After what could be a long session of texts and sermons, the catechumens would be blessed and dismissed before the main work of the Eucharistic offerings began; with them would go some others, such as baptized persons being disciplined for grave sins, and *energumens*, the mentally sick, who were thought to be demon-possessed.[74]

It is understandable that during the sporadic waves of persecutions of Christians by the Roman civil authorities, particularly in the second and third centuries, that church leaders were very cautious about revealing the locations for their gatherings to persons unknown to them. However, this practical accommodation to the political-cultural circumstances prevented the celebrations of the Lord's Supper in many respects from fulfilling its evangelistic or proclamation purpose. This does not mean that the casually curious outsiders, the inquirers, or even the catechumens should have been given the opportunity to *partake* of the elements – to participate – but rather that they should have been given the opportunity to see the Eucharist observed by the believing community. In permitting this, the developing early church would have further enhanced its proclamation of the gospel to those who needed so desperately to receive it. According to Werner Elert, from at least the middle of the second century onward, the Lord's Supper was concealed from anyone who had not fully completed the catechumen regimen and who had not been baptized:

> Admission (to the whole service) was not for just anybody. Origen points out that the Christians are not like the philosophers whom anybody may attend and listen to. The Christians on the contrary test every man first and instruct him privately (κατ' ἰδίαν) until he gives demonstration of trustworthiness and an orderly life. Only then is he admitted to their assembly as a "hearer." This goes only for the Service of the Word composed of hymns, lections, sermon, and prayers. Even this was obviously stoutly hedged about. Those outside were not denied the opportunity of hearing God's Word, but they must first prove their serious intention. Following the service of the Word came the celebration of the Eucharist. . . . Before the Eucharist began, however, the "hearers" had to leave the assembly, and not only they but also the catechumens, even though they were already being solidly instructed toward reception. *During*

---

[74] Stuart G. Hall, *Doctrine and Practice in the Early Church* (Grand Rapids: William B Eerdmans Publishing Company, 1992), p. 17.

> *the Eucharist the doors were guarded by deacons and subdeacons.*[75]

There is also archeological proof dating from the third century that at least some of the earliest homes were converted architecturally to accommodate not only assemblies of worship, but also the separation of those who could receive Communion from those who could not. And in this way the Supper became even more of a *mysterium* than a proclamation of the gospel:

> At Dura-Europos in Syria archaeologists discovered the remains of a home (ca AD 235), the interior of which had been renovated for use as a Christian place of worship. They found a separate room next to the sanctuary that was used for celebration of the Lord's Supper. The baptized would move from the regular meeting room to this room for the Communion part of the service. Persons who were not baptized were not permitted to enter this part of the building. Behind the closed and guarded doors the most sacred part of the service, the celebration of the Lord's Supper, followed.[76]

Two well-known sources for the mid-third century church's views on the Lord's Supper are the contemporaneous Cyprian of Carthage (ca AD 200 – 258) and Origen, initially of Alexandria (ca AD 185 – 251).[77] Especially with Cyprian, scholars have much material regarding the ante-Nicene church's Eucharistic practices. "His well-known *Letter 63* is 'the only ante-Nicene writing that deals exclusively with the celebration of the eucharist.' It has even been called 'the most notable document on the eucharist in the Christian literature for the first three centuries.' And is thus uniquely important for . . . knowledge of the life of the Church in the third century and for the history of dogma."[78] Cyprian's *Letter 63*, composed in AD 253, includes highly descriptive language about the celebration of Communion and what was deemed significant in his day. For example, in 9, 2 – 3:

> On the eve of the day when he suffered, he took the cup and blessed it and gave it to his disciples with the words: 'All of you, drink of this. This is the blood of the covenant, which will be offered for many for the forgiveness of sins. I tell you: I shall not drink again of this product of the vine, until I

---

[75] Werner Elert, *Eucharist and Church Fellowship in the First Four Centuries*, N. E. Nagel, trans. (Saint Louis: Concordia Publishing House, 1966), p. 75.

[76] Ernest Bartels, *Take Eat, Take Drink: The Lord's Supper Through the Centuries* (St. Louis: Concordia Publishing, 2004), p. 70.

[77] Dates given were sourced from Everett Ferguson, *Encyclopedia of Early Christianity* (New York: Garland Publishing, 1997, 1999 printing), pp. 306 and 835.

[78] Rordorf, et al, *The Eucharist of the Early Christians*, p. 156. Raymond Johanny adds concerning Cyprian that, the whole movement of Cyprian's thought is Eucharistic.

> drink new wine in the kingdom of my Father.' In this passage we find that the cup the Lord offered contained a mixture and that what he called blood was wine. We can see, then, that the blood of Christ is not offered if the wine is missing from the cup, and that the sacrifice of the Lord is not properly celebrated unless our gift and sacrifice correspond to the passion. Then again, how shall we drink new wine, product of the vine, with Christ in the kingdom of his Father unless in the sacrifice of God the Father and Christ we offer wine, and unless we mix the cup according to the tradition of the Lord?"[79]

Other examples from the hand of Cyprian connected with the Supper include:

> Those presbyters, contrary to the Gospel law . . . before penitence was fulfilled. . . dare to offer on their behalf and to give them the Eucharist. That is, they dare to profane the sacred body of the Lord. However, it is written, "Whoever will eat the the bread and drink the cup of the Lord unworthily, will be guilty of the body and blood of the Lord. [80]

And this particularly vivid example:

> He says that whoever will eat of His bread will live forever. So it is clear that those who partake of His body and receive the Eucharist by the right hand of communion are living. On the other hand, we must fear and pray lest anyone who is separate from Christ's body – being barred from communion – should remain at a distance from salvation. For He Himself warns and says, "Unless you eat the flesh of the Son of Man and drink His blood, you have no life in you.[81]

Cyprian's writings represent a more fully articulated theology of the Sacrament which is both sacrificial (or offertory) in focus and concerned with the reality of Christ's flesh and blood made manifest in the Eucharist. Here we also find the reference to Jesus' teaching in the Gospel of John, chapter 6:52 – 54. This text will grow in importance, applied more and more frequently in the centuries after Cyprian, to justify a sacramental theology that maintains the bread and the cup truly become, after the words of consecration, the body and blood of the Lord:

> The Jews then disputed among themselves, saying, "How can this man give us his flesh to eat?" So Jesus said to them, "Truly, truly, I say to you, unless you eat the flesh of the Son of Man and drink his blood, you have no life in you. Whoever feeds on my flesh and drinks my blood has eternal life, and I will raise him up on the last day.

---

[79] Rordorf, et al, *The Eucharist of the Early Christians*, p. 161.
[80] Bercot, *A Dictionary of Early Christian Beliefs*, p. 253.
[81] Ibid., p. 253

During those challenging yet also growing times for the church in the mid-third century, Origen was also at work. While far less prolific in this area than Cyprian, in his surviving writings there are a few brief statements which can be with certainty attributed to Lord's Supper theology and practice. "He indicates that the word *Eucharist* was used to designate the consecrated bread (*Contra Celsum* 8.57), and he alludes in passing to the care believers take in insuring that no fragment of that bread falls from their hands on to the ground when they receive it (*Hom. In Exod.* 13.3)."[82] Origen also declares concerning "Eucharistic consecration: 'we, giving thanks to the Creator of all, also eat the bread that is presented with thanksgiving and prayer over what is given; and it becomes through prayer a holy body and sanctifies those who partake of it with pure intention' (*Contra Celsum* 8.33)."[83]

While with Origen, as with his contemporary Cyprian, there are no extant texts indicating an appreciation of the Sacrament of the Supper as proclamation of the gospel, there is revealed, within the same text in which he describes the consecrated bread as the "Body of the Lord", an equal emphasis on the importance of God's word:

> I want to base my exhortation to you on examples drawn from your religious practices. You regularly attend the various mysteries, and you know how reverently and carefully you protect the Body of the Lord when it is given to you, for you fear that a fragment of it may fall to the ground and part of the consecrated treasure be lost. If it did, you would regard yourselves as culpable, and rightly so, if through your negligence something of it were lost. Well, then if you show such justifiable care when it comes to his Body, why should you think that neglect of God's word should deserve a lesser punishment than neglect of his Body.[84]

Another textual piece of evidence as to how the Supper was understood in the third century may be deduced from a surviving letter written from Firmilian, the Bishop of Caesaria of Cappadocia to Cyprian. While the letter is interesting because of its description of a self-proclaimed prophetess active in the year 230, the letter is even more telling in the way it describes the aspects of the Eucharist: "(She made) the

---

[82] Bradshaw, *Eucharistic Origins*, pp. 107 – 108.
[83] Ibid., p. 108.
[84] Rordorf, et al, *The Eucharist of the Early Christians*, p. 183.

Eucharist with a passable *invocation*, and she *offered sacrifice* to the Lord [not] without the sacrament of customary pronouncement."[85]

There are few sources to consult between the time of Cyprian and Origen and the Council of Nicea (AD 325) concerning the church's developing thinking about the Lord's Supper. "Cyprian is the last major witness to Eucharistic theology and practice in the third century. We know nothing of further developments in the second half of the century."[86] There is a brief quote from Dionysius of Alexandria (ca AD 262) that continues in the same vein as the previous mid-third century examples. Dionysius writes, "I do not think they will themselves be rash enough in such a condition to either approach the holy table or to touch the body and blood of the Lord." Yet there is nothing new in this statement, which was composed at least a decade after the deaths of Cyprian and Origen.

Within the space of sixty or so years from the occasion in Corinth which prompted Paul's letter and in particular his chapter 11:17 – 34 admonishment and exhortation on the Lord's Supper as proclamation, the theology and practice of the Sacrament was beginning to change. From the time of Ignatius in the early second century through the final decades of the third century and approaching the first ecumenical church Council of Nicea, the Pauline understanding of Communion as proclamation of the gospel was more and more superceded by the growing predominance of the twin doctrines of resacrifice and of thanksgiving (thus the term *Eucharist*, which lent its name to the now institutionalized liturgical rite). By the end of this period, the elements of bread and wine (cup) were understood to be transformed from ordinary physical substances into the true body and blood of the Lord Jesus – resort often being made to Jesus' words in John 6:52 – 54 to support their interpretation of Jesus' words in the biblical Supper accounts (this *is* my body. . .this *is* my blood).

These trends in the church's teaching and praxis involving the Supper were already beginning to shift the focus of the Communion celebration from something understood as deriving from the Lord and offered to believers, into something derived from the Lord that believers reoffered to God, with the intention as much being to

---

[85] Bradshaw, *Eucharistic Origins*, p. 114.
[86] Ibid.

'remind' the Father of Jesus' sacrifice as for the participants' own sakes. No longer were the symbolic elements, the actions of breaking and blessing, the sincere participation, and the words of institution viewed as accomplishing proclamation of the gospel. Instead, all these aspects of the Sacrament (along with the added emphasis on consecrating prayer and the authority of the bishop) were believed to constitute a mystical rite which reoffered, or physically recreated, with each observance, the atoning sacrifice of the Lord Jesus Christ.

No doubt this change trend in sacramental theology from its Pauline roots, toward the sort of teachings found in Cyprian and other church apologists and theologians some 200 years later, was certainly influenced by changes in the church's social demographics, the rise of state-sponsored persecution, increasing institutionalization, the influence of mystery cults, and even the simple misapplication or misinterpretation of some of the accepted New Testament texts. Yet whatever various influences and textual interpretations were involved, the theology and practice of the Lord's Supper as *proclamation of the death of the Lord until he comes* had, by the time of the Council of Nicaea, become the *resacrifice of the Lord and a repeated thanksgiving offering to the Lord* until he comes.

III

PROCLAMATION FORGOTTEN: THE LORD'S SUPPER AS EUCHARIST IN THE POST-NICENE CHURCH TO THE REFORMATION

I agree with the holy Roman Church and the Apostolic See, and I profess with my mouth and heart to hold as the faith concerning the sacrament of the Lord's Supper what the lord and venerable Pope Nicholas and holy synod by the authority of the gospels and the apostles have given to held and have ratified to me: Namely, that the bread and wine which are placed on the altar after the consecration are not only signs (non solum sacramentum), but also the true body and blood of our Lord Jesus Christ, and that sensually, not only in sign, but in truth (non solum sacramento, sed in veritate) they are handled and broken by the hands of the priest and crushed by the teeth of the faithful, swearing by the holy and one-in-substance Trinity and by the most holy gospel of Christ.

(*Berengar's Oath of 1059*)[87]

By the time Christianity was recognized as a *religio licita* through the Edict of Milan (AD 313), the practice of Lord's Supper observance in the multiplying churches was well established. Since the time of the Apostle Paul and the events in Corinth which had prompted his letter (1 Corinthians) and described the Supper as a proclamation of the Lord's death until he comes, the church moved further and further away from generation to generation in teaching and in celebrating its Pauline emphasis. Between AD 70 and AD 313 the Christian movement grew quite substantial and more influential in the Roman world, despite periodic waves of imperial or regional persecution. At the same time, the Supper celebration gradually moved from within the household agape meal setting into the context of the increasingly formalized liturgy of Lord's Day worship. These trends, coupled with other factors mentioned in the previous chapter, gave growing rise to a theology and practice of the Sacrament which emphasized resacrifice and a mysterious change of the elements of bread and wine into the body and blood of the Lord.

---

[87] Gary Macy, *Treasures from the Storeroom: Medieval Religion and the Eucharist* (Collegeville, MN: The Liturgical Press, 1999), p. 21.

The theology of Supper as resacrifice and as thanksgiving offered by the celebrant to God deeply impacted the praxis of the Eucharist during the weekly Sunday worship of congregations scattered throughout the Greco-Roman world and the Near East. While the legalization of Christianity as a religion within the Roman Empire brought about swift changes in ecclesiology and in such things as church architectural development, the trajectory of the church's sacramental theology regarding the Eucharist continued to move along the well-worn pathway of resacrifice and the real presence of Christ's body and blood at the point of the consecration of the elements. This is evident through a simple general survey of extracts from some of the premier theologians and doctors of the church. Ultimately, by the time Martin Luther raised his objections to the abuses he saw in the 16th century Roman Mass, the intertwined concepts of transubstantiation and resacrifice were deeply entrenched, following some 1,400 years of accretive development.

During the period immediately following the Council of Nicaea (AD 325) there arose a generation of outstanding biblical exegetes, theologians, and preachers. One among these, John Chrysostom (ca 347 – 407), trained in an Antiochene-style of exegesis, did seem to see something of the Supper's work in communicating the once-for-all death of Christ. Commenting upon 1 Corinthians 11:26 within a homily concerning 1 Cor. 11:17, he does speak of the Eucharist being given to the Church as a means of 'remembrance' of Christ's death. He says:

> Next, having spoken concerning that Supper, he (Paul) connects the things present with the things of that time, that even as on that very evening and reclining on that very couch and receiving from Christ himself this sacrifice, so also now might men be affected; and he saith, Ver. 26. "For as often as ye eat this bread, and drink this cup, ye proclaim the Lord's death till He come."
>
> For as Christ in regard to the bread and the cup said, "Do this in remembrance of Me," revealing to us the cause of the giving of the Mystery, and besides what else He said, declaring this to be a sufficient cause to ground our religious fear upon: - (for when thou considerest what thy Master hath suffered for thee, thou wilt the better deny thyself) – so also Paul saith here: "as often as ye eat ye do proclaim His death." And this is that Supper. Then intimating that it abides to the end, he saith, "till He come."[88]

[88] John Chrysostom, "Homily XXVII (1 Cor. XI. 17.)," in *Homilies on First and Second Corinthians, The Nicene and Post-Nicene Fathers*, vol. XII, Philip Schaff, ed. (Grand Rapids: Wm. B. Eerdmans Publishing Company, reprint July 1969), p. 161.

And yet this formidable preacher of the gospel and Antiochene exegete of biblical texts says nothing more about what it means that the Lord's Supper *proclaims* Christ's death until he returns. Instead, Chrysostom explains in various homilies concerning 1 Corinthians, 2 Timothy, and Hebrews, how the Supper can in fact be a true sacrifice, yet not *another* sacrifice:

> Christ is one everywhere, being complete here and complete there also, one Body. As then while offered in many places, He is one body and not many bodies; so also He is one sacrifice. He is our High Priest, who offered the sacrifice that cleanses us. That we offer now also, which was then offered, which cannot be exhausted. This is done in remembrance of what was then done. . . . It is not another sacrifice, as that of the High Priest in the Old Testament, but we offer always the same, or rather we perform a remembrance of a Sacrifice.[89]

And:

> The Offering is the same, whether a common man, or Paul or Peter offer it. It is the same which Christ gave to His disciples, and which the Priests now minister. . . . The Same who sanctified the one sanctifies the other also. For as the words which God spoke are the same as those the Priest now utters, so is the Offering the same. . . . And this is His Body, as well as that. . . . Christ is even now present, even now works.[90]

And again:

> The priest is the representative when he pronounces those words, but the power and the grace are those of the Lord. 'This is my Body,' he says. This word is the things that lie before us; and as that sentence 'increase and multiply,' once spoken, extends through all time and gives to our nature the power to reproduce itself; even so that saying 'This is my Body,' once uttered does at every table in the Churches from that time to the present day, and even till Christ's coming, makes the sacrifice complete.[91]

The sacrificial language associated with the Sacrament in Chrysostom is not surprising given the development for some three centuries prior to his time, of the twin constituents of resacrifice and real physical presence of Christ's body and blood. Dolores Greeley, in her dissertation, provides additional examples from Chrysostom concerning the real physical presence of Christ's body and blood and his emphasis upon the Supper as sacrifice. She also summarizes his Supper theology:

---

[89] Dolores Greeley, *The Church as 'Body of Christ' According to the Teaching of Saint John Chrysostom* (Dissertation. Notre Dame, IN: Unpublished), p. 88.
[90] Ibid.
[91] Ibid., p. 89.

> "Clearly then the victim that we offer in the host and in the cup is the same victim who was slain on Calvary." "Christ has entered heaven, having poured out His blood for us." Now although He no longer actively offers Himself in sacrifice as this would contradict his "sitting" at the right hand of God, yet His body and blood which are offered in the mysteries on our altar are truly a heavenly oblation. The blood, then, that was poured out for us, this is our sacrifice that we offer on the altar. Realism permeates Chrysostom's attempts to portray this truth. Pointing to the altar, he say, "Christ lies there slain." His body lies before us now." That which is in the chalice is the same as what flowed from the side of Christ. What is the bread? The Body of Christ."[92]

A contemporary of Chrysostom's, Gregory of Nyssa (d. 395), known as the youngest of the "three great Cappadocians,"[93] wrestled with how the element of the bread was changed into the body of Christ during the Eucharist. He describes his understanding of this conversion in his *Catechetical Oration 37*:

> We have good reason, then, to believe that now too the bread which is sanctified by the Word of God is transformed into the body of the divine Word. That body was virtually bread, and it was sanctified by the indwelling of the Word in the flesh. The means whereby the bread was changed in that body and converted into divine power operate precisely the same way now. In the former case, the grace of the Word sanctified the body which was constituted by bread and which, in a way, actually was bread. And in the latter case, similarly, the bread (as the apostle says) is sanctified by the Word of God and prayer (1 Tim. 4:5). The difference in the second case, however, is that it does not become the Word of God gradually by way of being eaten, but is immediately changed into the body by the Word – as the Word himself declared: 'This is my body' [Matt. 26:26].[94]

Gregory seems to be teaching an instantaneous transformation of the element of the bread in the Supper into the body of Christ. While he uses language indicative to the modern reader of a literal, physical change from bread into body, it must be borne in mind that during the fourth century a fully articulated doctrine of the transubstantiation of the common elements into the real body and blood of Christ did not exist.

Theodore of Mopsuestia (ca 350 – 428) is even more direct in declaring, not the value of the elements of bread and cup as *symbols* of Christ's passion, but rather as

---

[92] Greeley, *The Church as 'Body of Christ' According to the Teaching of Saint John Chrysostom*, p. 88.

[93] Everett, *Encyclopedia of Early Christianity*, p. 495.

[94] Maurice Wiles and Mark Santer, *Documents in Early Christian Thought* (Cambridge: Cambridge University Press, 1975, 12th edition 2005), p. 196

transformed into the body and blood of Christ *in some way*, and thus how the communicant should reverently interact with the portions he or she received:

> You should come up in great fear and with much love because of the greatness of the gift – fear because of its great dignity, love because of its grace. . . When you have received the body in your hands, you adore it. . . . With a great and sincere love you place it on your eyes, kiss it and address to it your prayers as to Christ our Lord. . . .[95]

During this era the importance of the prayer of consecration for the elements was on the rise. It was important to the practice of the Eucharist for the theologians of the church to identify when the common elements changed into the body and blood of Christ. Ambrose of Milan (d. 397) writes concerning the moment of the change in elements in his *De Mysteriis IX*:

> For the sacrament which you receive, is effected by the words of Christ. . . . The Lord Jesus himself declares: "This is my body." Before the benediction of the heavenly words another species is mentioned; after the consecration the body is signified. He himself speaks of his blood. Before the consecration it is mentioned as something else; after the consecration it is called blood.[96]

Rather than the words of Christ, as repeated by the Apostle Paul in 1 Corinthians 11:23 – 25, serving as an integral element with the symbols of bread and cup, and the participation of the faithful as proclamation of the gospel, these same words of institution were instead understood by Ambrose's time to have been given in order to accomplish the transformation of the elements themselves into the body and blood of Christ. For while Ambrose on the one hand writes, "As often as we receive, we proclaim the death of the Lord,"[97] he also unambiguously states that these words enable a resacrifice of the Lord upon the altar of the table. Frank Senn notes that "Ambrose is quite clear that the *sermo Christi* consecrates the bread and wine. As he states in *De Sacramento IV*, 14:[98]

> By whose words and by whose speech does the consecration take place? By those of the Lord Jesus. For all the rest that comes beforehand is spoken by the priest: God is praised, prayer is offered, he prays for the people, for

---

[95] Bradshaw, *Eucharistic Origins*, p. 142.
[96] Frank C. Senn, *Christian Liturgy: Catholic and Evangelical* (Minneapolis: Fortress Press, 1997), p. 245.
[97] Gerald Bray, ed. *1 – 2 Corinthians*, Ancient Commentary on Scripture, NT vol. VII (Downers Grove, IL: InterVaristy Press, 1999), p. 113. From Ambrose's *De Sacramento IV*.
[98] Ibid.

> kings, and so on. Then it happens that this venerable sacrament is consecrated. Then the priest no longer uses his own words. Instead he uses the words of Christ. Therefore the word of Christ confects the sacrament.[99]

Perhaps the greatest among the earlier post-Nicene church fathers, Augustine of Hippo (d. 430), agreed with his mentor Ambrose that the elements underwent their transformation at the moment in which the words of Christ (the words of institution) were declared by the officiating priest. "In *Sermon 227*, preached to the newly baptized, the bishop of Hippo states: 'That Body which you see on the altar, consecrated by the Word of God, is the Body of Christ. That chalice, or rather, what the chalice holds, consecrated by the Word of God, is the blood of Christ.' Or again, in *Sermon 234*, preached at Easter, Augustine says: 'The faithful understand what I am saying: they know Christ in the breaking of bread. For, not all bread, but only that which receives the blessing of Christ becomes the Body of Christ.' "[100]

Yet it must be admitted that debate has raged for centuries over Augustine's view of the nature of the presence of Christ in the Lord's Supper. Was his view of Christ's real presence in the Supper "physical" or "spiritual" in nature? The sermons excerpted previously seem to indicate that he believed in some form of conversion of the bread and the wine into the actual body and blood of Christ. Yet, he writes elsewhere of the change after consecration as being 'symbolic':

> . . .he used the language of both interchangeably. . . .He also spoke symbolically, saying that the elements were "visible signs of an invisible grace." When he used the term 'sacrament'' he explained himself by writing, "A sacrament is a sacred sign." Augustine claimed to believe that Christ's body was not actually present in the Sacrament, because he felt that according to His human nature Christ "is some place in heaven." According to His divine nature Christ is everywhere present. On one occasion Augustine represented Christ as saying, "You must understand what I have said in a spiritual sense. You are not going to eat this body which you see or drink that blood which those who crucify me are going to shed."[101]

As time went along, church doctrine and practice continued to be refined – by theologians and bishops certainly – but also by those who occupied the powerfully rising *cathedra* of the Pontifex Maximus of Rome. For example, Pope Gregory the

---

[99] Ibid.
[100] Senn, *Christian Liturgy: Catholic and Evangelical*, p. 245.
[101] Bartels, *Take Eat, Take Drink: The Lord's Supper Through the Centuries*, pp. 80 – 81.

Great's[102] Papacy, which he assumed on September 3, 590, is sometimes considered the first Roman episcopacy of the medieval era. And yet it was Gregory's statements regarding the Lord's Supper which would further the trend *away from* proclamation and *toward* sacrifice as the main motif in Communion. Ernest Bartels writes:

> Gregory the Great made a significant pronouncement regarding the Lord's Supper that continued to have an influence throughout the medieval period and beyond. Gregory said that **the Eucharistic sacrifice is the most solemn mystery of the church**. It fills the faithful with holy awe. **The sacrifice in the Lord's Supper is not a new sacrifice that is added to that of Jesus on the cross. It is a daily, unbloody repetition and perpetual application of that sacrifice.** The sacrifice in the Lord's Supper is the antitype of the Old Testament Mosaic sacrifice, and was foreshadowed by Melchizedek's unbloody offering of bread and wine. **The body of Jesus Christ is the subject of this sacrifice. As His body was present on the altar of the cross, so it is present on the altar of the church, and is offered to God through the priest. Offering the sacrifice is the exclusive prerogative of the priest. It is efficacious for all in the church, including those who have died in the faith.**[103]

In this statement, Pope Gregory the Great classifies officially the Lord's Supper as a "mystery" and as a "sacrifice," although not a *new* sacrifice. And Gregory unquestionably connects the physical body of Christ as it was constituted on the cross with the body of Christ present on the altar of the Eucharist. Here also is officially declared that the priest is the only officer of the church empowered to officiate at the Table. Finally, Gregory gives official sanction to use of the Lord's Supper as an offering to God on behalf of the faithful among the dead.

The excerpts from theological works and from homilies provided thus far, spanning the years between the second and the seventh centuries, give ample proof that the Lord's Supper, by this time known as the Eucharist, Communion, or the Mysteries, was not to any significant degree perceived of as a Sacrament of proclamation. The use of the Supper for proclaiming the gospel would not typically have had a place in works on the Sacrament or in the practical usage of the rite. Its theology and its observance were understood in terms of resacrifice and its bread and cup as undergoing transformation into the body and blood of Christ. Although the concept of Eucharist as resacrifice required an explanation for the physical presence of the

---

102 Pope Gregory the Great's dates are typically given as 540 – 604.

103 Bartels, *Take Eat, Take Drink: The Lord's Supper Through the Centuries*, pp. 107 – 108.

Lord's body and blood, no one had been able to thoroughly elucidate the nature of the change in elements that the church of that time held was taking place. The church lacked a sufficient explanation for this transformation or transmutation of the elements after the consecratory prayer – what later came to be called transubstantiation.

Such a theological exposition of this tradition in the Roman Church arose in the eighth century. "The church traces the concept of transubstantiation back to the great dogmatician, John of Damascus (perhaps ca. 675 – 750), whose doctrine of a real change became the common property of the Orthodox Church. John taught that the bread and wine become the body and blood of Christ, truly present in the Lord's Supper."[104] It is not as surprising that John of Damascus wrote concerning the doctrine of how the elements were believed to be changed into Christ's body and blood, so much as it is surprising that although the doctrine in practice and devotion had existed for at least five hundred years, no one had so clearly described it before!

> It is truly the Body, united with Godhead, which has its origin from the Holy Virgin; not as though that Body which ascended came down from heaven, but because the bread and wine themselves are changed into the Body and Blood of God. But if thou seekest after the manner how this is, let it suffice to be told that it is by the Holy Ghost, in like manner as by the same Holy Ghost, the Lord formed flesh to himself, and in himself, from the Mother of God; nor know I aught more than this, that the Word of God is true, powerful, and almighty, but in manner unsearchable.[105]

Although John of Damascus had provided the church of the time with an unequivocal statement on the transformation of the bread and the wine into the body and blood of Christ at the moment of consecration, not everyone was convinced. A century following John's determined statement in support of what came to be styled as transubstantiation, there raged a serious debate between those who supported the 'realistic' view and those who held to the 'spiritual' view of Christ's presence in the Supper. Ernest Bartels describes the two schools involved:

> Scholars vigorously disputed the manner in which Christ's body and blood were present in the Supper in the middle of the ninth century. This dispute revolved about the debate between Radbertus and Ratramnus, . . . Theologians

[104] Bartels, *Take Eat, Take Drink: The Lord's Supper Through the Centuries*, p. 94.
[105] Ibid., pp. 94 – 95.

> were divided primarily between two views from the ancient church. Some followed Ambrose, who held to a realistic sacramental view of the presence. Others followed Augustine, who taught a spiritual understanding of the presence in the Supper. Again, one is cautious in using terms like "real" and "spiritual" because spiritual things are not simply unreal. The terms are the result of conventional, academic use. [106]

The heated debate concerning the nature of Christ's presence in the Supper was ignited by Paschasius Radbertus (d. after 856) rather than by the theologian who might be expected, John of Damsascus. In A.D. 844, this French Benedictine monk "published a book entitled *On the Body and Blood of the Lord.* In this book, thought to be the first full treatise on the subject, he clearly taught the doctrine of transubstantiation, although he did not use that term."[107] Radbertus was unambiguous as to the nature of the change in the elements and the presence of Christ in the Supper. And he certainly believed that the prayer of consecration, by the Spirit's power, was the instrument for the transmutation of the elements. Bartels provides a summary of key statements from Radbertus' work:

> . . .the substance of bread and wine is effectively changed into the body and blood of Christ. This is the very body and blood of Christ who was born of the Virgin, crucified, and raised from the dead. After the elements have been consecrated by the priest there is nothing else in the Lord's Supper but "the flesh and blood of Christ." . . . The Holy Spirit brings about this miraculous change. As the Spirit created Christ's body and in the Virgin's womb without cohabitation, so whenever the Lord's Supper is celebrated He creates the body and blood of Christ out of the substance of bread and wine. . . ."[108]

Radbertus' transmutational theology of the elements of the Supper may seem to be a dramatic step further along the pathway toward the Roman Mass of the later centuries. Yet, his doctrinal statements are entirely consistent with the most literal interpretation of church documents and writings from prior generations. There is very little expounded in this ninth century work that had not previously appeared in the third through the eighth centuries. However, Radbertus achieved a more systematic description of a physical change and his work was successfully promulgated in the succeeding centuries, over and against the book refuting his doctrine, *De corpore et*

---

[106] Bartels, *Take Eat, Take Drink: The Lord's Supper Through the Centuries*, p. 109.
[107] Ibid.
[108] Ibid., p. 110.

sanguine Domini liber, written by his monastic superior, Ratramnus of Corbie. Ratramnus regarded the elements of the Supper as *mystic symbols of remembrance*.[109]

There is one development in the Roman Church of this period that has some bearing on the concept of the Eucharist as proclamation of the gospel. In 1014, official Papal approval was granted for the inclusion in the liturgy of the Mass a recitation of the Nicene Creed. Thus with the Great Prayer of Thanksgiving and the Nicene Creed, a profession, or proclamation of faith was inserted into the Catholic Church's celebration of the Eucharist.[110]

"As the church moved closer to the official position of transubstantiation, an eleventh century French scholar named Berengar of Tours (ca 1000 – 1088) caused a new controversy. On the basis of his study of Scripture and opinions of some church fathers, Berengar concluded that the doctrine of the Lord's Supper advocated by Radbertus two centuries earlier was superstition and contrary to the Bible, to the ancient fathers, and to reason."[111] The problem with the conclusion Berengar reached concerning a real "spiritual' presence of Christ in the Supper while repudiating Radbertus was that the followers of Radbertus "felt that Berengar's insistence on a spiritual rather than a physical or natural presence of the Lord in the sacrament undermined the very possibility of our salvation."[112] The Radbertus camp agreed with their theological father that only through the physical body and blood of Christ could salvation be imparted to participants.

Berengar of Tours was therefore summoned to Rome by Pope Nicholas II in order to defend his refutation of Radbertus and his theology of Christ's "spiritual" presence in the Supper. The outcome was a forgone conclusion. "The Papal Legate, Humbert, cardinal bishop of Silva-Candida, was chosen to draw up an oath for Berengar to

---

[109] Cited from the Christian Classics Ethereal Library, Philip Schaff , *The New Schaff-Herzog Encyclopedia of Religious Knowledge, Vol. IX: Petri – Reuchlin*, p. 402, http://www.ccel.org/s/schaff/encyc/encyc09/htm/iv.vii.liv.htm. "This does not, however, completely express his position, for he maintained at the same time that 'according to the invisible substance, i.e., the power of the divine Word, the body and blood of Christ are truly present' (*cap*. xlix.). This shows that Ratramnus was more than a symbolist, and that he believed in a real presence which was received by the faithful through the spirit of God."

[110] Louis Weil, "Proclamation of Faith in the Eucharist," in *Time and Community*, J. Neil Alexander, ed. (Washington, DC: The Pastoral Press, 1990), p. 282.

[111] Bartels, *Take Eat, Take Drink: The Lord's Supper Through the Centuries*, p. 111.

[112] Macy, *Treasures from the Storeroom: Medieval Religion and the Eucharist*, p. 22.

sign. The oath of Berengar is clear, blunt, and forceful."[113] *Berengar's Oath* was one of the documents in the Roman Church's history which was carefully preserved and included 'unofficially' in various canon law collections, "until a new code was issued in 1917."[114]

In 1063, the "abbot of Saint Stephen's Monastery in Caen became involved in the debate" with Berengar, who wavered in the wake of his forced acquiescence to the oath. Abbot Lanfranc (later Archbishop of Canterbury under William the Conqueror) asserted in his *Liber de Corpore et Sanguine Domini* that:

> We believe that through the ministry of the priest, the earthly substances on the Lord's table are sanctified by divine power in a manner that is unspeakable, incomprehensible, marvelous; and that [these substances] are changed into the essence of the Lord's body, even though the appearance of earthly elements remain.[115]

By the twelfth century, both the sacramental theology and the practical observance of the Lord's Supper was well on its way to resembling its later sixteenth century form – the form that was found to be so offensive to Luther, Calvin, Zwingli, and others. Gospel proclamation through celebrating the Sacrament, as Paul intended when he wrote to the Corinthians, was completely subsumed within the *mysterium* of bread and wine transmuted at the prayer of consecration into the true, physical body and blood of Christ. Proclamation of Jesus' once for all atoning death to the inward faith of the celebrants and to the outward gaze of the uninitiated was inverted. For now the intention of the officiating priest and of the celebrants themselves was to offer up to God a true resacrifice of the Lord Jesus.

Thomas Aquinas (1225 – 1274), generally considered greatest among the Medieval theologians of the Western Church, included in the third part (*Tertia Pars*) of his work, *Summa Theologica*, a series of questions and answers pertaining to the theology and practice of the Lord's Supper by the thirteenth century. Although there are two allusions to 1 Corinthians 11:26 involving the questions and answers, Aquinas does not discuss a theology of proclamation. In fact, both of these references

---

[113] Macy, *Treasures from the Storeroom: Medieval Religion and the Eucharist*, p. 22.
[114] Ibid., p. 21.
[115] Frank C. Senn, *Christian Liturgy: Catholic and Evangelical* (Minneapolis: Fortress Press, 1997), p. 251.

to 1 Corinthians 11:26 occur in Aquinas' discussion of the Eucharist, not as explicated answers for theological problems, but as objections to which he responds. For example:

> Obj. VI. St. Paul says, 'As often as you shall eat of this bread and drink of this chalice you shall show the death of the Lord' (1 Cor. 11, 26). Therefore Christ's passion and its fruit should be mentioned in the form of the consecration of the blood rather than in that of the consecration of the body.[116]

Aquinas' reply to this stated objection does not address the proclamatory aspect of the Sacrament and in fact does not even mention the 1 Corinthians 11:26 passage. There are, however, important examples in which this doctor of the Western Church describes the sacramental theology and the praxis of the Supper as of his time of writing (1265 – 1274) in concise and clear detail. A key example is found at the beginning of question 75, 1., concerning, "Whether the body of Christ be in this sacrament in very truth, or merely as in a figure or sign?" Note Aquinas' knowledge of and reliance upon prior theological masters of the church:

> Hilary says (*De Trin.* viii): **"There is no room for doubt regarding the truth of Christ's body and blood; for now by our Lord's own declaring and by our faith His flesh is truly food, and His blood is truly drink**." And Ambrose says (*De Sacram.* vi): "As the Lord Jesus Christ is God's true Son so is it Christ's true flesh which we take, and His true blood which we drink."
>
> I answer that, the presence of Christ's true body and blood in this sacrament cannot be detected by sense, nor understanding, but by faith alone, which rests upon Divine authority. Hence, on Luke 22:19: "This is My body which shall be delivered up for you," Cyril says: "Doubt not whether this be true; but take rather the Saviour's words with faith; for since He is the Truth, He lieth not."
>
> Now this is suitable, first for the perfection of the New Law. For, the sacrifices of the Old Law contained only in figure that true sacrifice of Christ's Passion, according to Hebrews 10:1: "For the law having a shadow of the good things to come, not the very image of the things." And therefore it was necessary that the sacrifice of the New Law instituted by Christ should have something more, **namely, that it should contain Christ Himself crucified, not merely in signification or figure, but also in very truth. And therefore this sacrament which contains Christ Himself**, as Dionysius says (*Eccl. Hier.* iii), is perfective of all the other sacraments, in which Christ's virtue is participated.

---

[116] Thomas Aquinas, *The Blessed Sacrament and the Mass*. Rev. F. O'Neill, trans., ed. (Fort Collins, CO: Roman Catholic Books, 1955), pp. 68 – 69. See also *Summa Theologica*, Tertia Pars: 73, 3, obj. 3.

> Secondly, this belongs to Christ's love, out of which for our salvation He assumed a true body of our nature. And because it is the special feature of friendship to live together with friends, as the Philosopher says (*Ethic.* ix), He promises us His bodily presence as a reward, saying (Matthew 24:28): "Where the body is, there shall the eagles be gathered together." Yet meanwhile in our pilgrimage **He does not deprive us of His bodily presence; but unites us with Himself in this sacrament through the truth of His body and blood. Hence (John 6:57) he says: "He that eateth My flesh, and drinketh My blood, abideth in Me, and I in him."** Hence this sacrament is the sign of supreme charity, and the uplifter of our hope, from such familiar union of Christ with us.
>
> Thirdly, it belongs to the perfection of faith, which concerns His humanity just as it does His Godhead, according to John 14:1: "You believe in God, believe also in Me." And since faith is of things unseen, as Christ shows us His Godhead invisibly, so also in this sacrament He shows us His flesh in an invisible manner.
>
> Some men accordingly, not paying heed to these things, **have contended that Christ's body and blood are not in this sacrament except as in a sign, a thing to be rejected as heretical, since it is contrary to Christ's words.** Hence Berengarius, who had been the first deviser of this heresy, was afterwards forced to withdraw his error, and to acknowledge the truth of the faith.[117]

F. O'Neill, summarizing Aquinas' views on the Eucharist as contained under question 83 maintains that Aquinas firmly held to doctrine of the Supper as true resacrifice. And Aquinas even resorts to 1 Corinthians 11:26 in support of this view. O'Neill writes:

> *The Mass therefore is a Complete Sacrifice and the same as Calvary.* First, because the same victim with the self same will to die once is made present. That is to say, the will that assumed the dread of punishment, the loathing and sorrow for sin, that bowed the back to the scourge, the head to the thorns, the shoulders to the Cross, opened the hands to the nails, and separated body and soul on the Cross is re-presented in the Mass because the Mass re-presents Calvary according to St. Paul (1 Cor. 11, 26): '*For as often as you shall eat this bread and drink this chalice you shall show forth the death of the Lord.*'[118]

---

[117] Aquinas, *The Blessed Sacrament and the Mass*, p. 15. This portion of the *Summa* was expanded from O'Neill's summary, using the edition available on-line through New Advent at: http://www.newadvent.org/summa/4075.htm.

[118] Aquinas, *The Blessed Sacrament and the Mass*, p. 136.

John Duns Scotus (1265/66 – 1308), writing just a short while after Aquinas, held the view that the Supper was a "sacrifice of the Church," offered up to God. Yet he disagreed with other Catholic theologians of his time in maintaining that the offering of the "Mass was not of equal efficacy with the sacrifice of the cross."[119] Scotus seems also to view the Lord's Supper as more of a commemoration, rather than a *reactualization* of Christ's Calvary offering. Frank Senn notes the following fragments from Scotus in support of this interpretation:

> The Mass consists both in representation of that offering made upon the cross and in pleading thereby: that is, pleading that through it God would accept the sacrifice of the Church. (When one pleads he usually does so by adducing something which is more acceptable to him whose favor is sought than is the entreaty of the petitioner himself.)
>
> The Mass is not equal in worth to the passion of Christ, although it has a special worth inasmuch as it is a special commemoration of the oblation which Christ offered on the cross.[120]

By the time Martin Luther took holy orders as an Augustinian monk, the Roman Catholic Church of the sixteenth century was steeped in some 1,400 years of thought and practice concerning the celebration of the Lord's Supper. The rich concept of the Supper as a proclamation of the death of the Lord until his return, instructed by the Apostle Paul to the factionalized believers in Corinth, was buried underneath the theology and praxis of the Mass – the Mass as a resacrifice of the true body and blood of Christ. And if there was any doubt whether this doctrine of Mass as sacrifice impacted matters beyond the writing of theological tracts and tomes, one need only be reminded that, "Pope Honorius III (Pope 1216 – 1227) ordered that when the Sacrament was taken from the church to the sick, the people should bow reverently and lights should be carried before it."[121]

The Eucharist as gospel proclamation to participants and the uninitiated might never have been recovered, what with the daunting, centuries-accumulated weight of church dogma in support of the Mass as resacrifice offered to God, were it not for the fact that an Augustinian monk in the early 16th century wrestled so violently with his own

---

[119] Senn, *Christian Liturgy: Catholic and Evangelical*, p. 255.
[120] Ibid.
[121] Bartels, *Take Eat, Take Drink: The Lord's Supper Through the Centuries*, p. 108.

sinfulness, and thus began to wrestle with the core theology of the gospel in the sacred Scriptures and its implications for the followers of Jesus and the forms of worship of the Church. In this emerging Reformation movement, Martin Luther managed to free the Lord's Supper from its unbiblical and traditional trappings by returning to its original basis – the foundational texts of the New Testament, including 1 Corinthians 11:23 – 26.

I attend to the import of the words, for Christ does not simply present to us the benefit of his death and resurrection, but the very body in which he suffered and rose again. I conclude, that Christ's body is really, (as the common expression is,) – that is, truly given to us in the Supper, to be wholesome food for our souls. I use the common form of expression, but my meaning is, that our souls are nourished by the substance of the body, that we may truly be made one with him, or, what amounts to the same thing, that a life-giving virtue from Christ's flesh is poured into us by the Spirit, though it is at a great distance from us, and is not mixed with us. ...

For as often as ye shall eat. Paul now adds what kind of remembrance ought to be cherished -- that is, with thanksgiving; not that the remembrance consists wholly in confession with the mouth; for the chief thing is, that the efficacy of Christ's death be sealed in our consciences; but this knowledge should stir us up to a confession in respect of praise, so as to declare before men what we feel inwardly before God. The Supper then is (so to speak) a kind of memorial, which must always remain in the Church, until the last coming of Christ; and it has been appointed for this purpose, that Christ may put us in mind of the benefit of his death, and that we may recognize it before men. Hence it has the name of the Eucharist. If, therefore, you would celebrate the Supper aright, you must bear in mind, that a profession of your faith is required from you.

(Jean Calvin, 1 Corinthians 11:23 – 29,
in *Commentaries on the Epistles of Paul the Apostle to the Corinthians,* volume 1)[122]

---

[122] Jean Calvin, *Commentaries on the Epistles of Paul the Apostle to the Corinthians*, vol. 1, John Pringle, trans. (Grand Rapids, MI: Christian Classics Ethereal Library, http://www.ccel.org/ccel/calvin/calcom39.html).

IV

PROCLAMATION REDISCOVERED: THE LORD'S SUPPER AS PROCLAMATION DURING THE REFORMATION

> *The second benefit of the Supper is, that it admonishes and incites us more strongly to recognize the blessings which we have received, and receive daily from the Lord Jesus, in order that we may ascribe to him the praise which is due. For in ourselves we are so negligent that we rarely think of the goodness of God, if he do not arouse us from our indolence, and urge us to our duty. Now there cannot be a spur which can pierce us more to the quick than when he makes us, so to speak, see with the eye, touch with the hand, and distinctively perceive this inestimable blessing of feeding on his own substance. This he means to intimate when he commands us to show forth his death till he come. (1 Cor. xi. 26) If it is then so essential to salvation not to overlook the gifts which God has given us, but diligently to keep them in mind, and extol them to others for mutual edification; we see another singular advantage of the Supper in this, that it draws us off from ingratitude, and allows us not to forget the benefit which our Lord Jesus bestowed upon us in dying for us, but induces us to render him thanks, and, as it were, publicly protest how much we are indebted to him.*
>
> (John Calvin, *Short Treatise on the Lord's Supper*, 1540)[123]

The Reformation began on October 31, 1517, with the posting of a document on the door of the Wittenberg Castle Church inviting disputation entitled, *The Ninety-Five Theses*. This first shot in the conflict of what was to become the Protestant Reformation and Catholic Counter-Reformation was originally intended to address grievances concerning the abuses of the Catholic Church with respect to the sale of indulgences and the profiteering of the Papal authorities. *The Ninety-Five Theses* made no claims for debate concerning the Roman Mass of the sixteenth century. However, it would not be long, once Pope Leo X (June 1520) issued his papal encyclical, entitled *Exsurge Domine* ("Arise, O Lord") refuting Luther, before the author of *The Theses* took aim at the theology and practice of the Latin Eucharist.

---

[123] John Calvin, *Treatises on the Sacraments*. Translated by Henry Beveridge (Grand Rapids: Reformation Heritage Books, 2002), p. 173. The section is numbered 18, and entitled "In the Supper We Are Reminded of Our Duty Towards God."

What was Luther's main objection to the Mass as it was celebrated in his time? Fundamentally it was the shift over the prior centuries from the Lord's Supper as producing a proclamation of the gospel into the hearts of the celebrants and as a testimony to those looking on, into a liturgical rite that implied that the celebrants were themselves making an offering *unto* God. While Frank Senn points out that, "the Mass that Luther attacked was less related to the theology than to practice, piety, and liturgical order,"[124] it is difficult to separate theology from its application into praxis. This is the point made by Norwegian theologian and preacher Carl Fredrik Wisløff (1908 –2004):

> Now when Luther maintains that the mass had been made into a "work" he does not mean by this word simply an external, ritual action. His contention takes into account the religiously serious striving which aims to attain something with God, but without faith. The mass as opus is not simply superstition, but is primarily legalism. With the term "work" reference is made quite inclusively to a spiritual attitude which does not stand face to face with God purely and simply to receive, but wants to present its piety to him.[125]

The interpretation that Luther's problem with the Roman Mass had to do with its promotion of legalism and thus taking away from the all-sufficient, once-for-all atoning sacrifice of Christ is borne out through the available written documents to which Luther was a primary contributor. For example, in *The Augsburg Confession* (1530) within Article III – "Of the Mass", there is a clear statement on the error Rome committed when it entertained the opinion that the Mass was propitiatory:

> There was added an opinion, which increased private Masses infinitely: to wit, that Christ by his passion did satisfy for original sin, and appointed the Mass, wherein an oblation should be made for daily sins, both mortal and venial. Hereupon a common opinion was perceived, that the Mass is a work that taketh away the sins of the quick and the dead, and that for the doing of the work. . . . Our preachers have admonished concerning these opinions that they do depart from the holy Scriptures, and diminish the glory of the passion of Christ. For the passion of Christ was an oblation and satisfaction, not only for original sin, but also for all other sins. . . . The Scripture also teacheth that we are justified before God through faith in Christ, when we believe that our sins are forgiven for Christ's sake. Now, if the Mass do take away the sins of the quick and the dead, even for the work's sake that is done, then justification

---

[124] Frank C. Senn, *Christian Liturgy: Catholic and Evangelical* (Minneapolis: Fortress Press, 1997), p. 268.
[125] Ibid., p. 270.

> cometh by the work of the Mass, and not by faith; which the Scriptures cannot endure.[126]

Within six years of the posting of his *Theses*, Martin Luther, in his, *The Adoration of the Sacrament* (addressed to the Bohemian Brethren in 1523), writes concerning the importance of a thoroughly scripturally based Lord's Supper theology and practice:

> In the first place, we have often said that the chief and foremost thing in the sacrament is the word of Christ, when he says: "Take and eat, this is my body which is given for you." Likewise also, when he took the cup, he said: "Take and drink of it, all of you, this is the cup of a new testament in a my blood which is shed for the forgiveness of sins. As often as you do this, do it in remembrance of me."
>
> Everything depends on these words. Every Christian should and must know them and hold them fast. He must never let anyone take them away from him by any other kind of teaching, even though it were an angel from heaven. They are words of life and of salvation, so that whoever believes in them has all his sins forgiven through that faith. . .[127]

"The Reformers' uncompromising repudiation of the sacrifice of the mass was the consequence of their conviction that it was dishonouring to Christ and incompatible with the New Testament doctrine of salvation. Accordingly, they felt bound to denounce the sarcedotalism of the mass in the strongest terms."[128] The *Godward* dynamics of the mass were entirely reversed from the original institution of the Supper as given by the Lord Jesus and repeated by the Apostle Paul to the Corinthians. The Lord's Supper was given by the Lord to acts as a means of grace within the celebrants and also as a means of gospel proclamation – to believers and nonbelievers alike.

Ulrich Zwingli (1484 – 1531), working for the Reformation during those early years contemporaneous with Luther, was inclined toward a non-bodily presence of Christ in the Supper. While his theology of the Eucharist developed over time (and perhaps he has been unfairly dismissed as a 'mere memorialist'), it is safe to assign to him a

---

[126] Philip Schaff, *The Creeds of Christendom Volume III, The Evangelical Protestant Creeds* (Grand Rapids: Baker Book House, 1998 reprint), pp. 36 – 37.
[127] Lee Palmer Wandel, *The Eucharist in the Reformation: Incarnation and Liturgy* (New York: Cambridge University Press, 2006), p. 101.
[128] Philip Edgcumbe Hughes, *Theology of the English Reformers* (Grand Rapids: William B. Eerdmans Publishing Company, 1965), p. 218.

belief in the spiritual presence of Christ at the Table. In his work, *Fidei expositio* (1531) he writes:

> To eat the body of Christ spiritually is equivalent to trusting with heart and soul upon the mercy and goodness of God through Christ, that is, to have the assurance of an unbroken faith that God will give us the forgiveness of sins and the joy of eternal salvation for the sake of his Son, who gave himself for us and reconciled us and reconciled the divine righteousness to us. For what can he withhold from us when he delivered up his only begotten Son?
>
> If I may put is more precisely, to eat the body of Christ sacramentally is to eat the body of Christ with the heart and the mind in conjunction with the sacrament.[129]

Zwingli is widely recognized for his spiritual presence and for his memorial emphasis with respect to the Lord's Supper. However, what is not as widely known is that his practical theology of the Eucharist includes its gospel proclaiming importance when used according to the biblical narrative. Further in Zwingi's *Fidei expositio* concerning the Supper, he argues:

> Now the Lord's Supper, too, does create faith (historical faith) in this way, that is, **it bears sure witness to the birth and passion of Christ. But to whom does it bear witness? To believers and unbelievers alike. For whether they receive it or not, it testifies to all that which is of the power of the sacrament, the fact that Christ suffered.** But only to the faithful does it testify that he suffered for us.[130]

Reformers such as Luther and Zwingli, and within a short time John Calvin, Martin Bucer (1491 – 1551), Philip Melanchthon (1497 – 1560), and John Knox (1514 – 1572) were inundated with Christians who were leaving the teachings and worship of the Catholic Church in favor of the Reformation. Yet these new congregants were so steeped in the liturgy of the Roman Church and for the most part so uneducated in the scriptural basis for faith and for the Sacraments, that the leaders of the Reformation recognized the need for new catechetical materials. Thus, for the first 150 years, from Luther's 1517 opening salvo to the days of the Westminster Assembly, the growing Protestant movement produced hundreds of confessions of faith and catechisms. One

---

[129] William Stacy Johnson and John H. Leith, editors, *Reformed Reader: A Sourcebook in Christian Theology*, vol. 1, 1519 – 1799 (Louisville, KY: Westminster/John Knox Press, 1993), p. 314.
[130] Ibid., p. 315.

of the earliest of these, insofar as it pertains to recapturing the biblical view of the Lord's Supper as proclamation of the gospel is *The First Confession of Basel* (1534):

> Article V, "Of the Sacraments of the Church"
>
> In this church the same sacraments are practiced, namely, baptism in entrance in entrance into the church (Matt. 3:11; 28:19; Acts 2:41, 42: 16:15, 33; Col. 2:12), and **the Lord's Supper, following later in life, to bear witness to faith and brotherly love**; even as it has been promised in baptism (Matt. 26:26 – 29; Mark 14:22 – 25; Luke 22:19 – 20; 1 Cor. 11:23 – 26).[131]

What did early Protestant celebrations of the Lord's Supper look like? A very helpful example from this period is the description provided of the worship setting for the Supper, explained within the framework of 1 Corinthians 11:26. Found in *The Bohemian Confession* (1535), Article 13 "The Lord's Supper," in part reads:

> Then, while all the rest of the people offer prayers, the ministers, repeating in truth the words of the Lord's Supper, urge the people to believe in the presence of the Body of Christ. They then distribute [the elements] as the people fall on their knees. **While this is going on the people make expressions of gratitude and eagerly preparing themselves that they may do this in accord with the word of Christ to do it in commemoration of Him. As Paul interprets this: "As often as you eat this bread and drink from this cup you proclaim the Lord's death until He comes" [1 Cor. 11:26].**[132]

An eyewitness account, published in France in 1556, sheds a great deal of light upon how the Communion service proceeded in the Pays de Vaud (a Reformed church heavily guided by the Genevan Reformation). Although much of the account of church life in Lausanne was written satirically for a French Catholic audience, its description of the Supper service is confirmed as accurate when collated with other sources from the period:

> Three or four times a year, according to the will of the authorities, two tables are set up in the church, each covered with a tablecloth, and a lot of hosts are set on the left, and three or four cups or glasses on the right, with lots of pots full of either white wine of red wine below the table. And after the sermon the preacher comes down from the pulpit and goes to the end of the table on the side where the hosts are, and with his head uncovered and standing places a

[131] James T. Dennison, Jr., "The First Confession of Basel (1534)," in *Reformed Confessions of the 16th and 17th Centuries in English Translation: Volume 1, 1523 – 1552* (Grand Rapids: Reformation Heritage Books, 2008), p. 290.
[132] Dennison, Jr., "The First Confession of Basel (1534)," pp. 324 – 325.

> piece in each person's hand, saying, "Remember that Jesus Christ died for you." Each person eats his piece while walking to the other end of the table, where he takes something to drink from one of the Lords, or another person deputized for the task, without saying anything, while sergeants with their heads uncovered pour the wine and provide additional hosts if they run out. Throughout all of this, somebody else reads from the pulpit in the vernacular with his head uncovered the gospel of Saint John, from the beginning of the thirteenth chapter, until everyone has taken their piece, both men and women, each one at their different table. . . and after this collation is done they all go dine.[133]

What is immediately apparent from this 1556 description of a typical Reformed Lord's Supper celebration is that the emphasis is placed upon the Word of God in connection with the Sacrament, and upon the participant's remembrance of Christ's death. The sermon preached and the Supper's proclamation of Jesus' death are united as adjacent elements of the liturgy. And the Communion elements are taken and consumed while the Gospel of John is being read. Thus, the sacramental *praxis* of the Reformed churches in the early days of the Reformation reflected their sacramental *theology*, their reading of 1 Corinthians 11:23 – 26, which they understood to connect Christ's words of institution with the eating of bread and drinking of wine involved in the Sacrament.

While the Reformation moved ahead vigorously in parts of Continental Europe, the Church of England was undergoing a significantly Reformed transformation in doctrine and practice under the Archbishop Thomas Cranmer (1489 – 1556), who succeeded Bishop Warham to the Canterbury See upon the latter's death in August 1532. Cranmer was uncompromising in his condemnation of the Catholic doctrine of the Mass, arguing forcefully against the very sacramental theology and praxis which had dominated the Catholic Eucharist since the third century. Examples from Cranmer include:

> The greatest blasphemy and injury that can be against Christ, and yet universally used through the popish kingdom, is this, that **the priests make their mass a sacrifice propitiatory, to remit the sins as well of themselves as of others, both quick and dead**, to whom they list to apply the same. Thus under pretence of holiness the papistical priests have taken upon them to be Christ's successors, and to make such an oblation and sacrifice as never creature made but Christ alone, neither He made the same any more times

[133] Philip Benedict, *Christ's Churches Purely Reformed: A Social History of Calvinism* (New Haven: Yale University Press, 2002), pp. 492 – 493.

> than once, and that was by His death upon the cross. . . . And that sacrifice was of such force that it was no need to renew it every year, as the bishops did of the old testament, whose sacrifices were many times offered, and yet were of no great effect or profit because they were sinners themselves that offered them, and offered not their own blood, but the blood of brute beasts; **but Christ's sacrifice once offered was sufficient for evermore.** . . .The papists, to excuse themselves, do say that they make no new sacrifice, nor none other than Christ made. . . And here they run headlong into the foulest and most heinous error that ever was imagined. **For if they make every day the same oblation and sacrifice for sin that Christ Himself made, and the oblation that He made was His death and effusion of His most precious blood upon the cross, for our redemption and price of our sins, then followeth it of necessity that they every day slay Christ and shed His blood.**[134]

Of course it was not unusual in the early days of the Reformation for those who published and preached against the Roman Catholic doctrine of the Mass to suffer loss of their pulpits and livings, imprisonment, and even martyrdom. This persecution was especially virulent in the days of Bloody Queen Mary in England. And one of those who suffered terribly for their commitment to biblical church practice and biblical Lord's Supper celebration was Nicholas Ridley. Ridley composed a work prior to his execution, entitled, *A Brefe Declaration of the Lordes Supper*, while being held prisoner at Oxford. Within *A Brefe Declaration*, Ridley looks to the Apostle Paul in 1 Corinthians 11, describing the Supper as a remembrance unlike any other known to man, and opposes the Catholic view of transubstantiation:

> Thus the Euangelistes & S. Paule haue rehearsed the words and worke of Christ, wherby he did institute & ordayne thys holy sacrament of hys body & blood, to be a perpetuall remembrance vnto his coming againe of him selfe. ... But this remembrance is of his body geuen for vs, and of his blood shedde for the remission of synnes. But this remembraunce which is thus ordained, as ye autor therof is Christe, bothe God and man, so by the almightye power of God, it farre passethe all kyndes of remembraunces, that anye other man is able to make eyther of hym selfe, or of anye other thing. ...
>
> Nowe on ye other syde, yf after the truth shalbe truly tried out, it shalbe founde, that the substaunce of bread is the naturall substaunce of the Sacrament, although for the chaunge of the vse, office and dignitie of ye bread, the bread in dede sacramentally is chaunged into the body of Christ, as the water in Baptisme is sacramentally chaunged into the fountayne of regeneration, 7 yet the naturall substaunce therof remayneth all one, as was before: if (I say) the true solucion of that former question (whervpon all these controuersies do hang) be, that the naturall substaunce of breade, is the materiall substaunce in the Sacrament of Christes blessed body: than must it

[134] Hughes, *Theology of the English Reformers*, pp. 218 – 219.

> nedes folowe of the former proposition (confessed of all that be named to bee learned, so farre as I doo knowe, in Englands) which is that there is but one materiall substance in the Sacrament of the body, and one onely lykewyse in the Sacrament of the bloude, that there is no such thyng in dede and in truthe, as they call Transubstantiation.[135]

In the *Confession of the Glastonbury Congregation* (1551), the product of pastor Vallérandus Poullain (1520 – 1557) and a refugee French Reformed congregation offered protection in England by Archbishop Cranmer, the Lord's Supper is beautifully described as "the Sacrament of Reconciliation, wherein according to Christ's institution the remembrance of His death is celebrated, and by the distribution of the broken bread and of the cup of blessing there is a communicating and imparting of the body and blood of Christ to all that communicate with true faith, for the sustenance of eternal life . . ."[136]

The Polish Reformed convert, John à Lasco (1499 – 1560), likely in collaboration with Marten Micron and ruling elder John Utenhove, created "a summary of Christian truth which was to be appropriated and understood by those applying to the Lord's Table."[137] This *Emden Examination of Faith* (1553) was used by the refugee Emden congregation as it sojourned in London (beginning ca 1551). Questions 33 – 35 have to do with the Lord's Supper. However, only question 33 is of specific relevance to the present study:

> Question 33. "What is the Lord's Supper?"
> Answer: It is an institution of Christ in which **through the eating of broken bread and the drinking of the cup, the Lord's death is proclaimed** (Matt. 26:26; Mark 14:22; Luke 22:19; 1 Cor. 11:23).[138]

Clearly these early Protestant congregations sought to strip the Roman celebration of the Eucharist of all its non-biblical accretions and return to the Pauline and Gospels' teachings as to importance and the use of the Lord's Supper. Yet sometimes the early

---

[135] Nicholas Ridley, *A Brief Declaration of the Lord's Supper* (London, UK: Seeley and Co. Limited, 1895, reprint), pp. 100, 108. The original typesetting of the 1586 edition has been preserved.

[136] Dennison, Jr., "Vallérandus Poullain (1551)," in *Reformed Confessions of the 16th and 17th Centuries in English Translation: Volume 1, 1523 – 1552* (Grand Rapids: Reformation Heritage Books, 2008), pp. 660 – 661.

[137] Dennison, Jr., "Emden Examination of Faith (1553)," in *Reformed Confessions of the 16th and 17th Centuries in English Translation: Volume 2, 1552 – 1566* (Grand Rapids: Reformation Heritage Books, 2010), p. 43.

[138] Ibid., p. 50.

catechisms and confessions were brief, and did not always provide the sort of exegetical explanations found in the treatises of the Reformers. How did the early Protestant congregations understand that their Supper celebrations "proclaimed the Lord's death"? How were their pastors exhorting this?

A good source to find answers to these questions in none other than John Calvin (1509 – 1564), who was hard at work in Geneva by this time, and had through successive editions of his *Institutes* (1536 – 1559), developed a systematic Reformed approach to the theology and practice of the Supper. It was an approach that countered the abuses of the Roman Mass, shared some commonalities with Luther and Lutheranism, and yet differed as to the nature of the presence of Christ, which Calvin firmly maintained was *real*, but *spiritual*. While Calvin briefly mentions 1 Corinthians 11:26 in his commentary, *The First Epistle of Paul to the Corinthians* (1546),[139] referring to the Supper as a "kind of memorial (*quoddam memoriale*), it is within his magisterial *Institutes of the Christian Religion* (Book IV. Ch. 17. 37) that the great Reformer provides his exegetical analysis of this text and its importance with respect to the Supper:

> We previously discussed how the Sacrament of the Sacred Supper serves our faith before God. But, **the Lord here not only recalls to our memory, as we have already explained, the abundance of his bounty, but, so to speak, gives into our hand and arouses us to recognize it.** At the same time he admonished us not to be ungrateful for such lavish beneficence, but rather to proclaim it with fitting praises and to celebrate it with thanksgiving. Therefore, when he gave the institution of the Sacrament itself to the apostles, he taught them to do it remembrance of him [Luke 22:19]. **This Paul interpreted as "to declare the Lord's death" [1 Cor. 11:26], that is, with a single voice to confess openly before men that for us the whole assurance of life and salvation rests upon the Lord's death, that we may glorify him by our confession, and by our example exhort others to give glory to him.** Here again **the purpose of the Sacrament is made clear, that is, to exercise us in the remembrance of Christ's death.** For the command to us to "**declare** the Lord's death till he come" [1 Cor. 11:26] in judgment **means nothing else than that we should by the confession of our mouth declare what our faith**

[139] John Calvin, *The First Epistle of Paul to the Corinthians*, John W. Fraser, trans., David W. Torrance and Thomas F. Torrance, eds. (Grand Rapids: Wm. B. Eerdmans Publishing Company, 1960, reprint 1968), p. 250. Calvin writes of verse 26 as Paul's "description of the way in which the memorial ought to be kept, viz. with thanksgiving. . . . But this knowledge ought to move us to praise Him openly, so as to let men know, when we are in their company, what we are aware of within ourselves in the presence of God."

> **recognizes in the Sacrament: that the death of Christ is our life**. Here is the second use of the Sacrament, which pertains to outward confession.[140]

For Calvin, every celebration of the Lord's Supper was a response to Paul's exhortation to proclaim, or declare, the Lord's death until he comes. The Sacrament promoted confession of faith in Christ and served as an exemplar toward the watching world. Calvin later adds, while refuting the Roman Catholic doctrine of the Mass as resacrifice of Christ's body and blood, that, "The Lord's Supper cannot be without a sacrifice of this kind, in which, while we proclaim his death [1 Cor. 11:26] and give thanks, we do nothing but offer a sacrifice of praise" (*Institutes*, IV. XVIII. 17).[141] Thus in addition to proclaiming the Lord's death, confessing faith in Christ, and glorifying Christ's work for a watching world, the Lord's Supper included an offering from the participants – but only an offering of praise, rightly due to the Lord, whose body and blood were symbolized and brought to remembrance in the Supper.

"When it comes to discussing the practical utility of sacraments Calvin has much to say. There is 'nothing more useful' in the Church than the Lord's Supper, and this is the reason why from the beginning the devil has sought to contaminate its observance by errors and superstitions."[142] Any accretions of liturgical showmanship or ceremonial actions not found in the instructions of Paul's epistle or within the pages of the Gospels are superfluous and dangerous in Calvin's view. Therefore he found much to argue with in the Roman Catholic practices of the Mass, as well as the centuries-old theology which lay behind its pomp and ceremony.

Yet in terms of the importance of the use of the Sacraments within their biblical confines, "Calvin is willing to transfer to the sacraments Paul's title for the Gospel, and to call them the *power of God unto salvation to everyone that believeth*."[143] Ronald Wallace, within his work on Calvin and the Sacraments, identifies Calvin's three aspects of their usefulness:

---

[140] John Calvin, *Institutes of the Christian Religion*, vol. 2 (John T. McNeill, ed., Ford Lewis Battles, trans. (Philadelphia: The Westminster Press, 1960), p. 1414.
[141] Calvin, *Institutes of the Christian Religion*, p. 1445.
[142] Ronald S. Wallace, *Calvin's Doctrine of the Word and Sacrament* (Grand Rapids: Wm. B. Eerdmans, 1953, 2nd ed. 1957), p. 240.
[143] Wallace, *Calvin's Doctrine of the Word and Sacrament*, p. 240.

> **Firstly, they assist spiritual growth by uniting us more fully to the Christ the more they are used by faith**. . . . This is the case when that which is offered is received by us in true faith. In the Supper our communion with Christ is "confirmed and increased; for, although Christ is exhibited to us both in Baptism and in the Gospel, we do not, however, receive Him entire but in part only."
>
> **Secondly, they confirm and increase the faith of believers**, which, once engendered, is so continually beset by temptation to doubt and by manifold difficulties that it requires to be continually supported and continually purged from unbelief. Those who possess Christ by faith must persevere in faith so that Christ may be a perpetual possession. The sacraments assist in such perfecting and perseverance of faith, and, in so doing, again assist growth in Christ.
>
> **Thirdly, the sacraments are a spur to practical Christian living.** The sacraments bring home to us so vividly the reality and intimacy of our union with the exalted Christ as to lead to practical conduct befitting those who enjoy such high privileges. **"There cannot be a spur which can pierce us more to the quick than when He makes us, so to speak, see with the eye, touch with the hand, and distinctly perceive the inestimable blessing of feeding on His own substance.**[144]

In addition to Calvin's rich descriptions of the importance of biblical Lord's Supper observance for the inward growth in grace of believing recipients, the Genevan Reformer understood and promoted the benefits of Communion celebrations for the outwardly expressed Christian ideals of the unity of the body and the nurture of brotherly love – those trademarks of the redeemed covenant family, united together under the blood of Christ. "The Lord's Supper," for Calvin, "is above all a feast of fellowship instituted 'especially that we should cultivate charity and concord together as becomes members of the same body.'" According to Calvin:

> **Christ intended the Supper "to be an exhortation** that which no other could urge or animate us more strongly both to purity and holiness of life and also to charity, peace and concord. For the Lord there communicated His body so that He may become altogether one with us and we with Him... **This unity is represented by the bread which is exhibited in the sacrament. As it is composed of many grains so mingled together that one cannot be distinguished from the other; so ought our minds to be cordially united as not to allow any dissension or division.**[145]

---

[144] Ronald S. Wallace, *Calvin's Doctrine of the Word and Sacrament* (Grand Rapids: Wm. B. Eerdmans, 1953, 2nd ed. 1957), p. 240.

[145] Ibid, p. 242.

Clearly, John Calvin sought to rediscover and then to propagate a biblical doctrine of the Lord's Supper, freed from the layers of tradition and embellishments infused into the Supper since the second century. The Lord's Supper was indispensable to the life of the church and the growth and sanctification of believers. Yet Calvin also strove never to divorce Communion celebration from the ministry of the Word – that is, he connected the verbal proclamation of the gospel with the visual proclamation of the Sacrament. For Calvin, there was an essential, non-negotiable partnership between the Word of God preached from the pulpit and the Word of God proclaimed visibly through the Lord's Supper. The biblical revelation of God was essential to provide the context for the prophetic symbols of bread and wine, and also to provide the correct Godward focus for the participants:

> **The sacraments should not be celebrated without a Word giving "a full explanation of the ordinance and clear statement of its promises".** There must be no "muttering and gesticulating like sorcerers" by ministers who "think to persuade Jessu Christ to come down into their hands". **If this Word is lacking, the "proper and principle substance of the Supper is wanting", for in the celebration of the sacraments the people must be led to "look not to the bare signs but rather to the promise thereto annexed",** and no one must be allowed to "stand gazing on the elements". Therefore a "voice must be distinctly heard throughout proclaiming that we must adhere to none but Christ alone", and **the visible ceremony must not be allowed so to obtrude on the consciousness of the participants that they become taken up with the dramatic and spectacular vividness of the ceremony taking place before their eyes rather than with the meaning of the simple action through which the Lord is seeking to speak to them**.[146]

Many others followed in Calvin's footsteps concerning what it meant to celebrate the Lord's Supper in a biblical manner. Theodore Beza's Confession (1560), known as, *A Brief and Pithy Sum of Christian Faith*, is considered "an abbreviated Calvin's *Institutes*. Beza (1519 – 1605) would settle in Geneva in 1559 as the first professor of Greek at the recently founded university and would become the noted successor to the Genevan star (Calvin) on the latter's death in 1564."[147] His work attached significance to the proclamation of Jesus' passion through the symbols, actions, participation, and words of institution of the Supper. He writes:

---

[146] Wallace, *Calvin's Doctrine of the Word and Sacrament*, pp. 242 – 243.
[147] Dennison, Jr., "Theodore Beza's Confession (1560)," in *Reformed Confessions of the 16th and 17th Centuries in English Translation: Volume 2, 1552 – 1566* (Grand Rapids: Reformation Heritage Books, 2010), p. 237.

> 35. *What things Properly Belong to the Sacraments, Having respect to the end for Which They Were Ordained*
>
> . . . **since the simple Word preached touches only one of the senses, the sacraments touch more (such as sight and other bodily senses).** They also are distributed with express ceremonies and are of great signification, so it is easy to be perceived how necessary it is for us to use the sacrament to increase and support our faith (Chrysostom, "Homily 83," on *Matthew*), which (after a manner of speaking) our finger and eye, and already by taste and feel in effect, the commodity of what we look for, [is] as though we had possessed it already. **Therefore, it is so far from us to denigrate the holy sacraments that we cannot (worthily, as it is our duty) extol and magnify the dignity and lawful use of the sacraments enough**. . . .
>
> . . .**The declaration of the death of Jesus Christ and consequently of all that He did for us, with thanksgiving for the benefits received and examining and proving ourselves, are the substance of the Supper (1 Cor. 11:25 – 26).**[148]

The Heidelberg Catechism (1563) as other Lutheran and Reformed catechisms before it, provided close instruction on the doctrines of Protestant Christianity, including theology and practice concerning the Lord's Supper. And in keeping with the Reformers' desire to return the Supper to its biblical basis, *The Heidelberg Catechism* often provided quotations from the Word of God in answer to the posed questions. For example, Question 77, which asks, "Where has Christ promised that he will thus feed and nourish believers with his body and blood, as certainly as they eat of this broken bread and drink of this cup?" Is answered using the 1 Corinthians Supper passage:

> In the institution of the Supper, which runs thus: The Lord Jesus, the same night in which he was betrayed, took bread; and when he had given thanks, he brake it, and said: 'Take, eat, this is my body, which is broken for you; this do in remembrance of me.' After the same manner also he took the cup, when he had supped, saying: 'This cup is the New Testament in my blood; this do ye often as ye drink it, in remembrance of me. For as often as ye eat the bread, and drink this cup, ye do show the Lord's death till he come.' And this promise is repeated also by St. Paul, where he says: The cup of blessing which we bless, is it not the communion of the blood of Christ? The bread which we break, is it not the communion of the body of Christ? For we, being many, are one bread, and one body; for we are all partakers of that one bread.[149]

---

[148] Dennison, Jr., "Theodore Beza's Confession (1560)," pp. 287, 297.
[149] Schaff, *The Creeds of Christendom*, pp. 333 – 334.

In order to provide interpretive clarity for *The Heidelberg Catechism*, one of its authors wrote a detailed exposition of its meaning. Zacharius Ursinus (1534 – 1583) created a *Commentary on the Heidelberg Catechism*. Ursinus explicates what the catechism means when using 1 Corinthians 11:26 with reference to Communion under the section entitled, "The Lord's Supper, Question 77:

> *As often as ye eat this bread*: The supper is, therefore, to be frequently celebrated, which we may also establish from its design, which is to celebrate the Lord's death.
>
> *Ye do shew the Lord's death*: Believe that Christ died, and that for you; then profess his death publicly before all.
>
> *Until he come*: This supper is, therefore, to be perpetuated unto the end of the world, nor is any other external form of worship to be expected. [150]

Former galley slave and exile John Knox, who sought refuge in Calvin's Geneva and quickly mastered Reformed theology and worship, in time virtually single-handedly exported the Calvinistic Reformation to Scotland. In doing so he also authored *The First Scots Confession* (1560), which says in Article XXI concerning the Supper:

> We utterly damn the vanity of those who affirm sacraments to be nothing else but naked and bare signs. . . .We spiritually eate the fleshe of Christ, and drinke his bloude; then we dwell in Christ, and Christ in us; we be one with Christ, and Christ with us."[151]

The section immediately afterward, Article XXII, "The Right Administration of the Sacraments", makes reference to "1 Cor. xi. 25, 26", and explains the meaning of "shaw furth" (καταγγέλλετε) as to extol, preach, magnify, and praise:

> . . .**The end and cause of *Christs* institution, and why the selfsame suld be used, is expressed in thir words, used, *Doe ze this in remembrance of me, als oft as ze sall eit this bread, and drinke this coupe, ze sall shaw furth,* that is, extoll, preach, magnifie, and praise *the Lord's death, till he cum.*** Bot to qhuat end, and in what opinioun the Priestes say their Messe, let the wordes of the same, their awin Doctouris and writings witness: To wit, that they, as Mediatoris betwixt *Christ* and his Kirk, do offer unto God the Father, a Sacrifice propitiatory for the sinnes of the quick and the dead. Quhilk doctrine, as blasphemous to *Christ Jesus*, and

---

[150] Zacharias Ursinus, *The Commentary of Zarcharias Ursinus on the Heidelberg Catechism*, G. W. Williard, trans. (Phillipsburg, NJ: Presbyterian and Reformed Publishing Company, 1852, undated reprint), p. 388.

[151] Senn, *Christian Liturgy: Catholic and Evangelical*, p. 365.

> making derogation to the sufficiency of his only Sacrifice, once offered for purgation of all they that sall be sanctified, we utterly abhorre, detest and renounce.[152]

Knox had a difficult situation on his hands when he left Geneva and began work in Edinburgh. Scotland had been thoroughly Catholicized over centuries of Roman influence, and had always been *cozy* politically with Catholic France. Knox genuinely loved the Supper, saying that, "The Lord Jesus, by earthy and visible things set before us, lifts us up to heavenly and invisible things." And perhaps as much as any of the Reformation's leading lights, Knox had to defend every doctrine he drew from Scripture against many centuries of Catholic tradition and certainly against widely accepted and cherished Roman liturgy. Nowhere was this more obvious for Knox than when pitting the Protestant Lord's Supper against the Roman Mass. Lee Palmer Wandel writes of Knox's theological and practical concerns in Supper observance:

> In *The Scots Confession*, John Knox distinguished between three different categories by which one could speak of the Eucharist: form, purpose, and meaning. He expressly opposed "the Roman Church" – simultaneously a nationalist and religious polemic – to the "true Kirk" in each of these three discrete categories. Failure to cleave to the Word of God in any one of the three categories was blasphemous; only the faithful adherence to Scripture in all three constituted the true sacrament.[153]

"Knox's successor at St. Giles', Robert Bruce, regarded the Supper also as the very foundation of the visible body of the church."[154] He engaged in passionate, powerful preaching on the importance of the elements, the actions, the participation, and the narrative of Jesus' passion as constituting *essential ceremonies* and signs testifying of the Lord's atoning death and the application of the benefits of that gruesome, substitutionary death to believers. One such sermon was delivered in 1589 at the Kirk in Edinburgh. Among the many things Bruce proclaimed about the importance of the Supper were these:

> Every rite or ceremony in the sacrament is a sign, and has its own spiritual signification, such as looking at the breaking of the bread, which represents to you the breaking of the body and blood of Christ. It is not that his body was broken in bone of limb, but that it was broken in pain, in anguish and

[152] Schaff, *The Creeds of Christendom*, p. 473.
[153] Wandel, *The Eucharist in the Reformation: Incarnation and Liturgy*, p. 189.
[154] Ross Mackenzie, "Reformed Theology and Roman Catholic Doctrine of the Eucharist as Sacrifice," in Journal of Ecumenical Studies, 15 no 3 Sum 1978, p. 429.

> distress of heart, under the weight of the indignation and wrath of God, which he sustained in bearing our sins. **Thus the breaking is an essential ceremony, the pouring out of the wine is also an essential ceremony; for, as you see clearly, by the wine is signified the blood of Christ, so by the pouring out of the wine is signified that his blood was severed from his flesh. The severing of these two makes death, for in blood is the life. Consequently, it testifies to his death. The pouring out of the wine, therefore, tells you that he died for you, that his blood was shed for you, so that this is an essential ceremony which must not be omitted. Likewise, the distribution, the giving and eating of the bread, are essential ceremonies.** And what does that eating testify to you? The application of the body and blood of Christ to your soul. . . . This conjunction between our body and the body of Christ is brought about by two special means: by means of the Holy Spirit and by means of faith.[155]

In spite of the feverish labors of the Protestant Reformers to reach a more biblical theology and practice of the Lord's Supper, aligned with the Apostle Paul's teachings in 1 Corinthians 11:17 – 34, the Roman Church maintained its traditional liturgy and its scholastic, sacerdotal, sacramental theology. Between 1545 and 1563, the Council of Trent convened to deliberate the nature of the Catholic Church and to formalize its responses to the Protestants on all the key points of dispute. "In session 13, on 11 October 1551, the Council finalized decrees and canons on the doctrines of the real presence and transubstantiation. Chapter 1 decreed the real presence:

> In the first place, **the holy council teaches and openly and without qualification professes that, after the consecration of the bread and the wine, our lord Jesus Christ, true God and true man, is truly, really and substantially contained in the propitious sacrament of the holy eucharist** under the appearance of those things which are perceptible to the senses. . .
>
> . . .Chapter 4 stated the doctrine of transubstantiation:
>
> But since Christ our redeemer said that is was truly his own body which he was offering under the form of bread, therefore there has always been complete conviction in the church of God – and this holy council now declares it once again – that, by the **consecration of the bread and wine, there takes place the change of the substance of the bread into the substance of the body of Christ our Lord, and of the whole substance of the wine into the substance of his blood.** And the holy **catholic church has suitably and properly called the change transubstantiation.**[156]

---

[155] Mackenzie, "Reformed Theology and Roman Catholic Doctrine of the Eucharist as Sacrifice," pp. 429 – 430.
[156] Wandel, *The Eucharist in the Reformation: Incarnation and Liturgy*, p. 221.

What had begun with the proposed disputations of Augustinian monk Martin Luther in 1517 as an effort to reform the Roman Church from within, quickly became a fracture of the Western Church into Catholic and Protestant. The differences which began over indulgences and the greed of the curates rapidly encompassed all areas of theology and practice which the Reformers deemed to be out of accord with Scripture. Instead of reform from within, a new branch of the Christian Church was born. And the theological, ecclesiological, and liturgical gap remains as wide today as in the 1500s. In response, the Roman Church continued to stand for its cherished theology of resacrifice and transubstantiation in the Roman Missal. Fresh on the heels of the Council of Trent's statements, Pope Pius V, in a catechism issued in 1566, declared:

> We therefore confess that the sacrifice of the mass is and ought to be considered one and the same sacrifice as that of the cross, for the victim is one and the same, namely, Christ our Lord, who offered himself, once only, a bloody sacrifice on the altar of the cross. The bloody and unbloody victim are two, but one victim only, whose sacrifice is renewed in the eucharist.... The sacred and holy sacrifice of the mass is not a sacrifice of praise and thanksgiving only, or a mere commemoration of the sacrifice performed on the cross, but also truly a propitiatory sacrifice, by which God is appeased and rendered propitious to us.[157]

As the years classified in history as the Reformation rolled into the years of the Puritans and then those of the Enlightenment, the rift between the Protestant recovery of biblical Lord's Supper observance on the one hand, and the Roman Catholic insistence upon their own traditions and praxis of the Mass on the other hand, continued, severely impacting worship, communities, and civil affairs throughout Europe and the areas now comprising the United Kingdom. Yet for those seeking to celebrate the Lord's Supper as Paul had exhorted in 1 Corinthians 11:23 – 25, and seeking in their celebrations to *proclaim the Lord's death until he comes* (1 Corinthians 11:26), the events of the Reformation era were a watershed. Among the Protestant churches, there was renewed hope and a growing assurance that their Communion theology and praxis were founded upon and contextualized by the Word of God.

---

[157] Mackenzie, "Reformed Theology and Roman Catholic Doctrine of the Eucharist as Sacrifice," p. 433.

Very well, then. When the Lord says, "This do in remembrance of Me," He gives us a memorial of His death—which plainly teaches us that the chief point of remembrance in our Lord Jesus is His death. He Himself regarded His death as the very center, heart and soul of what He would fix on our memories. Therefore those who say that His example is everything, or His teaching is everything, do greatly err—for when we remember Him, the first thing to be remembered is, "He has redeemed us to God by His blood." "Redeemer" is the name to which our memories must most tenaciously cling. His blood, His redemption, His atonement, His substitutionary sacrifice are always to be kept to the front.

"We preach Christ crucified," and you believe in Christ crucified. The reason of our success under God in this House of Prayer is that we have always preached Christ as the atoning sacrifice—the sinner's Substitute. And whosoever shall preach this boldly, clearly and thoroughly, putting it as the crown of the Gospel system, shall find God will bless His preaching. As for you, if you would have comfort and joy and peace, cling to the Cross. Look steadily to the accepted sacrifice. Never get away from your Lord Jesus. And when you remember Him, let His passion be the main thought which rises before you.

Next, notice another thing—this festival reminds us of the Covenant of Grace. Our Lord Jesus Christ, while He bade us remember Himself, said of the cup, "This cup is the new covenant in My blood." That is the word. Read "testament," if you prefer it. But I feel sure you are nearer the sense when you read "the new covenant in My blood." What, then? When I am to remember Jesus Himself, I am to take the cup which is the token of the Covenant. Ah, Beloved, you cannot know Christ thoroughly unless you understand the doctrine of the two Covenants and connect Him with the Covenant of Grace.

(Charles H. Spurgeon, "The Lord's Supper – A Remembrance of Jesus," Sermon #2038, *Metropolitan Tabernacle Pulpit*, August 19, 1888.)[158]

---

[158] Charles Haddon Spurgeon, "The Lord's Supper – A Remembrance of Jesus," Sermon no. 238, in Metropolitan Tabernacle Pulpit, August 19, 1888, (orig. publublished 1888, www.spurgeongems.org/vols34-36/chs2038.pdf), p. 6.

V

PROCLAMATION SEPARATED: THE LORD'S SUPPER IN PROTESTANT CHURCH PRACTICE SINCE THE REFORMATION

> *As the Eucharist forms the very heart of the whole Christian worship, so it is clear that the entire question of the Church, which all are compelled to acknowledge, the great life-problem of the age, centers ultimately in the sacramental question as its inmost heart and core. Our view of the Lord's Supper must ever condition and rule in the end our view of Christ's person and the conception we form of the Church. It must influence at the same time, very materially, our whole system of theology, as well as all our ideas of ecclesiastical history. Is it true that the modern Protestant Church in this country has, in large part at least, fallen away from the sacramental doctrine of the sixteenth century. All must at least allow, that there is some room for asking the question.*
>
> (Rev. John W. Nevin, D. D., late professor of theology, the Reformed Church, 1867)[159]

On April 29, 1647, the Cromwellian House of Commons of England's Long Parliament directed that six hundred copies of the Westminster Assembly of Divines' *Confession of Faith, with the Quotations and Texts of Scripture annexed*, be printed. Originally called together by Parliament to review and revise the *Thirty-nine Articles of the Church of England*, this assembly at Westminster fashioned a thoroughly Reformed and Presbyterian confession of the Christian faith. In chapter XXIX, *Of the Lords Supper*, the Westminster Divines began their confession concerning Communion upon the basis of Paul's 1 Corinthians 11:23 – 26 teachings, providing them in the margins as directed by the House of Commons. This beginning portion of chapter XXIX reads:

> Our Lord Jefus, in the night wherein he was betrayed, Inftituted the Sacrament of his Body and Blood, called the Lord's Supper, to be obferved in his Church, unto the end of the World, for the perpetual Remembrance of the facrifice of Himfelf, in his Death; the fealing all benefits thereof unto true Believers, their Spiritual nourifhment & growth in him, their further ingagement in, and to, all duties which they owe unto him, and, to be a bond,

[159] John W. Nevin, *The Mystical Presence. A Vindication of the Reformed or Calvinistic Doctrine of the Holy Eucharist*, (Philadelphia: S. R. Fisher & Co., 1867), p. 3.

> and pledge of their Communion with him, and with each other, as members of his myftical Body.[160]

This section of the *Westminster Confession of Faith* uses 1 Corinthians 11:23 – 26 as the basis for arguing that when the Lord's Supper is celebrated biblically by a congregation of Christians, the Lord's atoning death is brought to remembrance, all the benefits flowing from redemption are signified to believers, and a visible bond is displayed of their communion with the Lord and with other believers. Thus in this explication of Paul and his directions concerning the Supper, the importance of the Sacrament is clearly in its proclamation of the gospel to believers.

Nearly one year after the first publication of the *Westminster Confession of Faith*, on the 14th of April in 1648, the House of Commons, assembled in Parliament, made provision for the printing and distribution of six hundred copies of the *Larger Catechism* "with Scripture proofs, upon the advice of the Assembly of Divines." One of the original questions included in the work simply posed the question, "What is the Lords Supper?" The answer provided by the Westminster Assembly made use of 1 Corinthians 11:26 (and other textual proofs) and brought clarity to the Scots-English Presbyterian doctrine and practice of the Supper:

> A. The Lords Supper is a Sacrament of the New Testament, wherein, by giving and receiving bread and wine according to the appointment of Jefus Chrift, his death is fhewed forth, and they that worthily communicate, feed upon his body and bloud, to their fpirituall nourifhment and growth in grace, have their union and communion with him confirmed, teftify and renue their thankfulness and ingagement to God, and their mutuall love and fellowfhip each with other, as members of the fame myfticall body.[161]

This question and answer from *The Larger Catechism* is a summary of sacramental (specifically Supper) doctrine, composed for the same purpose as the catechisms and creeds from the heart of the early Reformation. It was designed to educate and to prepare new believers, or converts from Catholicism, in the meaning and the celebration of the Lord's Supper. Here again, as with the *Confession of Faith*, there is

---

[160] "The Confession of Faith," in *The Westminster Standards: An Original Facsimile*, with forward by William S. Barker (Audobon, NJ: Old Paths Publications, 1997 from an original 1648 ed.), pp. 49 – 50. Spelling as original.

[161] "The Larger Catechism," in *The Westminster Standards: An Original Facsimile*, with forward by William S. Barker (Audobon, NJ: Old Paths Publications, 1997 from an original 1648 ed.), p. 55. Spelling as original.

an emphasis on "showing forth" the death of Christ. Yet added to this important aspect of the Supper, are the concepts of spiritual nourishment and growth in grace (highlighting the Sacrament as a "means of grace"), as a testimony of faith, as an opportunity to offer thanksgiving, and as token of mutual love and fellowship between the participants, who together compose the *mystical body* of Christ.

By the middle of the seventeenth century, the Puritan influence, as well as that of other more austere Protestant groups, was beginning to be felt in England, Holland, and the new British settlements in North America. This movement made a great impact, even as the Presbyterian and Reformed theology was reaching its zenith in Europe and in Britain. The Society of Friends was especially hostile to celebrating the Lord's Supper with any frequency – believing that true communion was now accomplished through the indwelling Holy Spirit:

> . . . the Friends, their disparagement of the Sacraments has been rather due to an excessive supernaturalism (in the celebrations of the Roman Mass). The inwardness which they conceive as belonging to a religion enjoyed under the dispensation of the Holy Spirit implies a superiority to all external forms, the Lord's Supper included. **The Communion does not consist "in any symbolic breaking of bread and drinking of wine, but in that daily communion with Christ through the Holy Spirit, and through the obedience of faith, by which the believer is nourished.** [162]

Puritan Richard Vines (1600 – 1655), who appreciated the Lord's Supper, wrote concerning Paul's use of καταγγέλλετε with respect to Communion, within his, *The Passover: Its Significance, and the Analogy Between it and Christ our Passover,* that, "The Apostle, in alluding to their custom, uses a word in 1 Corinthians 11:26 (*as often as ye eat this bread and drink this cup, ye do show forth the Lord's death till He come*) that means "to commemorate "of "with thanksgiving and affection to set it forth."[163] Vines also wrote in his, *A Treatise of the Institution, Right administration, and Receiving of the Sacrament of the Lord's Supper*, that, " 'it [the Supper] is a solemn part of God's positive worship, to shew forth the death of Christ our Lord, not by meer historicall relation, but a practicall and publique profession of our faith, and

---

[162] Robert M. Adamson, *The Christian Doctrine of the Lord's Supper* (Edinburgh: T & T Clark, 1905), p. 95.

[163] Richard Vines, "The Passover: Its Significance, and the Analogy Between it and Christ our Passover," in *The Puritans on the Lord's Supper*, edited by Don Kistler (Morgan, PA: Soli Deo Gloria, 1997), p. 16.

acceptance thereof.' It is in the Supper that the church professes 'that God hath transferred the curse of the law to another, who underwent it', namely, Jesus Christ the Crucified."[164]

On December 24, 1669, that great Puritan theologian and preacher, John Owen (1616 – 1683), preached a marvelous sermon (more accurately, Communion 'meditation') in which he explicated his understanding of 1 Corinthians 11:26 as it applied to the Lord's Supper. For Owen, the celebration of the Lord's Supper *represented* the Lord's passion to believers and at the same time was a means of *profession* to others looking on. In doing this Owen operates within the same framework as the Westminster Divines in their catechisms and *Confession of Faith*. However Owen writes of another aspect more directly than did the Westminster Assembly. Owen includes an aspect of the Supper's proclamation as it professes Christ's death "unto others":

> One end, you see, of this great ordinance, is to show the Lord's death, – to declare it, to represent it, to show it forth, hold it forth; the word [καταγγέλλετε] is thus variously rendered. And in the especial ends of this ordinance it is that we have special communion with our Lord Jesus Christ.
>
> Now there are two ways whereby we show forth the Lord's death; the one is the way of representation to ourselves; and the other is a way of profession unto others...[165]

Owen continues in this particular discourse (*Discourse 4*), describing the "three ways whereby God represents Christ to the faith of believers" – by means of the written word of the gospel, by means of ministry and preaching of the gospel, and finally, "in particular by this sacrament, wherein we represent the Lord's death to the faith of our own souls." Under subheading iii, Owen describes the significance of the Sacrament in representing Christ to the faith of believers:

> The special way whereby we represent Christ unto our souls through faith, is in the *administration of this ordinance*; which I will speak to upon the great end of showing forth the death of the Lord.
>
> Now the former representations were general, this is particular; and I cannot at this time go over particulars. I bless the Lord, my soul hath many times

---

[164] Jon D. Payne, *John Owen on the Lord's Supper* (Edinburgh: Banner of Truth Trust, 2004), p. 70.
[165] Payne, *John Owen on the Lord's Supper*, p. 117.

> admired the wisdom and goodness of God in the institution of this one ordinance; that he took bread and wine for that end and purpose, . . .One end of the ordinance itself is, to represent the death of Christ unto us; and it represents Christ with reference to these five things: 1. It represents him with reference to God's *setting him forth.* 2. In reference to his own *passion.* 3. In reference to his *exhibition in the promise*. 4. To our *participation* of him by believing. And, 5.To his *incorporation* with us in union.[166]

John Owen also explained and emphasized the importance of the visual symbolism of the Supper within the section which followed concerning his point about the Sacrament as a way of profession unto others. In introducing this section on profession to others, Owen begins with two observations:

> i. That *visible profession is a matter of more importance than most men make of it*; as the apostle saith, Romans 10:10, 'With the heart man believeth unto righteousness; and with the mouth confession is made unto salvation.' Look how indispensably necessary believing is unto righteousness, to justification; – no less indispensably necessary is confession or profession unto salvation. . . .
>
> ii. There is in this ordinance a *special profession* of Christ. There is a profession of him against the shame of the world; a profession of him against the curse of the law; and a profession of him against the power of the devil. All our profession doth much centre, or is mightily acted, in this ordinance.[167]

Owen sees the Supper as containing a "special profession of Christ." As Communion is celebrated, proclamation of Christ's death is made against shame, the curse of the law, and the power of the Devil. As Payne observes concerning Owen's view of the Supper, "What the world needs more than anything else, Owen believes, is to have a glimpse of the church glorifying Christ and His death on the cross. Where better to proclaim it than at the Supper, a holy dramatization of Christ's body broken and blood shed for helpless sinners?"[168]

Thomas Watson (1620 – 1686) authored a work entitled, *The Mystery of the Lord's Supper*. Within the pages of this instructive work is found an explanation for the visual nature of the Sacrament that could have been penned by a learning style specialist of the present generation:

---

[166] Payne, *John Owen on the Lord's Supper*, pp. 120 – 121.
[167] Ibid., pp 122 – 123.
[168] Ibid., p. 70.

> Christ sets His body and blood before us in the elements. Here are signs, else we will not believe. . . . **Things taken in by the eye work more upon us than things taken in by the ear**. A solemn spectacle of mortality more affects us than an oration. **So, when we see Christ broken in the bread and, as it were, crucified before us, this more affects our hearts than the bare preaching of the Word.**[169]

Puritan minister John Flavel used 1 Corinthians 11:26 in his *An Exposition of the Assembly's Catechism* (1688), as the biblical basis for his explanation in answering Question 96, "What is the Lord's Supper?" In his subquestions and responses, numbers 11 and 12, he writes:

> Q. 11. What is the second particular use and end of this sacrament?
>
> A. It is to represent Christ to believers, **as an apt sign of him and his death; that is both memorative, significative, and instructive**.
>
> Q. 12. How is it a memorative sign of Christ?
>
> A**. It brings Christ to our remembrance, as his death and bitter sufferings are therein represented to us, by the breaking of bread, and pouring forth of wine; 1 Cor. xi. 26. For as often as ye eat this bread and drink this cup, ye do shew forth the Lord's death till he come.**[170]

And again in the same work in sub question 2, *Of the Elements, Action, and Subjects of it*, he alludes again to 1 Corinthians 11:26:

> Q. 2. Is not the bread in the sacrament turned into the very body of Christ itself, by transubstantiation?
>
> A. No, it is not; but the elements retain still their own proper nature of bread and wine, after the words of consecration; and are so called; 1 Cor. xi. 26. For as often as ye eat this bread, …[171]

Presbyterian minister Matthew Henry (1662 – 1714), following in the footsteps of others who had written guides to prepare Christians to come to the Lord's Table, published in June 1704 a work entitled, *The Communicant's Companion*. This book was designed to guide believers in all aspects of Lord's Supper observance, from preparing to come to the Table, to the importance of what took place during the

---

[169] Thomas Watson, "The Mystery of the Lord's Supper," in *The Puritans on the Lord's Supper*, edited by Don Kistler (Morgan, PA: Soli Deo Gloria, 1997), p. 128.
[170] John Flavel, "An Exposition of the Assembly's Catechism," in *The Works of John Flavel*, vol. VI (Edinburgh: Banner of Truth Trust, 1820, reprint 1997), p. 286.
[171] Flavel, "An Exposition of the Assembly's Catechism," p. 287.

ordinance, to the benefits obtained from communing, and even to one's proper response and practice of the faith after the celebration. These "communicant's companions," or "communicant's manuals" were a very common and popular feature among Christians of the 17th century through the middle of the 19th century. Many of these were printed and used by those of the Anglican persuasion. Those of Anglican origin were often more of the devotional style. For example, in *The New Weeks Preparation for a Worthy Receiving of the Lord's Supper*, this statement concerning preparation for the Supper is made: "Our esteem or disesteem (of this holy sacrament) will best be seen by our preparing or not preparing for it as we ought. There is something of a preparation of heart, mind, and ways, required of all religious offices, much more for this, which is the flower and perfection of all."[172] Presbyterians and other branches of the Reformed faith used them as well, yet in more of a catechetical vein. Henry's *Communicant's Companion* addresses 1 Corinthians 11:26 in explaining what it means to say that the Lord's Supper in a "confessing ordinance":

> In the ordinance of the Lord's Supper we are said to show forth the Lord's death, 1 Cor. xi. 26, that is,
>
> 1. We hereby profess our value and esteem for Christ crucified; ye show it forth with commendation and praise: so the word sometimes signifies. The cross of Christ was to the Jews a stumbling-block, because they expected a Messiah in temporal pomp and power. It was to the Greeks foolishness, because the doctrine of man's justification and salvation by it, was not agreeable to their philosophy. . . They who put him to such an ignominious death, and loaded him with all the shame they could put upon him, hoped thereby to make every one shy of owning him, or expressing any respect for him; but the wisdom of God so ordered it, that the cross of Christ is that which above any thing else Christians have cause to glory in. . . .
>
> This, then, we mean, when we receive the Lord's Supper; we thereby solemnly declare that we do not reckon the cross of Christ any reproach to Christianity: and that we were so far from being ashamed of it, that, whatever constructions an unthinking, unbelieving world may put upon it, to us it is the wisdom of God and the power of God; it is all our salvation and all our desire. . . .
>
> 2. We hereby profess our dependence upon, and confidence in Christ crucified. As we are not ashamed to own him, so we are not afraid to venture our souls, and their eternal salvation with him, believing him "able

---

[172] Edward Wickstead, *The New Weeks Preparation for a Worthy Receiving of the Lord's Supper, as Recommended and Appointed by the Church of England* (London: Thomas Wilson and Sons York, 1740), pp. v – vi.

> to save to the uttermost all that come to God by him;" and as willing as he is able, and making confession of that faith. . . .
>
> This, then, we mean, when we receive the Lord's Supper; we confess that Jesus Christ is Lord, and we own ourselves to be his subjects, and put ourselves under his government; we confess that he is a skillful physician, and own ourselves to be his patients, resolving to observe his prescription; we confess that he is a faithful advocate, and own ourselves to be his clients, resolving to be advised by him in everything. In a word, in this ordinance we profess that we are not ashamed of the gospel of Christ, nor of the cross of Christ, in which the his gospel is all summed up, knowing it to be "the power of God unto salvation to all them that believe," and having found it so ourselves.[173]

Another important figure in the continuation of a Pauline approach to proclamation through the Lord's Supper from the Puritan era into the modern era is John Willison (1680 – 1750), a minister of the gospel for Brechin Parish Church, and later South Church Dundee. Willison is significant in that his ministry and sacramental teaching spanned the transition from the late 17th to the mid 18th century. His work, *A Sacramental Catechism*, first published in 1720, subtitled as "a Familiar Instructor for Young Communicants," included detailed material on all aspects of the Supper. In one of the work's subsections, entitled, "Concerning the Sacramental Words," Willison applies 1 Corinthians 11:26 to the praxis as well as the theology of Communion:

> Q. What is the meaning of the words which Christ spoke with respect to the whole sacrament: **"For as often as you eat this bread and drink this cup, you show forth the Lord's death till He comes"?**
>
> A. It is as if He said, "See that you make conscience of coming to this holy table, of coming frequently; for every time you do it in a right manner **you keep up the memorial of your Lord and Savior's death** in a way that is pleasant to Him" – seeing that He has appointed this as a standing ordinance in the Church to continue till His coming in judgment, when He will call His servants to account concerning their observing His injunctions, and this among the rest.[174]

And:

---

[173] Matthew Henry, *A Communicant's Companion* (Philadelphia: Presbyterian Board of Publication, 1843, The Evangelical Reprint Library, reprint 1969), pp. 47 – 49.
[174] John Willison, *A Sacramental Catechism* (1720, reprinted, Morgan, PA: Soli Deo Gloria Publications, 2000), p. 103.

Q. What is meant **by showing forth the Lord's death** in the sacrament, which seems to be laid down as our main business in this ordinance?

A. We may be said to represent, show forth, and commemorate the death of Christ in the sacraments in three ways: with respect to ourselves, with respect to the world, and with respect to God.

Q. How are we to show forth the death of Christ with respect to ourselves?

A. **As the external elements and signs of the Lord's Supper give a plain representation of the death and sufferings of Christ to eye of the body**, so in partaking of these elements we ought to set the things represented by them (the death of Christ, with the matchless love He therein expressed) before the eyes of our minds and understandings, in order to beget a fresh remembrance of that dying love and to raise our faith and hope in a crucified Savior.

Q. How are we to show forth Christ's death in the sacrament with respect to the world?

A. By owning hereby, **in the most public manner, that we are the disciples of a crucified Jesus, not ashamed of our Master or His ignominious death, but declaring before all that we glory in Him, and rely upon the merits of His death here shown forth as the only hope of our salvation**, and that we have no Savior besides Him.

Q. How are we to show forth Christ's death in the sacrament with respect to God?

A. In two ways:

1. We are to show it forth to a loving and merciful God in **a way of thanksgiving and praise,** ascribing all glory to Him for such a noble ransom and sacrifice as He has provided for us.

2. We are also to show forth Christ's death in the sacrament to a just and sin-avenging God in **a way of faith and prayer**, pleading the sacrifice with God as a screen and defense against the sword of justice and curse of the law, and presenting it as the ground of all our hopes and expectations.[175]

Willison understands *proclamation* (show forth) in 1 Corinthians 11:26 to comprise all of the aspects included in Paul's Lord Supper instruction. The impact of this

[175] John Willison, *A Sacramental Catechism* (1720, reprinted, Morgan, PA: Soli Deo Gloria Publications, 2000), pp. 109 – 110.

proclamation of the gospel through the Supper reaches the participants inwardly, testifies outwardly to the world, and assists in offering praise and thanksgiving to God. Put another way, memorial, commemoration, or remembrance is accomplished in the Supper of the Lord Jesus' death. This is accomplished through the instruments of the visual elements of bread and cup as they represent the death and sufferings of Christ. For the participating believer, who comes in faith and prayer, the visual symbols and the declarative words of institution guide an offering of thanksgiving and praise unto God for his salvation gift. Meanwhile, all of the above serve to testify or proclaim to the watching world, in a very public manner, the death of Christ and the participating believers' faith in him.

Another 17th to 18th century transition figure preaching and teaching on the Lord's Supper was the Anglican bishop of Asaph from 1704 to 1708, William Beveridge (1637 – 1708). Beveridge was an avid student of the earliest period of church history and recognized by his fellow churchmen as an advocate of recapturing ancient church practice for his own times. Preserved within a collection of his theological works, published some time after his death, is a sermon preached upon 1 Corinthians 11:29, in which Beveridge argues for the importance of the Lord's Supper:

> But how shall we know how often we are bound to receive this holy Sacrament? There are two ways to know it: from the practice of the holy Apostles and primitive Christians; and then from the reason of the thing, and the end of the institution.
>
> First, We find the holy Apostles, who perfectly understood our Lord's mind, administering and receiving this holy Sacrament whensoever they met together upon a religious account; yea, so as that it seems to have been the principal end of their meeting, especially upon the Lord's Day: for it is written, "that upon the first day of the week (Acts 20.7), when the disciples came together to break bread, Paul preached to them, ready to depart on the morrow." From whence we may observe, that they received this Sacrament at least every first day of the week, which is the Lord's Day; and that the main end of their meeting upon that day, was not to hear sermons, but to break bread; only the Apostle being to depart on the morrow, took that occasion of preaching to them. And the same custom obtained, not only in the Apostles' times, but for many ages after; so that the primitive Christians looked upon

> this sacrament as the chief part of their public devotions; insomuch as they never held any religious assemblies, without the celebration of it; . . .[176]

Beveridge preached concerning 1 Corinthians 11:26, during this sermon on verse 29, that just, "as the Jews, as oft as they offered any bloody sacrifices, foreshewed the Lord's death until his first coming; so Christians, as the Apostle tells us, "as oft as they eat this bread, and drink this cup, they shew forth the Lord's death till His coming again."[177] Perhaps it is not so surprising that a leader within the Anglican Church of the early 18th century would argue for the centrality of Communion. However, it must be remembered that Beveridge was a close student of the practices and writings of earliest decades of the ancient church. He derived his view of the Lord's Supper from his understanding of Apostolic practices and available records concerning primitive Christianity.

Shortly after the time of Willison's and Beveridge's contributions to the teaching of the Lord's Supper as proclamation of the death of Christ, one of the greatest preachers and theologians of the 18th century was making an impact, not in Europe, Scotland, or England, but across the Atlantic Ocean in the growing colonies of North America. Jonathan Edwards (1703 – 1758), considered alongside Whitefield and Wesley as central to the first Great Awakening, was also keenly aware of the importance of the Lord's Supper. Interestingly, Edwards saw in the *proclamation* of the Supper a covenantal profession – i.e. a profession or exhibition by both parties in the covenant of redemption, God as redeemer and the participants as those he has redeemed. In his 1746 work, *An Humble Inquiry into the Rules of the Word of God concerning the Qualifications requisite to a Complete Standing and Full Communion in the Visible Christian Church*, section ix, Edwards writes extensively of the theology and practice of the Supper:

> There is in the Lord's Supper a mutual solemn profession of the two parties transacting the covenant of grace, and visibly united in that covenant; the Lord Christ by his minister, on the one hand, and the communicants (who are professing believers) on the other. The administrator of the ordinance acts in the quality of Christ's minister, acts in his name, as representing him; and stands in the place where Christ himself stood at the first administration of

---

[176] William Beveridge, *The Theological Works of William Beveridge, D. D.*, vol. VI., Sermons CXXIX – CXLVI (Oxford: John Henry Parker, 1845), p. 23. These quotations are excerpted from "Sermon CXXX. The Worthy Communicant."
[177] Ibid.

> this Sacrament, and in the original institution of this ordinance. Christ, by the speeches and actions of the minister, makes a solemn profession of his part in the covenant of grace: he exhibits the sacrifice of his body broken and his blood shed; and in the minister's offering the sacramental bread and wine to the communicants, Christ presents himself to the believing communicants as their propitiation and bread of life; and by these outward signs confirms and seals his sincere engagements to be their Saviour and food, and to impart to them all the benefits of his propitiation and salvation. And they in receiving what is offered, and eating and drinking the symbols of Christ's body and blood, also profess their part in the covenant of grace; they profess to embrace the promises and to lay hold of the hope set before them, to receive the atonement, to receive Christ as their spiritual food, and to feed upon him in their hearts by faith. Indeed, what is professed on both sides is the *heart*; for Christ in offering himself professes the willingness of *his heart* to be theirs who duly receive him; all the communicants, on their part, profess the willingness *of their hearts* to receive him, which they declare by their significant actions.... Thus the Lord's Supper is plainly a mutual renovation, confirmation, and seal of the covenant of grace: both the covenanting parties profess their consent to their respective parts in the covenant of grace.... And there is in this ordinance the very same thing acted over in profession and sensible signs, which is spiritually transacted between Christ and his spouse in the covenant that unites them....[178]

Edwards describes the Lord's Supper as a mutual profession of the covenant of grace between God (through the officiating minister who stands and acts in Christ's name) and the believing participants in the celebration. And the ordinance comprises for both covenantal parties the profession, the actions, and the sensible signs or symbols of the bread and the wine which are involved. Edwards understood the importance of the words of institution as a contextualizing framework for the actions and elements of the Supper's profession. And yet in describing the Lord's Supper so vividly as a covenantal profession, he recalls those covenantal signs and actions which marked the initiation or the re-confirmations of all the prior covenantal ceremonies made between God and his people. Thus, the actions of both the covenanting parties and the symbols God chooses to use are essential for the Supper to accomplish its own means of proclaiming the gospel.

Continuing further with Edwards concerning the Supper as to the actions and symbols:

> **The actions of the communicants at the Lord's table have as expressive and significant a language as the most solemn words.** When a person in

[178] Adamson, *The Christian Doctrine of the Lord's Supper*, pp. 105 – 106.

> this ordinance *takes* and *eats* and *drinks* those things which represent Christ, **the plain meaning and implicit profession of these his actions** is this, 'I take this crucified Jesus as my Saviour, my sweetest food, my chief portion, and the life of my soul, consenting to acquiesce in him as such, and to hunger and thirst after him only, renouncing all other Saviours and all other portions for his sake.[179]

How very clearly did Edwards comprehend the covenantal parameters and basis for the Lord's Supper. The words of the gospel concerning the institution of the Supper and concerning the betrayal and atoning death of Christ are essential. The symbolic elements of the bread and the wine are essential. The actions of taking, eating, and drinking are essential. And the offering of persons – first that of God in Christ, and then that of the believing participants – are essential. Thus the great colonial American preacher and theologian, Jonathan Edwards understood the Pauline, 1 Corinthians 11:23 – 26 celebration of the Lord's Supper.

And of course, Edwards understood that this proclamation function of the Supper – both inward and outward – was made efficacious only by means of faith. And in his continuing debate over church membership and Communion with Rev. Solomon Williams, Edwards made the case for the importance of faith for proper communicating in the Supper. In his, *Answer to Solomon Edwards*, he wrote of faith and the Supper:

> What *inward* thing does the outward taking or accepting the body and blood of Christ represent, but the *inward* accepting of Christ's body and blood, or an accepting him in the heart? And what *spiritual* thing is the outward feeding on Christ in this ordinance the sign of, but a *spiritual* feeding on Christ, or the soul's feeding on him? Now there is no other way of the soul's feeding on him but by that *faith* by which Christ becomes our spiritual food, and the refreshment and vital nourishment of our souls.[180]

Jonathan Edwards represents the height of achievement in describing the biblical theology and the pastoral praxis of the Lord's Supper. He built upon the foundation of 1 Corinthians 11:23 – 26 and he inherited the rediscovery of the Pauline Eucharist brought about by Luther, Calvin, the Westminster Divines, and John Owen. Edwards, in both his theological thought and his pastoral wisdom, had distilled a description of the celebration of the Lord's Supper to its primary purpose – proclaiming the

---

[179] Adamson, *The Christian Doctrine of the Lord's Supper.* pp. 106 – 107.

[180] Ibid., p. 107.

covenant of grace, the gospel fulfilled in Christ Jesus' death – and the means of that proclamation – through the words, symbols, actions, and participation by the Redeemer and the redeemed.

The nineteenth century brought new strains of theology and reflection into the ways the church understood the Lord's Supper. Many of these trends, such as Rationalism, Romanticism, Existentialism, and Biblical Criticism, were disruptive in terms of maintaining a Pauline biblical celebration of the Supper as proclamation of the gospel. And yet there continued to be some theologians and pastors who wrote and taught the Supper in the narrow path passed on to them by the leading lights of the 16th, 17th, and 18th centuries.

Perhaps in the end it was not so much the loss of teaching concerning the Pauline practice of the Lord's Supper, as it was instead a decline in the number of those Christians who embraced and practiced it. Apparently the decline in interest in the importance of celebrating the Lord's Supper in the 19th century was not confined to those in the pews. "As the shepherds go, so do the sheep," it is often said. A decline in pastoral leadership concerning using the means of grace through Communion, and proclaiming the gospel by its use, are evident in the introduction provided in 1848 by T. R. Sulivan, the editor of a book entitled, *Sermons on Christian Communion*: "Designed to Promote the Growth of the Religious Affections, by Living Ministers." He writes pertaining to the intended goal of the volume that:

> The design of this publication is, then, partly, to heighten the interest in the communion. But since interest in the communion is only a means of grace in connection with preaching, – the great appointed means of keeping faith alive and fruitful in the world, – it is hope also that it may react upon the pulpit, through a response to the call for a style more persuasive and affecting. In the language of Sydney Smith, – **"The forms which the Gospel exacts are few, and instituted for the only purposes for which forms ought to be instituted, to awaken attention to realities." Preaching the word is only impressing through the ear those very realities which the communion symbolizes through the eye. Practically to regard the occasion** (*preaching and Communion*) **as a stand-point at the outset of the Christian's race, and the departing-place of the Christian's ever-renewed progress, might secure to the ministry the double benefit of greater unity of effort and more individual earnestness.** "The want is, – everywhere in the pulpit the want is of that *simple* and *deep religious sensibility* which would give a vitality and charm to many a discourse that has sense enough and truth and

> wisdom enough in it, but yet is perfectly dead, and leaves the hearer dead, for want of that living earnestness in the preacher."[181]

Perhaps the compiler and editor of this 1848 volume understood the problem of his generation. Ministers of the time (speaking in broad-brush strokes) had begun to diminish the value of the Lord's Supper as a means of proclaiming the gospel. A "compartmentalization" was beginning to set in between the means of grace in preaching the gospel, and the means of grace in proclaiming the gospel through the Lord's Supper. This separation in thought and in practice of the means of grace placed virtually all emphasis (for the preacher and the congregants) upon verbal proclamation as the only biblical necessity for weekly biblical Lord's Day worship. At the same time, the Supper was typically celebrated infrequently and not viewed as an extremely important supplement to preaching. The Sacrament was usually neglected, although it offered a visual proclamation of the gospel.

Often the Lord's Supper in the 19th century was perceived to simply be liturgical vestige, and empty religious rite or form, lacking any real spiritual benefit to the celebrants. Sullivan's collection of sermons concerning Communion from ministers alive and preaching in his generation was an effort to bring the gospel-proclaiming power of the Lord's Supper back into view, and to help both pastors and church members to awaken to its potential when paired with the gospel preached from the pulpit. The sermons chosen for this volume were quite carefully considered. And one of the sermons included, preached by Ephraim Peabody at King's Chapel (founded in 1686) in Boston, MA, and entitled, "The Lord's Supper to be Observed," sought to address the mistaken and unbiblical idea that the Lord's Supper was an empty ritual, devoid of power, and an unnecessary hold over from olden times. About halfway through his sermon on 1 Corinthians 11:26 and the Lord's Supper he states:

> But still, many are perplexed with difficulties; and one of the chief ones arises out of the marked tendency of the age to do away with forms. It is a mere form, it is said – and what is its use? It is not like any moral duty – I can observe it and still not be a better man. It is a mere form, and it is a hindrance and a fetter to the spirit.

---

[181] T. R. Sullivan, ed. *Sermons on Christian Communion* (Boston: Wm. Crosby and H. P. Nichols, 1848), pp. vii – viii.

> It is admitted, that to him to whom it is a mere form, devoid of spiritual significance, it is worthless, and perhaps worse. A mere form, a dead form, is but solemn, idle trifling with the holiest realities. But a form need not be dead. Let it bring vividly before me divine truth and heavenly graces, and by so doing help to awaken my mind to them, and the form has become to me instinct with spiritual life and that of infinite values. It is only through outward forms that one mind becomes manifest to another, or exerts power over it. A form! What is it? . . . Through that form, a ray of light, which else for me had been extinguished, is made to stream down through the dark gulf of ages into my soul. – So the Lord's Supper is a form. But call it not a mere form. So long as it speaks, as it has always spoken, of the holy submission, the forgiving tenderness, the divine beneficence of him whom we communicate, so long as it has power through its associations to touch our hearts, to awaken penitent thoughts and holier resolves, it is no longer a mere form, – it is spirit and it is life.[182]

Originally written in 1846, about the time of Sullivan's effort to revive earnestness with respect to the Lord's Supper observances of the 19th century, a professor of theology in the seminary of the Reformed Church named Robert W. Nevin, D. D. authored an apologetic work in defense of the Calvinist, Reformation doctrine of the Lord's Supper. His book, entitled, *The Mystical Presence: A Vindication of the Reformed or Calvinistic Doctrine of the Holy Eucharist*, contained in its chapter II, a telling narrative of the decline of theology and practice of Communion in the mid-19th century:

> It cannot be denied that the view generally entertained of the Lord's Supper at the present time [1840s], in the Protestant Church, involves a wide departure from the faith of the sixteenth century with regard to the same subject. The fact must be at once clear to every one at all familiar with the religious world as it now exists, as soon as he is made to understand in any measure the actual form in which the sacramental doctrine was held in the period [the Reformation] just mentioned.
>
> This falling away from the creed of the Reformation is not confined to any particular country of religious confession. It has been most broadly displayed among the continental churches of Europe, in the form of that open, rampant rationalism, which has there to so great an extent triumphed over the old orthodoxy at so many other points. But it is found widely prevalent also in Great Britain and in this country [U.S.]. It is especially striking, of course, as has been already remarked, in the case of the Lutheran Church, which was distinguished from the other Protestant confession, in the beginning, mainly by its high view of the Lord's Supper, and the zeal it showed in opposition to what it stigmatized reproachfully as sacramentarian error. In this respect, it can hardly be recognized indeed as the same communion. The original name

[182] Sullivan, *Sermons on Christian Communion*, pp. 339 – 340.

> remains, but the original distinctive character is gone. Particularly this is the case, with a large part at least, of the Lutheran Church in our own country. We cannot say of it simply, that it has been led to moderate the old sacramental doctrine of the church, as exhibited in the *Form of Concord*; it has abandoned the doctrine altogether. Not only is the true Lutheran position, as occupied so violently against the Calvinists in the sixteenth century, openly and fully renounced; but the Calvinistic ground itself, then shunned with so much horror as the very threshold of infidelity, has come to be considered as also in unsafe contiguity with Rome. . . .
>
> But it is not the Lutheran Church only, which has fallen away from its original creed, in the case of the Lord's Supper. Though the defection may not be so immediately palpable and open to all observation, it exists with equal certainty, as was said before, on the part of the Reformed Church. It does so for the most part in Europe; and in this country the case is, to say the least, no better. . . . Along with this, of course, must prevail an unsacramental feeling generally, by which the Lord's Supper also is shorn of all its significance and power. . . .
>
> Methodism, in this way, may be said to wrong the sacraments, . . . almost as seriously as the Baptist system itself. The general evil, however, reaches still farther. Even those denominations among us which represent the Reformed Church by true and legitimate descent, such as the Presbyterian in its different branches, and Reformed Dutch, show plainly that they have fallen away, to some extent, from the original faith of the church, in the same direction.[183]

In response to the "falling away" from the Reformation doctrines of the Lord's Supper he witnessed in his own day, Nevin urged a return to the "old Reformed view, the communion of the believer with Christ in the Supper (as it) is taken to be specific in its nature and different from all that has place in the common exercises of worship. The sacrament, not the elements of course separately considered, but the ordinances as the union of elements and word, is held to be such an exhibition of saving grace, as is presented to the faith of the Church under no other form." Nevin quotes Dr. John Owen on the uniqueness of the ordinance of Communion for the church, and then makes a second primary point. "In the old Reformed view, the sacramental transaction is a *mystery*: . . . 'Not without reason,' says Calvin, 'is the communication, which makes us flesh of Christ's flesh and bone of his bones denominated by Paul a great mystery. Later in the chapter Nevin observes this description of the Supper as involving *mystery* in other writings. 'The *mystery* of our coalition with Christ,' says the Gallic Confession, 'is so sublime, that it transcends all

---

[183] John W. Nevin, *The Mystical Presence: A Vindication of the Reformed or Calvinistic Doctrine of the Holy Eucharist* (Philadelphia: S. R. Fisher & Co., 1867), pp.105 – 108.

our senses and also the whole course of nature.' 'The *mysteriousness*,' we are told by Dr. Owen, 'is beyond expression; the *mysterious* reception of Christ in this peculiar way of exhibition.' "[184]

Included in Nevin's volume on the state of Lord's Supper doctrine and practice in his era are a collection of examples of recent theologians and pastors' writings concerning the Eucharist. These are intended to illustrate the lack of "mystery" or presence of Christ then widely held in the Protestant Church. One such example is an excerpt from a Rev. John Dick, D. D., from his, *Lectures on Theology*, "Lectures XCI and XCII":

> That the bread and wine were no more than a representation of the body and blood of Christ; or in other words, the sign pointed to denote the benefits that were conferred upon mankind in consequence of the death of Christ: that therefore Christians derive no other fruit from the participation of the Lord's Supper, than mere commemoration and remembrance of the merits of Christ, and that there is nothing in the ordinance but a memorial of Christ. . . . There is an absurdity in the notion, that there is any communion with the body and blood of Christ, considered in themselves; that he (Calvin) intended any such thing; or that it could be of any advantage to us. When our Church therefore says, that 'the body and blood are as really, but spiritually, present to the faith of believers in that ordinance, as the elements themselves to our their outward senses.' And that they 'feed upon his body and blood to their spiritual nourishment and growth in grace,' it can mean only, that our incarnate suffering Saviour is apprehended by their minds, through the instituted signs; and that by faith they enjoy peace and hope; or it means something unintelligible and unscriptural.[185]

Despite the laudable efforts of Sullivan, Nevin, and other faithful ministers and theologians of the 19th century, there continued to be a general movement away from the great biblical truths associated with the Lord's Supper which had been rediscovered in the 16th century Reformation and fostered in the 17th and early 18th centuries. At the same time there remained a cadre of scholars and pastors from the Protestant Church who would from time to time publish, teach, or preach on the importance of the Supper as proclamation of Jesus' death and as a testimony of the covenant of grace.

---

[184] Nevin, *The Mystical Presence: A Vindication of the Reformed or Calvinistic Doctrine of the Holy Eucharist*, pp. 118 – 119.

[185] Ibid., pp. 111 – 112.

Presbyterian and Princeton Seminary professor of systematic theology A. A. Hodge sought to assist his students in mastering *The Westminster Confession of Faith*. Like many who had gone before him, he authored a commentary of the Westminster Divines' work, entitled, *The Confession of Faith* (first published in 1869). In addressing the Confession, chapter XXIX, sections II –VI concerning the Lord's Supper, Hodge declared:

> (c.) The distribution and reception of the elements. This is an essential part of the ordinance, which is not completed when the minister consecrates the elements, not until they are actually received and eaten and drunk by the people. Christ says, "This do in remembrance of me." Paul adds, "For as often as ye eat this bread, and drink this cup, ye do shew forth the Lord's death till he come." Luke xxii. 19; 1 Cor. xi. 26. **So that the essence of the sacrament consists in the eating and the drinking.**[186]

Robert Lewis Dabney, a Southern Presbyterian professor at Union Theological Seminary, also composed a Systematic Theology work designed to aid his students, which engaged in teaching Reformed theology along the same organization as the Westminster Confession of Faith. Although his *Lectures in Systematic Theology* (1878) does not explicate 1 Corinthians 11:26, Dabney does treat the issue of the use of elements and actions and their agreement with the purpose of the Sacrament:

> We hold that the Lord's Supper is a means of grace; and the scriptural conception of this phrase explains the manner in which the sacrament is efficacious to worthy communicants. It sets forth the central truths of redemption, in a manner admirably adapted to our nature sanctified; and these truths, applied by the Holy Ghost, are the instruments of sanctification and spiritual life, in a manner generically the same with, though in degree more energetic, than the written and spoken word.[187]

One 19th century Presbyterian minister of the gospel, the Rev. Stephen Porter, went so far as to propose that the church adopt the practice of daily Communion, as most likely was practiced in the early days of the church deduced from the earliest gatherings described in the Book of Acts (2:42 – 46). Porter was burdened by the belief that the Supper was such an effective means of grace and equipping for revival in the church and for empowering outreach, that he published an entire book on the

---

[186] A. A. Hodge, *The Confession of Faith* (Edinburgh: The Banner of Truth Trust, reprint 1978), p. 359.
[187] Robert Lewis Dabney, *Lectures in Systematic Theology* (Grand Rapids, Baker Book House, reprint 1985), p. 814.

concept, entitled *A Daily Walk with God, In His Own Ordinances, or, The Bible Standard of Duty, As Exemplified in the Primitive Christians.* The work went through at least five editions, the fifth in 1869.

In 1896, Francis Beattie, accomplished theologian and Presbyterian churchman, published his commentary upon the *Confession of Faith* and catechisms of the Presbyterian faith. Within this work, *The Presbyterian Standards*, Beattie addresses aspects of the Lord's Supper from *The Westminster Confession of Faith*, in which "The End or Design of the Lord's Supper" is explained:

> In some respects this is the most difficult point to explain in connection with the doctrine of the supper. . . .
>
> 1. The Lord's supper shows forth and commemorates the sufferings and death of Christ in the church and to the world until he comes again. It is thus a memorial service, looking back to his sufferings and death as a sacrifice upon the cross for our sins. It is also a prophetic ordinance, looking forward to, and reminding us of, his coming a second time without sin unto salvation.
>
> 2. The Lord's supper is designed to signify and seal the benefits of Christ and the covenant of grace to believers. . . . All the blessings which flow from the death of Christ for us are set forth in the supper; and by the blessing of Christ through the Spirit to the worthy recipient he obtains, by means of this sacrament, and has sealed to him thereby, the blessings exhibited to him in the ordinance to his spiritual nourishment and growth in grace. . . .
>
> 3. The sacrament of the supper is designed to express the believer's thankfulness, and to be constant and repeated pledge of his engagement to be the Lord's. By this sacrament believers testify and renew their gratitude to God for all his wonderful mercy and grace towards them, in the gift of salvation which is in Christ. . . .
>
> 4. The sacrament of the Lord's supper is a means of communion with Christ, and of fellowship between believers. . . . Because believers are in union with Christ, and one in him, they have fellowship with each other. They are members of Christ's mystical body, so that their mutual love and fellowship are thereby assured.[188]

Perhaps it is fitting to close the era of the 19th century and its relative decline in Pauline Lord's Supper appreciation and practice with another example of a well-loved minister who was thoroughly devoted to faithful Lord's Supper practice. Charles Haddon Spurgeon (1834 – 1892) frequently preached impassioned sermons

---

[188] Francis R. Beattie, *The Presbyterian Standards* (Greenville, SC: The Southern Presbyterian Press, 1997), pp. 326 – 328.

of the nature and efficacy of the Lord's Supper. He also wrote a Communion hymn, "Amidst Us Our Beloved Stands", and published a book of Communion meditations entitled, *Till He Come*, the title obviously derived from 1 Corinthians 11:26. It is reported in the "Prefactory Note" to Spurgeon's Communion volume that, "For many years, whether at home or abroad, it was Mr. Spurgeon's constant custom to observe the ordinance of the Lord's supper every Sabbath-day, unless illness prevented." Among Spurgeon's Communion meditations, is one he delivered for a Lord's Supper celebration at Mentone. His text was 1 Corinthians 10:16, 17, entitled "Communion with Christ and His People":

> It is a lamentable fact that some have fancied that the simple ordinance of the Lord's supper has a certain magical, or a least physical power about it, so that, by the mere act of eating and drinking this bread and wine, men can become partakers of the body and blood of Christ. It is marvelous that so plain a symbol should have been so complicated by genuflexions, adornments, and technical phrases. Can anyone see the slightest resemblance between the Master's sitting down with the twelve, and the mass of the Roman community? The original is lost in the super-imposed ritual. Superstition has produced a sacrament where Jesus intended a fellowship. Too many, who would not go the length of Rome, yet speak of this simple feast as if it were a mystery dark and obscure. They employ all manner of hard words to turn the children's bread into stone. It is not the Lord's supper, but the Eucharist; we see before us no plate, but a "paten"; the cup is a "chalice", and the table is an "altar." These are incrustations of superstition, whereby the blessed ordinance of Christ is likely to be again overgrown and perverted. What does the supper mean? It means communion: *communion with Christ, and communion with one another.*[189]

The Protestant Church and the Sacrament of Communion were buffeted throughout the first half of the 20th century by the forces of skepticism, the rise of post-modernist thinking, and even the excessive confessional compromises attempted through the ecumenical movement (i.e. World Council of Churches, etc.). Everything previously accepted from the Bible's record was subject to investigation, doubt, and disregard – from miracles to prophecies to the great workings of the Holy Spirit.

How did the Reformed theologians of the mid-20th century understand and apply 1 Corinthians 11:26 to the Lord's Supper? Dr. L. Berkhof writes of this text with respect to the Supper in his *Systematic Theology* (1938) that, "The concluding words

---

[189] C. H. Spurgeon, *Till He Come: Communion Meditations and Addresses by C. H. Spurgeon* (London: Passmore & Alabaster, 1896), pp. 313 – 314.

of 1 Cor. 11:26, 'For as often as ye eat this bread, and drink this cup, ye proclaim the Lord's death till He come," point to the perennial significance of the Lord's Supper as a memorial of the sacrificial death of Christ; and clearly intimate that it should be celebrated regularly until the Lord's return."[190] Later within the same section of his work, Berkhof returns to 1 Corinthians 11:26, describing the Lord's Supper as a "symbolical representation of Christ's death."[191] And he explains that this means:

> The central fact of redemption, prefigured in the sacrifices of the Old Testament, is clearly set forth by means of the significant symbols of the New Testament sacrament. The words of institution, "broken for you" and "shed for many", point to the fact that the death of Christ is a sacrificial one, for the benefit, and even in the place, of His people.[192]

Just a few decades later, the professor of systematic theology at the Free University of Amsterdam, G. C. Berkouwer, authored a work focused upon the theology and practice of the Sacraments. In this work, from the "Studies in Dogmatics" series, Berkouwer uses the 1 Corinthians 11:26 passage in support of the 'eschatological' importance of the Supper's proclamation. This eschatological interpretation of the 1 Corinthians 11:26 was a popular stock and trade for theologians and commentators throughout the second half of the 20th century and remains prevalent with respect to this passage down to the present. Berkouwer comments with reference to 1 Corinthians 11:26 and the Supper's eschatological dimension that:

> When Paul writes that in the Lord's Supper we proclaim the Lord's death "till he comes," he is not only setting a temporal limit to the celebration of the Supper but is also indicating its eschatological orientation now. Precisely in the proclamation of Christ's death, the celebration extends toward the fulfillment in the Kingdom. In the Lord's Supper, the Church stands between the death of Christ and his new presence. "The glory of this event that puts all others in the shadow (what Jesus has done through his death), makes it the duty of the Church to proclaim his death. . . .In this eschatological relation between the Supper and the return of Christ the significance of the Lord's Supper for the Church is decisively determined. . . . The slightest neglect of the Supper must therefore be condemned, for therein the community of believers loses its connection with the past (the death of Christ) as well as its

---

[190] L. Berkhof, *Systematic Theology* (Grand Rapids: Wm. B. Eerdmans Publishing Co., reprint Dec. 1979), p. 650.
[191] Ibid.
[192] Ibid.

> outlook on the fulfillment. Furthermore, therein the "calling of the Church" is affected, and in the neglect of the Supper its whole historical life is at stake.[193]

Reflecting upon the state of things in the church with respect to the Lord's Supper in the late 1950s, Donald Baillie (once Professor of Systematic Theology in the University of St. Andrews), describes the differences between his boyhood days and those of the time of his writing:

> When I look back to my childhood and boyhood in the Highlands of Scotland . . . I can never forget that in those days and in that environment the sacrament of the Lord's supper meant a very great deal in the life of a faithful community. It was surrounded by an atmosphere of mystery and awe and holy reverence. The emphasis on its solemnity was indeed so extreme and one-sided that only a small minority of the regular church-goers, in Highland Presbyterianism, ever took the step of becoming communicants at all: the rest of the people, while faithfully attending public worship, and even the communion service, considered themselves unworthy to sit at the Lord's table and to receive the sacred symbols of His body and blood, 'lest they should eat and drink judgment on themselves'. Moreover every celebration of the Lord's supper was preceded by several days of preparatory services, beginning on the Thursday, which was treated as a fast, and going through the Friday and Saturday, so that the actual communion service on Sunday morning was the climax of what was called a 'communion season'; and it was followed by services of thanksgiving on the Sunday evening and even on the Monday morning. All this was possible of course because communion was celebrated in any one parish only once or twice a year. That infrequency may seem strangely out of accord with the high value placed upon the sacrament, and with the principles of our forefathers at the Westminster Assembly who declared that celebration should be frequent. But in those days in the Scottish Highlands it was not uncommon for the most ardent spirits to secure greater frequency of communion for themselves by attending the 'communion seasons' of other parishes up to a considerable distance. I am not contending that all was well in this conception and practice of communion (far from it!). But at least it was a real sacrament, holy, supernatural, sanctifying, a great and potent means of grace to the most devout members of the Church.
>
> **I cannot close my eyes to the fact that to most people in the tradition to which I belong the sacrament means less now.** Is that true of all the Protestant Churches? Have they all lost something of its meaning and power? Or may we venture to hope that after a period of loss we are recapturing some of it now? . . . there are many others whose sacramental approach is profoundly Christian and to whom Holy Communion means everything. . . .

---

[193] G. C. Berkouwer, *The Sacraments* (Grand Rapids: William B. Eerdmans, 1969), p. 192.

> **Could many of us Presbyterians say that kind of thing about this sacrament which from the very beginning in the New Testament was the central service of the Christian Church?** And if not, why not? Can we be quite content about the situation? It is of course true that our tradition has always refused to make the sacraments more central than the Word. But **it has always in its great days refused to separate the Word and the sacraments from each other.**[194]

Baillie captured in this introduction to his fourth lecture, "The Real Presence," the essence of the change in theology and practice of Lord's Supper observance that had occurred over a sixty-year period, from the late 19th to the middle 20th century. While he wrote primarily about the lack of devotion on the part of Presbyterians toward the Supper, he also recognized it in the other Protestant denominations of his day. And, while he expressed a hope that there was a Communion renewal beginning to take shape, he also voiced ongoing concern for his own Presbyterian community. A major concern for Baillie was not just the lack of interest or devotion on the part of many Protestants concerning the Supper's practice. It was also the perception among its ministers and theologians that the Word of God through the act of preaching could be so widely separated from the Sacraments – especially the Lord's Supper. In a 1954 work, *Dynamics of Worship: Foundations and Uses of Liturgy*, translated into English in 1967, Richard Paquier recorded his observations of this tendency in the Reformed Church. Yet to Paquier's thinking, this imbalance between Word and Sacrament dates back to the very founding of the Reformation:

> It is true that Augustine said, *Accedit verbum ad elementum, et fit sacramentum*, but in this instance these were not the same terms of reference as those suggested by the Lutheran formula: *Wort und Sakrament*. In fact, through its reaction against a solid and condensed sacramentalism, the Reformation has found itself, *volen nolens*, with a one-sided exaltation of the word to the detriment of the sacraments; and the Reformed churches have often lost sight of their organic link, and, therefore, of the specific character of the sacrament.
>
> Word and sacraments, therefore, are equally an integral part of divine revelation and of the worship life of the church. Christ preached the word of God and the gospel of the kingdom to his hearers in order to enlighten them. But, he also gave his person and his life to men in order to deliver them from

---

[194] D. M. Baillie, *The Theology of the Sacraments* (London: Faber and Faber, 1957), pp. 91 – 92.

> the power of darkness. He preached numerous parables, but he touched the sick with his fingers; he laid hands on them.[195]

This separation of the gospel proclamation of the Lord's Supper from the act of preaching always leads to a diminution of the Sacrament of the Supper. It produces a perception among the congregations that the celebration of the Lord's Supper is *optional* and certainly secondary to preaching as a means of God's grace. It is this detrimental separation between Word and Sacrament that continued throughout the 20th century and now pervades the 21st. This problem is so pervasive, it has even occasioned debate within the Orthodox tradition:

> This "rupture" between word and sacrament has pernicious consequences also for the doctrine of the sacraments. In it, the sacrament ceases to be biblical and, in the deepest sense of the word, *evangelical*. It was no accident, of course, that the chief focus of interest in the sacraments for western theology was not their essence and content but rather the conditions and "modi" of their accomplishment and "efficacy."[196]

F. J. Leenhardt, perhaps overstating the denigration of the Supper that takes place in Protestantism in favor of the Word of God written and spoken, begins his first chapter, "Word and Sacrament," in the book *Essays on the Lord's Supper*, with this summary of the challenge Protestants face:

> The PROBLEM of the relationship of Word and Sacrament is of course not a new one. It could be said that it arose from the confrontation of Catholicism and Protestantism – or rather perhaps from antagonism between Roman and non-Roman Catholics and the Protestantism current amongst us. Two different conceptions underlie this opposition, and these may be related respectively to their dominant note by saying: on the one side, the Church of the Word; on the other, the Church of the Sacrament.
>
> It does not seem to me possible, on the basis of doctrine and of the facts themselves, to doubt that Roman Catholicism gives to the Sacrament a position which, if not exclusive, is at least preponderant. This is not the place to establish or discuss the grounds of this affirmation. It is equally incontestable that Protestantism gives to the Word a place, which, if not exclusive, is at least preponderant; but this incontestable preponderance of the Word raises several difficulties concerning the problem of relationship with Christ. In claiming the title Church of the Word, Protestantism does not relate itself only to the sources and norms of its faith which it finds in the holy

---

[195] Richard Paquier, *Dynamics of Worship: Foundations and Uses of Liturgy*, (Philadelphia: Fortress Press, 1967), p. 29.
[196] Alexander Schmemann, *The Eucharist: Sacrament of the Kingdom* (New York: St. Vladimir's Seminary Press, 1987), p. 67.

> Scriptures as the Word of God. It intends to affirm, more or less explicitly, that its faith refuses to the Sacrament what it accords exclusively to the Word, that it recognizes the Sacrament to be of no vital importance, either on the theological or practical level.[197]

Returning for a moment to Donald Baillie, who well understood the implications of separating the Word from the Sacrament, and yet maintained throughout his work on Communion that words were essential – both in celebrating the rite and in the preaching accomplished prior to the Eucharist. In writing of the Lord's Supper as a *memorial feast*, Baillie notes:

> None of the great Churches has ever reduced it to this alone, but each has always regarded this as part of its meaning. The Lord's supper must always be, among other things, in remembrance of Jesus Christ and particularly of His passion, and all its other meanings must depend upon this historical reference; for it is an historical reference – the Church's corporate memory of the episode of the cross of Christ. . . . St. Paul says, 'As often as you eat this bread and drink this cup, you do show the Lord's death until He come.' He may have meant the action of taking and breaking the bread and pouring out the wine is a dramatic representation of the death of Christ, who, as he says elsewhere, had been publicly portrayed or placarded, as crucified, before the eyes of the Galatians. But some scholars think the Greek word translated 'ye do show' or 'portray' ought to be given its more natural sense and translated 'You do announce' or 'proclaim' or even 'recite'. Thus the sentence may mean: 'whenever you celebrate the Lord's supper, you recite the story of the passion', If so, it would indicate that in St. Paul's time it was the custom to recite the whole story at the Lord's table, and this might well account for the fact that the part of the Gospel story which narrates the final scenes is out of proportion fuller and more detailed than all the rest of the story;. . .[198]

One of the strongest voices in the latter half of the 20th century for the Lord's Supper's Pauline use in proclaiming the gospel was Joseph R. Shultz, who served as dean of Ashland Theological Seminary. Shultz authored a book entitled, *The Soul of the Symbols*. Shultz certainly embraced the 20th century's eschatological emphasis in the Supper, but he also recognized the huge gospel proclamatory value for its use in the Christian church as well. In his chapter "The Eucharist," Shultz deals with 1 Corinthians 11:23 – 26 and its imperatives for the body of Christ:

---

[197] Oscar Cullman, F. J. Leenhardt. *Essays on the Lord's Supper*, Translated by J. G. Davies (Richmond, VA: John Knox Press, 1958), p. 32.

[198] Baillie, *The Theology of the Sacraments*, p. 103.

> For every time ye eat the bread, and drink the cup, ye proclaim the death of the Lord until He comes." . . .The term "proclaim" here is nearer the truth than "show," and may even be given as "announce" or "recite." Whichever term is selected, the sense of the text is that the Eucharist is a "proclamation," Professor Torrance describes the proclamation as "The Church on earth is given in its Eucharistic worship to *echo* the eternal intercession of Christ." This living echo of Calvary is the intercession of the Church. The Eucharist is the resounding "Amen" within the Christians faith, the counterpart on earth to the eternal intercession of Christ in heaven. The proclamation of the Church is "Alleluia, blessing and honor and glory and power be unto him who sitteth upon the throne, and unto the Lamb for ever and ever" (Rev. 5:13).
>
> The fellowship of Christians proclaims the Gospel in the world. In heaven is the reconciling Son before the Father interceding for man; on earth is the Church showing forth His reconciliation and proclaiming His mercy and grace. **The proclamation in the Eucharist dare not be only to the Church, but also as a witness to the world. Just as the world comes to know God's love through the Christian Agape, so the world come to know God's redeeming sacrifice through the Christian Eucharist. The Christian message to all mankind is proclaimed in the Eucharist.**[199]

It is worth noting, that even within the Catholic Church, the concept of Eucharist as proclamation is being discussed in the modern era. In 1985, a small book was printed entitled, *Eucharist as Proclamation*, authored by Erasto Fernandez. Fernandez begins by acknowledging that prior to Vatican II, "everyone thought of the Eucharist as nothing more than a sacrifice." Then with the Vatican II initiatives, Catholics were instructed to think in terms of "Celebrating the Eucharist," rather than simply "going to Mass." The Roman Church's emphasis for the celebration of the Lord's Supper had shifted from "sacrifice" to "celebration." Fernandez writes, however, that while there have been advantages to this new approach to Communion, it has not achieved the level of involvement from celebrants that would be most desirable. Thus, Fernandez' order, the Blessed Sacrament Fathers, took for their mission project the theme of "Eucharist as Proclamation." Elaborating on this further, Fernandez writes:

> In recent years, however, especially in places where the celebration aspect of the Eucharist has been fully utilized and explored and benefited from, there is emerging a new way of looking at the Eucharist, precisely because the approach to Eucharist as celebration can be somewhat limited and limiting. This other way is Eucharist as Proclamation. . . . The proclamation aspect . . . calls for a total and more lasting engagement of the entire person – at the

---

[199] Joseph R. Shultz, *The Soul of the Symbols: A Theological Study of Holy Communion* (Grand Rapids: William B. Eerdmans, 1966), pp. 140 – 141.

> Eucharist and outside too. And so, more and more we find ourselves turning from the Eucharist as celebration to the Eucharist as proclamation – at least among those who wish to derive the maximum from their Eucharists.[200]

More recently, there have been some serious efforts in published Protestant works, intending to bring back an emphasis on the celebration of the Lord's Supper – both as it relates to the Word preached, and as it relates to Eucharist proclamation of the gospel. For example, David Peterson, in D. A. Carson's 1993 work, *Worship*, discusses the situation in 1 Corinthians 11 and the problems associated with the Lord's Supper. He works through the verses of the pericope then comes to verse 26:

> In vs. 26 Paul asserts that eating the bread and drinking the cup is a means of proclaiming the Lord's death until he comes, a means of reminding one another of the significance of his sacrifice. By their disregard for one another they were *negating the very point of that death* – 'to create a new people for his name, in which the old distinctions based on human fallenness no longer obtain.'[201]

What does Peterson then glean from his analysis of 1 Corinthians 11:17 – 34?

> Although the terminology of edification is not used in 1 Corinthians 11, the issue of *edifying the church* is undoubtedly prominent. The Lord's Supper, which has so often throughout church history been understood as a means of deepening personal communion of believers with their Lord, is clearly meant to focus the eyes of the participants on *one another* as well as on God. We do not simply meet to have fellowship with God but to minister to one another as we express our common participation in Christ as our Savior and Lord. It is the 'horizontal' significance of the Lord's Supper that is so often played down in contemporary practice. Yet, according to Paul, those who disregard their responsibility to welcome and care for fellow believers in the local congregation cannot worship or serve God acceptably![202]

As was previously discussed, communicant's manuals as well as published Communion sermons or meditations were popular tools for Christians from the mid-17th century through the mid-19th century. It seems there is a definite need for a revival of these sorts of tools in the present day if Lord's Supper celebrations are to be renewed in the Protestant Church. In 2000, one such effort was made, a collection

---

[200] Erasto Fernandez, *Eucharist As Proclamation* (Albatross Books, 1987), pp. 3, 66.

[201] D. A. Carson, *Worship: Adoration and Action* (Grand Rapids: Baker Book House, 1993), pp. 81 – 82. David Peterson, "Worship in the New Testament."

[202] Ibid., p. 82. David Peterson, "Worship in the New Testament."

of Lord's Supper messages derived from the sincerely pastoral labors at weekly Communions by Peter J. Leithart. This paperback, entitled, *Blessed Are the Hungry*, revives a once common Christian literary and devotional genre. References in several places to 1 Corinthians 11:26 may be found in Leithart's work. Two examples will suffice for illustration:

Excerpted from "Sweet Words":

> At least since Augustine, the sacraments have been understood as "visible words." James Jordan has suggested that the Supper is more appropriately called an "edible word," but even so the analogy of the Word and Sacrament stands. This notion of sacramental "words" picks up on the thread of imagery we have been examining here, that is, the biblical connection between receiving God's Word and eating it. Paul makes it clear that the celebration of the Supper is, in some manner, a proclamation of the death of Christ, an act of preaching (1 Corinthians 11:26). The Supper is the gospel made food, and in this transformation of proclamation into meal, the Supper replicates the history of Jesus Himself:[203]

Excerpted from "The Way Things Really Ought to Be: Eucharist, Eschatology, and Culture":

> At the Lord's table, we eat bread and drink wine together *to proclaim the Lord's death until He comes*. Here, a wide-angle exploration of the Eucharist casts fresh light on one of the traditional, "deeper" questions of Eucharistic and liturgical theology. Paul writes that the Supper proclaims the death of Jesus until He comes (1 Corinthians 11:26), but how is this the case? Liturgists have sometimes attempted to locate some act in the rite of the Supper that corresponds to the death of Jesus: some suggest the fraction (breaking of bread) correlates with the breaking of Jesus' body, while others note the separation of bread and wine as a sign of sacrificial death, while others refer this to the repetition of the words of institution. I find these efforts strained, since it is all but impossible to make a meal look like death by crucifixion. Breaking bread and pouring out wine has, by an act of imaginative faith, been understood as an enactment of the crucifixion, but more appropriate media for such a portrayal are conceivable, as Thomas Aquinas recognized: *Carnes animalium occisorum expresse repraesentent Christi passionem*. . . . Since the Supper is the communal meal as a whole, the fact that we eat together and the way we do it, that is what "proclaims the Lord's death."[204]

---

[203] Peter J. Leithart, *Blessed Are the Hungry: Meditations on the Lord's Supper* (Moscow, ID: Canon Press, 2000), p. 70.
[204] Leithart, *Blessed Are the Hungry: Meditations on the Lord's Supper*, pp. 179 – 180.

Leithart's Communion meditations using Paul's exhortation to the Corinthians, about the Supper as proclamation of the gospel return us at the beginning of the 21st century to the main question for this entire inquiry. For now a case is being advanced for a proper balance between Word preached from the pulpit and Word made visible in the Supper. And while the proper *balance* is sought out among the Protestant churches, the proper *understanding* and *use* of the Supper may also be rediscovered. Everything the Lord gave and instructed concerning the Sacrament is necessary to accomplish what the Apostle revealed – proclamation of Jesus' death until he comes. Christ designed the Supper to serve as a Gospel Feast.

Just two years after Leithart's, *Blessed Are the Hungry* was published, 2002 witnessed several new works in the area of Lord's Supper renewal and its proper place and function in the worship and life of the church. Keith Mathison took a constructive approach to the matter by seeking to bring back John Calvin's sacramental doctrines and infuse them into this generation's Supper celebrations. His book was entitled, *Given for You.* Mathison takes a serious look at 1 Corinthians 11:26 and finds it to be compelling for weekly Eucharist celebration in the local church:

> According to Scripture, the Lord's Supper is also a proclamation of the death of Christ (1 Cor. 11:26). This is the same message that Paul says is the heart of his gospel message (1 Cor. 2:1 – 3). Is the church not called to proclaim the death of Christ? Do believers not need to be continually reminded of this message, to hear this gospel? The heart of the preached word is Jesus Christ and him crucified. The heart of the visible word is the same – the death of Christ. IF the Lord's Supper truly is the proclamation of Christ's death, as Paul says it is, why would any Christian not want this proclamation to be part of every gathering for worship?[205]

Mathison is quite right to equate the preaching of the gospel from the pulpit with the visible and tactile proclamation of the same atoning death of Jesus Christ through the celebration of the Lord's Supper. And Mathison adds another important thought later in this volume. While considering Calvin's attitude about the balance between Word

---

[205] Keith A. Mathison, *Given for You: Reclaiming Calvin's Doctrine on the Lord's Supper* (Phillipsburg, NJ: P & R Publishing, 2002), p. 294.

and Supper, Mathison writes, "The preached word and the visible word are complementary, not contradictory."[206]

Covenantal Worship: Reconsidering the Puritan Regulative Principle, was written by R. J. Gore, Jr. In this work, Gore makes a similar plea to Mathison's – for balance in Protestant worship between the ministry of the Word and the celebration of the Lord's Supper. While making his appeal for balance in Word and Sacrament, as well as weekly Communion observance, Gore appeals to apostolic practice, the Lord's own instruction, and the insights of modern liturgical scholarship:

> If it is necessary to balance word and symbol, it is critical to balance Word and Sacrament. If there is anything that modern liturgical scholarship agrees on, it is that the Lord's Supper should be celebrated every Lord's Day as the church gathers to worship the risen Lord. We have seen Calvin's emphasis that true worship is worship involving both the Word and the Table. As von Allmen notes, the most basic reason that weekly communion is essential is that, "Christ instituted it and commanded the Church to celebrate it." Indeed, there is evidence that the New Testament church did just that. The implications of apostolic practice, as well as the liturgical history of the church, indicate that weekly communion should be the norm and not the exception.[207]

Gore argues in this work that the Reformed tradition would benefit from re-examining the regulative principle of worship, which according to Gore has been influenced by Puritan approaches to worship over those of Calvin and the earlier Continental Reformers. While everyone will not agree with Gore, and while his argument for frequent Communion from modern scholarship or ancient tradition may not be that persuasive, he does have a point when he takes us to the words of Christ and Paul, and to the evident practice of the first century church.

Further calls for rediscovering, recovering, or in Mark Hicks' case, revisioning the Lord's Supper were published in 2002, a strong year for works on this subject. Hicks' book, *Come to the Table: Revisioning the Lord's Supper*, maintains a commitment to the Reformed understanding of the Word and Sacrament and the balance that must be

---

[206] Mathison, *Given for You: Reclaiming Calvin's Doctrine on the Lord's Supper*, p. 297.
[207] R. J. Gore, Jr. *Covenantal Worship: Reconsidering the Puritan Regulative Principle* (Phillipsburg, NJ: P & R Publishing, 2002), p. 157.

maintained. Hicks was moved by the Pauline 1 Corinthians 11 passage and the problems addressed in Corinth to rethink the Table as a place of gospel equalization. That is, that the gospel does its redeeming work and the image of that unity in the redeeming blood of Christ is the appearance of all sorts of people, made one family partaking together of the Supper. How does Hicks see Lord's Supper celebration going forward?

> When the supper is abstracted as an independent act of worship (one of five as a checklist), it loses its connectedness with the Word and the worship event. I am an advocate of the Reformed tradition where the supper and the Word are bound together not only theologically but in practice. The supper is a concrete proclamation of the Word, but it is exactly its concrete character (bread and wine) which must be explained and applied. The supper needs to be joined with a preached Word from God so that not only the alien will appreciate its significance, but that the church will be reminded and will remember the work of God in Jesus Christ for them. The gospel should be proclaimed when the supper is served. . . .The church should not adjust the supper to the alien . . ., but proclaim the gospel through the supper and Word so that the alien learns the traditions of faith and redemption.[208]

Dan Schmidt, another author on the Supper from the past decade, includes an entire chapter in his work, *Taken by Communion: How the Lord's Supper Nourishes the Soul*, devoted to the Supper as proclamation. Schmidt points out right away in addressing 1 Corinthians 11:26 that "Christianity insists on proclamation." While all other religions teach self-improvement, self-righteousness, or inner peace, the Christian faith is unique in its possession of a gospel – good news, and this gospel "needs to be shared." Schmidt details more of what it means for our Communion celebrations to "proclaim":

> Communion encourages us to remember; it exhorts us to proclaim. We are neither passive consumers of what appears before us nor paying customers expecting to have our senses sated. We come to be confronted, changed, taken. We affirm in communion that the death of Jesus is essential, and we declare our desire for "becoming like him in his death" (Phil. 3:10). By proclaiming the Lord's death, we announce agreement with necessary change. My life, we say, is of little consequence; I give it gladly and freely to the

---

[208] John Mark Hicks, *Come to the Table: Revisioning the Lord's Supper* (Abilene, TX: Leafwood Publishers, 2002), p. 174.

> Lord. In the transaction of faith, we sign the waiver releasing our hold on life. It now belongs to God, to do with as he will.[209]

What does it mean in this era to *recover* the Lord's Supper? That is the question addressed by Leonard J. Vander Zee in, *Christ, Baptism and the Lord's Supper: Recovering the Sacraments for Evangelical Worship*. Vander Zee writes that when Paul says "we proclaim the Lord's death, he means that in the absence of the historical Christ, the sacrament binds us to him through remembrance of what he said and did surrounding his death." In describing how celebrations of the Supper recall Christ's great "paschal mystery," Vander Zee adds that, "We live, and we eat and drink this meal under the shadow of the cross. . . .It brings us into fellowship with the "lamb that was slain."[210]

And yet although there is a tone of suffering and death in the remembrance and proclamation of Christ's atoning sacrifice in the Supper, there is also the joy of the believers' coming resurrection and reunion at the return of Christ. Vander Zee continues:

> Just as the Supper unites us with the historical Jesus in his death, resurrection and ascension, it also unites us with Jesus, who dwells at the Father's right hand in glory. Just as it thrusts us back in time, it pushes us forward to the end of time. The sacrament unites us with the body of the ascended and glorified Christ in a way that anticipates our future union with him.[211]

A more modest recent effort, designed in fact to assist new converts or younger communicants with the Sacrament, is Richard D. Phillips', *What Is the Lord's Supper?* This useful work is part of the series on the basics of the Reformed Faith Series from Presbyterian & Reformed Publishing. Phillip's booklet and others like it are precisely the sort of resources that are needed in this 21st century if the Supper is going to regain its place alongside preaching as a means of proclaiming the gospel.

---

[209] Dan Schmidt, Taken By Communion: How the Lord's Supper Nourishes the Soul (Grand Rapids: Baker Books, 2003), p. 118.
[210] Leonard J. Vander Zee, *Christ, Baptism and the Lord's Supper* (Downers Grove, IL: InterVarsity Press, 2004), p. 217.
[211] Ibid.

Pastors and congregations today need help to return to a biblical understanding of the Lord's Supper as rightfully both Communion and *Gospel Feast.*

It is not at all surprising, with the rising interest throughout Protestantism in invigorating Lord's Supper theology and practice, and given the popularity of *multiple-views* books on common points of difference among denominations, that Zondervan published, *Understanding Four Views on the Lord's Supper* in 2007. Within John H. Armstrong's introduction to this helpful book, he writes of the significance of the Supper:

> There is no real doubt about this simple historical fact – through the centuries this meal has been the central and characteristic action of the church at worship. If the church is a community that remembers Jesus as Lord, then the chief way this has been done in public worship has been through this Supper. And this remembrance is not designed for sentimental reflection but as a divinely invoked "recalling" of the historic event of Christ's life and work, particularly his passion, resurrection, and ascension.[212]

Armstrong also makes the case for frequent Communion in the pages of his fine introduction to this volume. And he addresses the eschatological importance of Paul's phrase in 1 Corinthians 11:26, that we are to "proclaim the Lord's death until he comes." As Armstrong's exhortation for frequent Supper celebration arises from the 1 Corinthians 11:26 text, it is quoted here:

> Paul writes in 1 Corinthians 11:26, "For whenever you eat this bread and drink this cup. . . . " The word *whenever* appears to be open-ended. It means that simply that you may take the meal as often as conscience and common practice determine. Churches differ in their customs, but one thing we do know – the earliest Christians took the Supper very often. It is possible that in some settings they took it almost every day. It seems fairly obvious when we read the historical records that initially they took it every Lord's Day. Paul's counsel does not determine the precise number of times the church should take the meal, but it places no limits on frequent celebration either.
>
> A common argument I've encountered among some evangelical Protestants is that frequent celebration will make the Supper ordinary or less important. I have always found this argument weak, if not outright appalling. How can you remember the Lord's death too frequently? How can I express my devotion

---

[212] John H. Armstrong, "Do This in Remembrance of Me." In *Understanding Four Views on the Lord's Supper* (Grand Rapids: Zondervan, 2007), p. 15.

> and love for Christ too much? The problem in making it too ordinary may lie in our hearts, not in how often we actually come to the table.[213]

The very year (2007) that *Understanding Four Views on the Lord's Supper* was published, theologians of the Lutheran tradition published an important collection of scholarly articles, some specifically related to the topic of the Lord's Supper as gospel proclamation. The volume, was entitled, *The Preached God: Proclamation in Word and Sacrament*. One of the articles included in this volume is especially compelling, given one of the goals of Supper renewal is better balance between Word and Sacrament. How do pastors in practical, real-world worship settings connect Word and Sacrament? Through more preaching of the Sacraments. That is the title of this article within *The Preached God*. And how is this accomplished?

> So let us talk of preaching the sacraments. Our talk must be of *preaching* the sacraments, not merely talking about them. This means at the first instance preaching the sacraments as the *gospel*, not as springboards for ethical exhortation (though they may be that too) since that is not where our problem lies. The task is to preach the sacraments as a gospel Word for us, a Word which cuts into our lives, puts the old to death and raises up the new. So preaching the sacraments cannot be just explaining them or even just talking about what they are supposed to do, though some of that may incidentally be involved. If preaching, as I have already tried to suggest, is doing the text to the hearer, then in this case the "text" is the sacramental deed, the visible, tangible Word, and preaching must then be the somewhat exacting and tricky task of doing the visible Word to the recipient in such a way that the audible and visible simply go hand in hand, or better, hand in glove.[214]

Forde's description of what it means to *preach the Sacraments*, is a very fitting model for ministers to follow today if congregations are going to embrace sacramental renewal in the local churches. And this would be the proper way to think about, connect, and practically apply gospel proclamation in the Supper with the gospel proclaimed from the pulpit.

Two other very recent works, one from the Baptist tradition and the other from the Scots Presbyterian tradition, take up the concept of gospel proclamation through the Lord's Supper, specifically engaging with 1 Corinthians 11:26 and Paul's use of

---

[213] Armstrong, "Do This in Remembrance of Me." In *Understanding Four Views on the Lord's Supper*, p. 22.

[214] Gerhard O. Forde, *The Preached God: Proclamation in Word and Sacramen,* Mark C. Mattes and Steven D. Paulson, eds. (Grand Rapids: William B. Eerdmans, 2007), pp. 100 – 101.

καταγγέλλετε (*proclaim*) with reference to the Lord's Supper. Malcolm Maclean, in his, *The Lord's Supper* volume writes that: "The meal is also a proclamation that says something to those looking on." Macleod notes that it is probable the early Christians did not sit in silence at the Supper. An account of what happened to Jesus was narrated, either from recollection or from written accounts. He also notes that Jesus gave instructions during the first Lord's Supper. It was this combination of ritual (taking the bread and wine) and Word (reading the accounts) that Paul referred to by 'proclaim'. . . . This combination of word and action suggests that the Lord's Supper is an act of prophetic symbolism.[215]

A compilation of articles on the Lord's Supper from the Baptist tradition concludes this historical overview of the church's understanding of the Lord's Supper with reference to gospel proclamation. The most recent volume as of this writing, *The Lord's Supper: Remembering and Proclaiming Christ Until He Comes* (2010) is a fresh look at the Lord's Supper from a variety of nuances. James M. Hamilton, Jr., writing in this volume an article entitled, "The Lord's Supper in Paul: An Identity-Forming Proclamation of the Gospel," explains the meaning of, "For as often as you eat this bread and drink the cup, you proclaim the Lord's death until he comes":

> This means that in eating the bread and drinking the cup the Corinthians were by faith claiming for themselves the benefits of the death of Christ and identifying themselves with the body of Christ – the church. To proclaim the Lord's death is to celebrate His life-giving sacrifice of Himself, looking back to the cross, and at the same time forward to His return – "until he comes" (11:26). . . . In the Lord's Supper, we are proclaiming the Lord's death: heralding that Jesus died for our sins.[216]

Hamilton later turns his attention to the question of frequency and the Supper, and in his reply connects Communion observance with the totality of biblical services of worship. "If it is objected that this (weekly Communion) would diminish its significance, my reply is simply that those who make this argument typically do not claim that weekly observance diminishes the significance of preaching the Word, the

---

[215] Malcolm Maclean, *The Lord's Supper* (Ross-shire, Scotland: Christian Focus Publications, 2009), pp. 34 – 35.
[216] James M. Hamilton, "The Lord's Supper in Paul: An Identity-Forming Proclamation of the Gospel," in *The Lord's Supper: Remembering and Proclaiming Christ Until He Comes*, edited by Thomas R. Schreiner and Matthew R. Crawford (Nashville: B & H Publishing, 2010), p. 92.

prayers of God's people, the singing of Psalms, hymns, and spiritual songs, and I doubt they would be disappointed to have weekly baptisms! The same practices and attitudes that keep preaching, praying, singing, and baptizing from having their significance diminished could surely be applied to the weekly celebration of the Lord's Supper."[217]

The original admonitions, instructions, and exhortations which the Apostle Paul applied to the congregation of believers in Corinth, Greece more than 1950 years ago, "For as often as you eat this bread and drink of the cup, you proclaim the Lord's death until he comes," has impacted every generation of Christians from the first century to the present day and will continue to do so "until he comes." 1 Corinthians 11:26 has been understood and interpreted in a variety of ways since its creation to address a pastoral concern by Paul. This historical survey of its application to the life and worship of the Christian Church since its inception has demonstrated that the original impact of Paul's exhortation – proclaiming the Lord's death until he comes – has often been submerged under the twin theological and praxis emphases of resacrifice and transubstantiation.

After some 1,400 years of Lord's Supper celebrations which understood the Sacrament as an offering of Christ's true body and blood upon the altar, *by the priest unto God*, a rediscovery of the importance of Pauline Lord's Supper celebration occurred in the 16th century at the hands of Martin Luther, Ulrich Zwingli, John Calvin, and many others within the Protestant movement.

Following a flowering of exhortations from the Reformation era, and well into the 17th and 18th centuries for regular biblical Lord's Supper celebrations which proclaimed the death of Christ and thus his benefits by faith to the participants, the Supper again fell into neglect among the Protestant churches, increasingly viewed as a mere form, or an empty, unnecessary ritual. As Hughes Old observes in the concluding chapter of his recent volume, *Holy Communion in the Piety of the Reformed Church*, "in the centuries that followed the Reformation, profound insights came to light in the eucharistic piety of the Reformed church, but, in the twentieth

[217] Hamilton, "The Lord's Supper in Paul: An Identity-Forming Proclamation of the Gospel," in *The Lord's Supper: Remembering and Proclaiming Christ Until He Comes*, p. 101.

century, these insights were largely forgotten or ignored. It is to be hoped that in the twenty-first century these insights will be rediscovered and appreciated."[218] Old, the great scholar of Reformed worship, is writing about Eucharistic piety, but the same can be demonstrated to be true with respect to the Supper as gospel proclamation!

Recent scholarly and practical works have sought to recover a biblical, Pauline theology and praxis of the Lord's Supper in Protestant churches which will, in fact accomplish, "proclaiming the Lord's death until he comes." The Lord's Supper is in the process of being rediscovered or recovered as the *Gospel Feast*. As it is a purpose of this volume to apply its findings to the needs of the local church, the final two chapters will address the sacramental theology now needed and the practical application of that theology to worship in the church.

---

[218] Old, *Holy Communion*, p. 857.

VI

PROCLAMATION RESTORED: GOSPEL PROCLAMATION THROUGH THE LORD'S SUPPER TODAY – A GOSPEL-CENTERED WAY FORWARD

"As often as ye eat this bread and drink this cup, ye do proclaim the Lord's death till he come" (11:26). The word is really "preach," here: "ye do preach the Lord's death." There is one moment of your life above all others when you are preaching a sermon – that is when you meet around the Lord's table. You are preaching to the powers of darkness, "proclaiming the Lord's death" which has vanquished them. Also, to the Lord in heaven who looks down and sees your heart, you are witnessing your trust in His atoning work. When we meet around His table, we are feasting upon Him as He is received into our hearts by faith; as our heads are bowed in worship around His table we are sharing in fellowship with the living Lord, and are telling Him what He means to us.

(Alan Redpath, *The Royal Route to Heaven*, 1960)[219]

My purpose in pursuing this extensive exegesis and historical survey concerning 1 Corinthians 11:26 was to arrive at a more refined understanding of what Paul is teaching when he interprets the regular, ongoing celebrating of the Lord's Supper as "proclaiming the Lord's death until he comes." And in seeking to acquire a deeper theological and pastoral comprehension of Paul's meaning when using the Greek word καταγγέλλετε with reference to the Lord's Supper, I also sought to apply those theological and pastoral insights to the worship of the body of Christ in our local churches today.

There is no need, nor is it my purpose to change, amend, or adjust the documents of my particular branch of the Protestant Church – that of Presbyterian and Reformed. The precision of the *Westminster Confession of Faith*, the *Larger and Shorter Catechisms*, and the marvelous language of the *Heidelberg Catechism* are more than adequate statements on the importance of the Lord's Supper. In answer to question #66 of the *Heidelberg Catechism* concerning the Sacraments we read this phrase: "The sacraments are holy visible signs and seals, appointed of God for this end, that by the use thereof, he may the more fully declare and seal to us the promise of the

---

[219] Alan Redpath, *The Royal Route to Heaven: Studies in First Corinthians* (Westwood, NJ: Fleming H. Revell Company, 1960), pp. 135 – 136.

gospel." *The Westminster Confession of Faith* speaks of "signs and seals of the covenant of grace," and of the Supper as the "perpetual remembrance of the sacrifice of Himself in His death." And the *Westminster Larger Catechism* summarizes quite well the visible and symbolic aspects of the Supper in question #168:

> Question 168: What is the Lord's Supper?
>
> Answer: The Lord's Supper is a sacrament of the New Testament, wherein, **by giving and receiving bread and wine according to the appointment of Jesus Christ, his death is showed forth**; and they that worthily communicate feed upon his body and blood, to their spiritual nourishment and growth in grace; have their union and communion with him confirmed; testify and renew their thankfulness, and engagement to God, and their mutual love and fellowship each with other, as members of the same mystical body.

And then our tradition may also look to the brilliance of Calvin's theology of the real spiritual presence of Christ in the Supper, and the means by which its celebration lifts up the participants into the heavenly places. Or we may also resort to perhaps that greatest of theologians of the past on the Supper, Jonathan Edwards, and his marvelous explanation of the meal in terms of covenantal proclamation by both the Redeemer and his redeemed. Through its visual proclamation of Jesus' atoning death for our eternal salvation, the Communion celebration is very much also the *Gospel Feast.*

Yet despite these wonderful statements concerning the importance of the Lord's Supper, I find that what is needed in my pastoral work is further elaboration on what it means to "show forth," or proclaim the Lord's death until he comes. And I'd also like to visualize what that looks like in the covenant worship of my church. I maintain that everyone in the Christian faith needs to have a deeper understanding of what Jesus does by his Spirit when the Eucharist is celebrated according to Scripture and received by believing people.

And so that brings me again to the purpose of this work – answering the questions posed in the introduction. The first question, "How is it that since Paul addressed his letter to the church in Corinth in the first century, with so many generations of theologians, churchmen, and pastors at work, that so little weight has been given to the significance of the Lord's Supper as a means of proclaiming the gospel?" which seems to have been answered through the historical survey of the ways this passage has been interpreted and applied to Lord's Supper practice during the past 1,950 or so years. The importance of the Lord's Supper as proclaiming the gospel diminished during the early days of the persecuted, then state-recognized Church and continued through the Middle Ages, typically to be overshadowed by the church's fascination with the Supper as an offering unto God – a resacrifice of Christ's true body and blood upon the altar.

The biblical importance of Paul's teaching in 1 Corinthians 11:23 – 26 was rediscovered, or if you will, recovered, in the early years of the Protestant Reformation, fostered in the two centuries that followed, and then gradually forgotten again, as the Supper lost its significance to most Protestant theologians, pastors, and congregants. Yet it is my hope in this current generation and by God's grace, that the Lord's Supper will again be understood by the body of Christ as the Lord's other means of proclaiming the gospel, alongside that of preaching.

The second question I posed, "Has the church in all its multi-colored local manifestations and differentiated denominations deprived itself of a crucial biblical principle which could transform the celebration and the impact of the Lord's Supper?" must be answered in the affirmative. In many Protestant traditions the Supper is viewed purely as memorial and possessing no equivalent place in worship alongside that of preaching, praying, baptizing, singing, or giving. Even within my own Reformed tradition, the preaching of the Word is given such priority that the Supper of our Lord is often but an afterthought in the worship of the local church. And of course in the Catholic, Orthodox, and Anglican traditions, the sacrificial nature of the Supper is given priority over everything else.

And the third and final question of interest in this work, "And, if the church has deprived itself of a crucial principle, or at least a sharper understanding of that principle, what is it and how can it be recaptured and applied to the worship of the church today?" may now be answered in this chapter and the one to follow, through distilling the principle of "Supper as gospel proclamation," and applying it in practical ways to the worship of the local congregation. This is the reason I sometimes use the terms *Gospel Feast* or *Gospel Feasting* as equivalents for the Lord's Supper.

According to the results of the exegetical work in chapter 2, we can safely conclude that the Apostle Paul interpreted Jesus' command to *perpetually keep the sacrament until his return*, as a *means of proclaiming the gospel*. There is admittedly nothing *new* or *novel* in this conclusion. However, we have drawn some elaborative interpretations from this exegetical finding which will provide a great deal of help to working pastors in thinking about what all this means and why it is important.

Principle One: The Lord's Supper constitutes another means, alongside preaching, of proclaiming the death of Jesus Christ, that is, the gospel. *This applies to believers and to the as of yet unsaved onlookers.*

Of primary importance with respect to 1 Corinthians 11:26 and the biblical use of the Lord's Supper is what Paul means when he states that the Eucharist *proclaims* the Lord's death. This is the heart of what faithful celebrations of the Lord's Supper accomplish. The atoning death of the Lord Jesus Christ on behalf of sinners is visually represented and declared. This proclamation of the Lord's death in the Supper is accomplished through all aspects the Lord commanded his Church to employ in the Sacrament. Thus, the symbols or elements of bread and cup, the actions of breaking, pouring, and distributing, and the receiving by believing participants – all of it contextualized by the words of institution – comprise the act of proclamation. The Lord's Supper is in fact a regular visual proclamation of Jesus' death and also a prophetic symbol, reminding us of his promised return. It is in in the truest sense, a Gospel Feast.

The question for shepherds of God's flock is what the implications of this are with respect to worship. In the first place, preachers are called to proclaim the Lord's death above all things in their work of building God's kingdom and fulfilling the Great Commission of Matthew 28:18 – 20. What does the Apostle Paul say to the Corinthians earlier in the same epistle from which our Lord's Supper derived?

> And I, when I came to you, brothers, did not come proclaiming to you the testimony of God with lofty speech or wisdom. **For I decided to know nothing among you except Jesus Christ and him crucified.** And I was with you in weakness and in fear and much trembling, and my speech and my message were not in plausible words of wisdom, but in demonstration of the Spirit and of power, so that your faith might not rest in the wisdom of men but in the power of God (1 Corinthians 2:1 – 5).

Thus, the goal of all earnest preaching is to proclaim the death of the Lord Jesus Christ and what that death accomplished for those who believe in Jesus according to faith. Biblical theologians have demonstrated that when Paul writes in this way, he is using a sort of inspired shorthand for preaching Jesus' incarnation, life, ministry, suffering, death, resurrection, and ascension into heaven. As preachers, we must embrace the biblical truth that *the Lord's Supper constitutes another means of proclaiming the death of Jesus Christ and his victory over sin, death, hell, and Satan. Gospel proclamation by means of preaching from the pulpit and gospel proclamation by means of celebrating the Eucharist accomplish the same kingdom, Great Commission purposes. They should never be separated, but instead should be deeply entwined together in the worship life of the local church.*

Principle Two: The Lord's Supper is a visual testimony, profession or proclamation of the unity of the body of Christ.

A second theological principle necessary for biblical praxis of the Supper is derived from the context of the situation among the believers in the Corinthian congregation. We know that Paul's concern even in bringing up the Lord's Supper was the result of reports he had received that in the body life of the Corinthian Christian community, their divisions or factions were actually denying their proclamation of the gospel in the Supper. Thus we may rightly conclude that another aspect of biblical gospel proclamation which takes place in the celebration of *the Supper is a visual testimony or profession of the unity of the body of Christ* – that is, a public profession of the communion the believing participants have with God through Christ *and* the communion they have with one another as the redeemed family, a kingdom and priests to our God, ransomed and washed in the blood of the Lamb.

Principle Three: The Lord's Supper goes beyond past remembrance or memorial, proclaiming Christ's present work and his eschatological promise.

A third theological principle we have observed through our exegesis and through recent theological reflection on the 1 Corinthians 11:26 text is that the Lord's Supper goes beyond past remembrance or memorial. It also has *a genuine eschatological aspect*, deriving from the end of Paul's brief exhortation, "you proclaim the Lord's death *until he comes*." The Lord's Supper celebration, if administered according to

Paul's directive, has the power to exhibit past redemption, present intercession, spiritual presence, and enabling grace, alongside the prophetic aspect of displaying the future blessed hope of Jesus' glorious return.

The other aspects of the Lord's Supper also testify to the gospel of God's grace in Christ, even if they lie outside of the immediate text of our current inquiry. We can say that the Eucharist is indeed, as derived from the Greek, a doxological offering of thanksgiving and praise unto God. This is the only aspect of the Supper which is *Godward*, in the sense that the Sacrament was instituted by Christ with the intention of affecting the participants in remembering, proclaiming, and receiving grace. Thus is most respects it is a *manward* directed Sacrament, for his benefit and help, not as the Roman Church would have it – a *Godward* offering or re-offering of Christ's body and blood. The *manward* or *outward* direction of the Lord's Supper celebration lends itself to its purpose as a tool for gospel proclamation.

With regard to this *outward*, proclamatory aspect of the Lord's Supper, those of us who pastor congregations should immediately grasp the potential for the Sacrament's use as a strengthening adjunct or partner to preaching the gospel. While the Supper is not open to participation by nonbelievers or seekers, it nevertheless is a visual proclamation of the gospel. Even those who do not partake, yet remain during the celebration are presented with the signs and seals and the words of institution which declare the saving passion of the Lord Jesus Christ. For some, the visual impact of the symbols, contextualized by the Lord's words, may be used by the Holy Spirit to bring about saving faith. As John Koenig declares:

> ". . .the celebrative meals of thanksgiving referred to in the New Testament often drew nonbelievers to church gatherings. Verbal expressions of the good news about Jesus were of course decisive for conversion – surely no eucharist took place without them (1 Cor. 11:26) – but the actual turning to faith of many curious onlookers and seekers after righteousness must have come when they were able to see the gospel enfleshed in real human communities, especially during worship at table. . . . William Tully rightly insists that eucharistic services in our day ought to be considered services of evangelism. On the other hand, we have no evidence that visitors to eucharistic meals in

> New Testament times partook of or expected to partake of the ritual eating and drinking prior to baptism.[220]

There are so very many aspects to the gospel proclamation accomplished when the Lord's Supper is celebrated. It is a far-too-long neglected partner for the Word of God preached from the pulpit. And no matter what the text may be that we are about to preach on any given Lord's Day, if we have brought the celebration of the Supper into the covenant worship of God's local congregation, then we can be assured that the power of the cross of Christ will be lifted high for all to see – publicly proclaimed through the bread and the cup, the breaking and pouring, the giving and receiving, and the words of our Lord.

---

[220] John Koenig, *Feast of the World's Redemption: Eucharistic Origins and Christian Mission* (Harrisburg, PA: Trinity Press International, 2000), p. 255.

The third corollary of a covenantal theology of the Supper is that the celebration of the Lord's Supper is proclamatiom – a witness to the world. It is καταγγελιών, to use the biblical term (cf. 1 Cor. 11:26).

At the heart of a covenantal theology of worship is the idea that when God has heard our cry for help and delivered us from our misery, then we owe to God a witness to his mercy and his mighty acts for our salvation. We have often spoken of this, for it is a motivating obligation to tell the congregation, as well as to the whole of creation, what God has done for us. This is why the recounting of holy history is essential to worship. We tell the story as both memorial and thanksgiving, which is a witness. This witness not only strengthens the faith of the faithful but also inspires the faith of the doubtful. The giving of the witness is essential to evangelism because it is proclamation. ...

In other words, the very act of participating in the sacred feast is a profession of faith.

(Hughes Oliphant Old, *Holy Communion in the Piety of the Reformed Church*, 2013)[221]

---

[221] Hughes Oliphant Old, *Holy Communion in the Piety of the Reformed Church*, Jon Payne, ed. (Powder Springs, GA: Tolle Lege Press, 2013), pp. 70 – 71. Old's comments occur within his discussion of the covenantal and sacramental dimensions of Calvin's Eucharistic theology.

VII

PROCLAMATION IMPLEMENTED: THE PRACTICE OF LORD'S SUPPER GOSPEL PROCLAMATION IN TODAY'S CHURCHES

> *In the Lord's Supper, we are proclaiming the Lord's death: heralding that Jesus died for our sins. The gospel has more power to humble than any other force in the world. It places all on equal footing before the cross. This humbling power of the gospel then enables us to proclaim the Lord's death as we live out the self-inconveniencing love for others modeled by Jesus, even unto death.*[222]

Now it is important for us to take the exegetical and historical work that has been done, distilled into a practical, pastoral theology of the Lord's Supper as proclamation of the gospel (the *Gospel Feast*), and apply it to regular ministry in our local churches. How should we proceed? What means are available to us as working pastors?

The first key **Principle One: The Lord's Supper constitutes another means, alongside preaching, of proclaiming the death of Jesus Christ, that is, the gospel.** *This applies to believers and to the as of yet unsaved onlookers. Gospel proclamation by means of preaching from the pulpit and gospel proclamation by means of celebrating the Eucharist accomplish the same kingdom, Great Commission purposes. They should never be separated, but instead should be deeply entwined together in the worship life of the local church.* And so we must ask, "How do we put this principle into practice in our churches?"

In the first place I should state that this does not mean that the Sacrament of the Lord's Supper is *superior* to preaching as a means of proclaiming the gospel of Jesus Christ. Romans 10:17 is very clear that, "faith comes by hearing and hearing through the word of Christ." But it does mean that our Reformed tendency to elevate the art and power of preaching such that the Supper is of little use is also unbiblical.

---

[222] Hamilton, "The Lord's Supper in Paul: An Identity-Forming Proclamation of the Gospel," in *The Lord's Supper: Remembering and Proclaiming Christ Until He Comes*, p. 101.

It should be quite obvious at this stage in our investigation that the exhortation in the 1 Corinthians 11:17 – 34 pericope, as well as the practice of the earliest New Testament congregations, was to join the preaching of the Word verbally with the proclamation of the gospel through the Supper. Take the account in Acts for example, *And they devoted themselves to the apostles' teaching and the fellowship, to the breaking of bread and the prayers* (Acts 2:42, 46).

The practical outgrowth of this principle put into practice leads us to these recommendations for local pastors and their ministry of the gospel:

1. The best use of the Lord's Supper is as a partner with the Word preached to accomplish gospel proclamation. Therefore it is to every church's benefit to celebrate the Lord's Supper with the same frequency as the Word is preached. Weekly Communion is thus the preferred frequency.

2. In order to strengthen the bond between preached proclamation and sacramental proclamation of the gospel, every effort should be expended to connect the themes from the sermon and text to the visual gospel of the Supper celebration. This can be accomplished within the sermon as the pastor deems appropriate. However, for others it will be more suitable to connect the sermon to the Supper during the transition from the pulpit to the Table. The exhortation offered during the celebration of the Supper should always emphasize the gospel and that Communion is a gospel meal or feast.

3. Another way to assist the pastor in making this connection – and more importantly, for the congregation participants to see the gospel connection – is to prepare in advance a devotional, or brief commentary for the bulletin or a bulletin insert, which connects the preached text with the Lord's Supper. In Appendix I, you will find a few examples gleaned from many parts of the Bible as to how this can be done. (These may also be written for use in weekly church newsletters or pastoral letters.) A companion volume is also available, containing biblical devotions for the Lord's Supper, entitled, *Gospel Feasting: 104 Lord's Supper Devotions from the Old and New Testaments.*

4. Exhortations and even the closing prayer from the conclusion of the Supper may be worded so as to reflect the main points made in the sermon and its application to your flock.

5. As the Supper celebration proclaims the gospel alongside the sermon, nonbelievers or seekers should be invited specifically to remain during the Supper. The Table should be fenced against their partaking. However, they should be addressed at the end of the fencing in words such as, "Nevertheless, we invite you to remain during this part of our worship and we pray that God will use these visual words you see before you as another means to bring you to saving faith in the gospel of Jesus Christ. We long for the Spirit of Christ to bring you eternal salvation and invite you to share in this Gospel Feast."

6. In order that the impression is not given that the Supper is merely an add-on after the preached Word, adequate time should be given in each service for the celebration of the Eucharist and for contextualizing its observance with the proclamation of the gospel in the sermon.

7. I recommend if your congregation has not been exposed to a high view, or rather a closer to balanced view, of the visible Word partnered with the preached Word, that you engage in either evening classes, Sunday school teaching, or other appropriate venues to prepare your congregants and help them to get the most out of celebrating Communion as a local manifestation of God's redeemed covenant family.

8. Preach about the blessings of Communion on a regular basis. Consider making your recorded Communion sermons or even Table exhortations available in print, on mp3, or on your church's website. And don't rule out the idea of publishing your Lord's Supper sermons, even your devotions, in an inexpensive format for distribution to your congregation. This was often the practice in the days of the Reformation and during the 17th – 19th centuries.

Principle Two: The Lord's Supper is a visual testimony, profession, or proclamation of the unity of the body of Christ.

1. The Lord's Supper is a proclamation of the gospel as it unites people of diverse backgrounds, races, economic standings, or capabilities, making them into one adopted family in Christ. This aspect of the Supper's proclamation should be a regular part of our preaching, teaching, and pastoral ministry among our congregations. The problem of divisions and disregard for other brothers and sisters who are different in some way is not unique to the Corinth, Greece church of 1,950 years ago. Addressing this aspect of gospel proclamation in the Supper is best done through regular reference to the importance of recognizing the body of Christ in the Supper. Let me give you a practical pastoral illustration of what this sometimes looks like:

> Recently I was involved in working with our presbytery's shepherding committee in helping another church through a crisis between its senior pastor and assistant pastor. The church developed factions, following one or the other of these two men (frighteningly like the 1 Corinthians' situation). Without going into all the details, both the senior and the assistant pastors eventually resigned. Yet the divisions remained, sharply dividing this flock with a called congregational meeting scheduled immediately after the Lord's Day worship in order to approve the senior pastor's resignation. I was asked to lead at the Lord's Supper prior to this congregational meeting. As I was fencing the table, and reminding everyone present about being mindful of their brothers and sisters in Christ – I recalled what Jesus said about leaving your gift at the altar and going to be reconciled with your brother. How could I permit that divided body of Christ to come to the Lord's Table in the state of division they were in?
>
> And thus it occurred to me that what need to take place right there on the spot – if God's grace would allow – was gospel reconciliation between these factions. The alternative was to simply *go through the motions* of having the Sacrament and risk the celebration on that Lord's Day being no different than the ones they were having in Corinth in the Apostle Paul's time. And so, I stopped the fencing after reminding the participants about *going and being reconciled to their brothers and sisters*, and about the recent divisions in their flock, and asked them all to take a few minutes to greet one another in the Lord Jesus, to speak a genuine word of blessing, and wherever necessary, to reach out in confession and forgiveness to begin reconciliation with those with whom they had an offense.
>
> This took five or six minutes, but it was amazing what God chose to do in that short time. And we resumed the Lord's Supper celebration as it should properly, biblically be celebrated, as one redeemed family in the blood of the Lord Jesus Christ. This was truly a Gospel Feast for everyone present and

> served to draw believers together, rather than drive them apart. This is one of the ways in which the Spirit of Christ will work in our Communion celebrations.
>
> There will be times when pausing the Lord's Supper to encourage reconciliation will not only be appropriate but necessary to fulfill the law of Christ and maintain the integrity of the gospel's proclamation in the Supper.

2. The next suggestion pertains to all aspects of the Supper from a pastoral viewpoint, however this is a good place to take it up for consideration. One of the great trends now long lost in the 17th and 18th centuries was the use of communicant's manuals. These were designed to help communicants prepare to come to the Lord's Table. It was preached and taught in those days, and so congregants knew that it was important to prepare to receive the Lord's Supper, and then also to seek to live as Christians more faithfully after receiving Communion.

Of course, we have lost much of this *Communion piety* approach to receiving the Lord's Supper. Yet, regular instruction is necessary, perhaps now more than ever, as to how to prepare (or as they used to say, *keep short accounts*) by means of prayer and meditation on God's Word to receive the Supper. Included in this instruction must be the importance of maintaining brotherly love in keeping with Jesus' command and the Apostles' instruction.

I believe it will be highly useful and graciously edifying for the Protestant congregations we serve in this generation to have available a variety of contemporary communicant's manuals written and distributed. See appendix II for further discussion.

Principle Three: The Lord's Supper goes beyond past remembrance or memorial, proclaiming Christ's present work and his eschatological promise.

1. It happens so very often when we are at the Table of the Lord. We have all done it. We have had a busy week. Our sermon series has been moving through the Book of Job or perhaps Judges, and we are preoccupied with an ailing congregation member or the end of the year budget process. We come to our exhortation at the Table, the accompanist has perhaps played some rather somber background piece, and we fail to remind the communing members that the Lord's Supper is not only a

backward-looking remembrance, it is also a signpost of eschatological hope – blessed hope in the return of Christ.

It is our task, as much as we may have tendency to forget, that we are proclaiming through the Eucharist, our Lord's death *until he comes*. The only way I know of to improve in this regard of the Supper is to plan ahead. We must decide before we engage in leading the service of worship what aspect of the Supper proclamation – past, present, or future – we will emphasize on that particular Lord's Day. But let us be sure to exhort the certain hope found in the Supper celebration, just as surely as we remind our congregants of the awful atoning death. And by the way, let us also not forget to remind our churches of Christ's *real presence* with us by the Spirit during the Supper.

2. I have found it helpful in emphasizing the *until he comes* aspect of the Supper, to read from texts not typically used in the Communion liturgy or exhortations. For example, there are within the New Testament Scriptures, examples in which Christ's death is closely connected with his glorious return (i.e., 1 Thessalonians 4:13 – 18; Romans 6:7 – 9; 1 Corinthians 15:12 – 28). And of course the primary text of this present investigation, beautifully and succinctly connects Christ's atoning death with his pending return.

In conclusion, let me again plead with all ministers of the Christian faith to revisit your understanding of the Lord's Supper according to the words of the Apostle Paul as he interpreted what he had received from the Lord:

> For I received from the Lord what I also delivered to you, that the Lord Jesus on the night when he was betrayed took bread, and when he had given thanks, he broke it, and said, "This is my body which is for you. Do this in remembrance of me." In the same way also he took the cup, after supper, saying, "This cup is the new covenant in my blood. Do this, as often as you drink it, in remembrance of me." *For as often as you eat this bread and drink the cup, you proclaim the Lord's death until he comes.*

In closing may I also suggest, as this is a practical chapter for the sake of improving and enriching Lord's Supper gospel proclamation in our churches, that the training of ministry students in our Protestant and Reformed seminaries be strengthened with reference to the Sacrament of the Eucharist. My own seminary experience, while highly enriching and a good preparation for ministry, offered only one class in the training of the order of worship. The Lord's Supper was but one short portion within this class, devoted to the broader topic of Christian liturgy. Is it any wonder that ministers in our day rarely think of the Lord's Supper as a Gospel Feast? Now is the time for the body of Christ to return to that richer, more biblical understanding of the Supper as *kerygmatic*. Such an understanding was rediscovered by Calvin during the Reformation, as Hughes Old notes:

> Calvin's celebration of the Lord's Supper had a very distinct evangelistic dimension. In other word, it was at the Lord's Supper, and the services in the preparation for the Lord's Supper, that the evangelistic appeal was made.
>
> Some may prefer to speak of the *kerygmatic* dimension of the sacrament because, for them, the word "evangelism" has been hopelessly compromised by revivalism. Whatever word we choose it must do justice to the text: "for as often as you eat this bread and drink this cup you proclaim the Lord's death until he comes." Call it proclamation or call it evangelism; it amounts to the same thing. …
>
> The locus of evangelistic preaching [in Calvin's Geneva] was the celebration of the Eucharist.[223]

With an expectant return to Paul's 1 Corinthians 11:25 – 26 exhortation, this powerful use of the Supper as proclamation can be recovered yet again in our own generation. Let this then be my plea for those who train future generations of ministers of the gospel and future teaching theologians that the curriculum for all MDiv, MA, and MAR students be expanded to include a class whose sole purpose is to teach and to train seminary students in the theology and the practice of the Sacraments of our Lord Jesus Christ. In doing so, may the gospel be faithfully proclaimed – not only through the Word preached, but also through the visual signs, seals, and actions of the Lord's Supper. May our 21st century churches once again eat and drink deeply and richly at Christ's *Gospel Feast*!

---

[223] Old, *Holy Communion*, p. 136.

1st, We must pray that we may be prepared for this solemnity (the Lord's Supper) before it comes. Whatever is necessary to qualify us for communion with God in it, is spoken of in Scripture as God's gift; and whatever is the matter of God's promise, must be the matter of our prayers; for promises are given, not only to be the ground of our hope, but also to be the guide of our desire in prayer. Is knowledge necessary? "Out of his mouth cometh knowledge and understanding," and at wisdom's gates we must wait for wisdom's gifts, rejoicing herein "that the Son of God is come, and hath given us an understanding." Is faith necessary? That is not "of ourselves, it is the gift of God." Him, therefore, we must attend, who is both the author and the finisher of our faith. To him we must pray, Lord, increase our faith: Lord, perfect what is lacking in it: Lord, fulfill the work of faith with power. Is love necessary? It is the "Holy Ghost that sheds abroad that love in our hearts, and circumciseth our hearts to love the Lord our God." To that heavenly fire we must therefore go for this holy spark, and pray for the breath of the Almighty to blow it up into a flame. Is repentance necessary? It is God that gives repentance, that takes away the stony heart, and gives a heart of flesh; and we must beg of him to work that blessed change in us. "Behold the fire and the wood," the ordinance instituted, and all needful provision made for our sacrifice, "but where is the lamb for a burnt-offering?" Where is the heart to be offered up to God? If God did not provide himself a lamb, the solemnity would fail. To him therefore we must go to buy such things as we have need of against the feast, that is, to beg them; for we buy without money and without price, and such buyers shall not be driven out of God's temple, nor slighted there, however they are looked on in men's markets.

(Matthew Henry, *The Communicant's Companion*, 1828.)[224]

---

[224] Matthew Henry, *The Communicant's Companion* (New York, NY: Crocker & Brewster, 1828), pp. 136 – 137.

APPENDIX I

EXAMPLES OF LORD'S SUPPER DEVOTIONS FOR USE IN WORSHIP BULLETINS CONNECTING PREACHED TEXTS WITH THE CELEBRATION OF COMMUNION

As the preached Word of God is the primary means for gospel proclamation and conversion, while the Lord's Supper is a primary *visible* means for gospel proclamation, it is highly effective to connect these two biblical means of proclamation during the weekly service of worship. Obviously, specifics and context of each biblical text chosen for the Sunday service will result in a wide variety of themes, principles, and applications for the weekly Lord's Supper devotion. These devotions should be printed in the order of worship bulletin, provided on a separate insert, or issued during the week in the church's newsletter or pastoral letter. If desired, all of these means may be employed each week.

If the church maintains a website, or if the pastor writes his own columns for a blog, Communion devotions are a wonderful means of sharing the importance and the joyfulness of the Sacrament to an even wider audience than the local congregation. These technological tools assist pastors and church leaders in teaching and also in reaching the unchurched who may be curious about the Lord's Supper. Using some of the basic concepts in this book of Supper as Gospel Feast, the pastor can also communicate the good news of Jesus Christ through the Eucharistic biblical passages and through explanation of the importance of the symbols of bread and of the cup.

The format for the Communion celebration devotions typically begins with a straightforward presentation of the theological principles in the text and their importance for the communicant. They may or may not include (depending upon the author's preferences, time, and space available) a sample prayer to assist the participant in preparing themselves for the Supper.

Included in this section are sample devotions based upon both Old and New Testament texts, formatted both with and without prayers. The brevity of these devotions should make it easy to adapt them to various sizes of bulletins and other spacing requirements. It is hoped that the accompanying examples will spur others in ministry to write their own Supper devotions, contextualized to their local kingdom settings and in response to specific pastoral needs within the congregation.

For those who are interested in a larger collection of these devotions, or who are looking for a devotional communicant's manual for their churches, there is also available a volume containing 104 examples covering many of the books of the Old and the New Testaments. The book is entitled, *Gospel Feasting: 104 Lord's Supper Devotions from the Old and New Testaments*, and was written as a companion to *The Gospel Feast*.

**Nota Bene*: These devotions, written for use in the author's congregation, utilize the older style of capitalization of the pronouns whenever they refer to any of the persons of the Trinity.

The Tree of Life, Jesus Christ, and the Supper

And out of the ground the Lord God made to spring up every tree
that is pleasant to the sight and good for food.
The tree of life was in the midst of the garden,
and the tree of the knowledge of good and evil.
(Genesis 2:9)

Principle: God in His goodness provided for His image-bearer Adam every possible good thing, so that there was nothing he lacked in the garden of Eden. According to Genesis 2:9, this included access to eat from the tree of life, which we read in Genesis 3:22 would have enabled Adam to live forever.

Yet there was another tree in Eden. It was the tree of the knowledge of good and evil. Deceived by the serpent, both Adam and Eve disobeyed God's single requirement of them, that they not eat from this particular tree, *for in the day that you eat of it you shall surely die*. Through their disobedience Adam and Eve were separated from fellowship with God and incurred the curse promised them as a result of their sin.

We read at the end of Genesis 3 that the Lord God *drove them out of the garden of Eden to work the ground from which he was taken. He drove out the man, and at the east of the garden of Eden he placed the cherubim and a flaming sword that turned every way to guard the way to the tree of life.* This was actually a merciful act on God's part because had He not done so, man would have remained cursed and separated from God for eternity.

Instead, God in His mercy provided *another* means of access to eternal life — a means of access that not only brings life, but also brings a reversal of the curse. Through Jesus Christ, God's one and only Son, we once again have access to the tree of life, for Jesus is the way, the truth, and the life for all those who truly trust in Him. With the return of Jesus in His glory, the book of Revelation, in chapter 22 promises a restored paradise for redeemed believers in which a river is described flowing from the *throne of God and of the Lamb*. On either side of this river, the Apostle John is shown *the tree of life with its twelve kinds of fruit, yielding its fruit each month.*

As we eat the Lord's Supper together, we are reminded it is only through our Spirit-birthed faith intimacy with Jesus that we may taste eternal life. Jesus is both our *access* to, and in His fullness and blessings, the *essence* of the tree of life. And every covenantal blessing provided to Adam in his original state prior to the Fall is now restored to our inheritance through our redemption in Christ.

Prayer: Gracious and loving heavenly Father, Creator and Sustainer of all things, we thank you that although our first parents Adam and Eve, and we ourselves, sinned against you and were cut off from the tree of life, You restored our access to everlasting life through Jesus, Your Son. We thank you that as Jesus Christ hung on that awful tree He became really and true the new tree of life for all who believe in His name.

As we receive the Lord's Supper, may Your Spirit give us a foretaste of the everlasting life we will one day enjoy in fullness. May the sweetness of born-again life be tasted by faith as we share together in the bread and in the cup. In Jesus' name. Amen.

God's Presence and the Supper

And they (Adam and Eve) heard the sound of the Lord God walking in the garden in the cool of the day, and the man and his wife hid themselves from the presence of the Lord God among the trees of the garden. But the Lord God called to the man and said to him, "Where are you?"
(Genesis 3:8 – 9)

Principle: Prior to Adam and Eve's disobedience in eating the fruit from the Tree of the Knowledge of Good and Evil, the image-bearers of God enjoyed complete communion with their Creator and experienced His presence in the Garden of Eden. Their sin in violating the single prohibition God gave them to keep brought them both shame and fear. Instead of the wonderful fellowship with the Lord they had previously enjoyed, now they perceived that their communion with God was broken by their willful sin. And yet, the Lord God, fully knowing already what they had done, nevertheless sought them out. In the verses that follow, God deals with the Fall of mankind through Adam by declaring not only the curse, but also His plan to redeem His creation — to *reverse the curse*.

Jesus Christ later came in fulfillment of God's promise as the second Adam. And where the first Adam failed and brought upon all of the creation the great curse, the second Adam obeyed His Father perfectly, died upon the cross, and now is in the process of utterly reversing the curse. As a result of Christ's work, believers in Him are once again granted the astounding privilege of communion with God! This privilege is most evidently displayed and intensified for us as we come together and celebrate the Lord's Supper.

Far from being an empty, symbolic ritual, Communion is celebrated in union with Christ and with our redeemed brothers and sisters according to the faith. This Sacrament reminds us of what Christ did to save us. And yet it also encourages us by the Holy Spirit that Jesus also made us children of God and co-heirs with Him in all the riches of the heavenly places. As a child of the living God, we are invited to dine with the Lord each time that we partake of the bread and cup while gathered for Sabbath worship.

After their fall into sin, when Adam and Eve heard the sound of the Lord walking in the garden and God's voice seeking them out, they hid themselves in fear and in shame. But thanks be to God in Christ that we who believe in Jesus' name no longer have to hide in fear and shame from the Lord. In fact, instead of running away from His presence, we now eagerly seek Him through prayer, through the faithful preaching of His Word, and through the celebration of the Sacraments of baptism and the Lord's Supper, all means of God's glorious and generous grace!

Prayer: O great Lord God, how amazing it is to me that You, from the very beginning of the creation, have desired intimate fellowship with the men, women, and children you have made in Your image. Father, I am even more astounded and thankful that even though the first Adam sinned against You and brought separation between all mankind and Yourself, You continued to call out to him, saying, "Where are you?"

Through the covenant of redemption and the finished work of Jesus Christ Your Son, You also reached out and sought after me. Through the gift of faith You restored communion with me, cleansing my willful sins and my inherited sin, by the blood of Jesus. Gracious and merciful Father, prepare me now to celebrate this restored communion with You around the table with my adopted brothers and sisters in Christ. Remind me and refresh me through the powerful working of Your Spirit, using these simple elements of bread and the cup. May I always be thankful for the love You poured out for me through the blood of Jesus, represented in the Lord's Supper. Amen.

The Covenant and the Supper

Now the Lord said to Abram, "Go from your country and your kindred and your father's house to the land that I will show you. And I will make of you a great nation, and I will bless you and make your name great, so that you will be a blessing. I will bless those who bless you, and him who dishonors you I will curse, and in you all the families of the earth shall be blessed."
(Genesis 12:1 – 3)

Principle: The God of the universe is also the God of the covenant. The Lord enters into relationship with His people by means of covenants, just as we read in God's dealings with Abram (Abraham). Yahweh, the living God, always initiates the covenants He makes. In Abraham's case, the Lord requires him to leave behind all that he has ever known in exchange for a promised land that he knows nothing about. As part of God's covenant, He makes certain promises of blessing to those who are faithful to Him. The promises of God to Abraham included; making of him a great nation, a divine blessing, a great name, a curse on his enemies, and a blessing for all the families of the earth through him.

When God chose to formalize His relationship with Abraham through a covenant ceremony (see Genesis 15:5–6), we read that, he *believed the Lord, and he counted it to him as righteousness*. Abraham's relationship with Yahweh was not based upon anything Abraham had done, or anything special about his person. His covenant bond with God was based upon God's choosing and through the living faith Abraham exercised toward his God.

The promises God made to Abraham, which he trusted in through the gift of faith, were ultimately fulfilled in the person and work of Jesus Christ. As Jesus fulfilled the Abrahamic Covenant, He also fulfilled what we understand to be the Covenant of Redemption, which God the Father and God the Son entered into before the Fall and even before the world was made. In fulfilling all of the covenantal promises of Yahweh, Jesus indeed blessed *all of the families of the earth* through the gift of salvation to all who truly believe in Him.

When Jesus told the disciples on the night He was betrayed that the cup of blessing *that is poured out for you is the new covenant in my blood* (Luke 22:20), He was announcing to them that the Covenant of Redemption and the Abrahamic Covenant were about to be fulfilled through His shed blood upon the cross. The command of Jesus to the Apostle Paul, *Do this, as often as you drink it, in remembrance of me* (1 Corinthians 11:25), teaches us that as followers of Christ, we are to gather as the covenant people of God to remember, and to celebrate the realization of the covenant promises through Jesus Christ.

Prayer: Thank you heavenly Father, that You desire to have fellowship with me and all those You call Your people by means of covenants. Praise and honor and glory and blessing to You and to Your Son for together providing for my redemption from sin before the world existed! Lord Jesus Christ, thank You for your atoning sacrifice, whose blood sealed my salvation and brings me the precious and priceless blessings of the covenant! Thank You Holy Spirit, for enabling me to see with the eyes of faith, as did my father Abraham, the reality and certainty of God's promises! And thank You, wonderful Spirit, for applying to me the benefits and blessings which flow from Jesus Christ! Help me now to see with the eyes of faith, the fulfillment of the covenants and promises of God through Christ, in the visible symbols set before me in the Lord's Supper.

Empower me to rejoice in Your never ending faithfulness to me and to everyone You have washed in the cleasing blood of Jesus. I give You thanks and praise that although I was a wild branch, You took Me unto Yourself and grafted me into the fruitful tree of Christ. How marvelous it is that You have placed me among Your holy people. In Jesus' name I pray. Amen.

Melchizedek and the Supper

After his return from the defeat of Chedorlaomer and the kings who were with him,
the king of Sodom went out to meet him at the Valley of Shaveh (that is, the King's
Valley). And Melchizedek king of Salem brought out bread and wine.
(He was priest of God Most High.) And he blessed him and said,
"Blessed be Abram by God Most High,
Possessor of heaven and earth;
and blessed be God Most High,
who has delivered your enemies into your hand!"
And Abram gave him a tenth of everything.
(Genesis 14:17 – 20)

Principle: Many of the greatest theologians throughout history have attempted to identify all of the *types* or *shadows* of Jesus Christ located within the Old Testament Scriptures. Clearly, God chose in various ways to prepare His people for the coming of His Son through the incarnation. He did this by means of persons and ceremonies that would depict Jesus' future offices and work.

In the case of Melchizedek, this mysterious kingly and priestly figure, there is no doubt that a type or shadow is intended for Christ. Some argue that Melchizedek is in fact an Old Testament *Christophany*, a pre-incarnate appearance of Christ Himself! We know that God intends us to learn from Melchizedek something about Christ because it is clearly revealed for us in the Epistle to the Hebrews, chapter 7: *For this Melchizedek, king of Salem, priest of the Most High God, met Abraham returning from the slaughter of the kings and blessed him, and to him Abraham apportioned a tenth of everything. He is first, by translation of his name, king of righteousness, and then he is also king of Salem, that is, king of peace. He is without father or mother or genealogy, having neither beginning of days nor end of life, but resembling the Son of God he continues a priest forever.*

It is then to this king of righteousness and peace — to this priest of God Most High — that Abram, the man of faith, comes and receives both bread and wine, and particularly divine blessing. One cannot help but see this important event in Abram's life as a time of worship of and communion with God, through the priestly ministry of Melchizedek.

And so it is when we come seeking to worship the Most High God, that we do so through the ministry of Jesus Christ, King of righteousness and peace, the great High Priest, who always lives to intercede for us. Communion with God Most High is mediated to us by the Spirit of God through the work of Christ and represented to us by bread and wine. Through our faithful participation in worship and communion at the Lord's Table, we receive divine blessing and grace.

Prayer: Heavenly Father, God of Abraham, Isaac, and Jacob, and my God, thank you for providing a great High Priest in your service, to make propitiation for my sins. I am completely unworthy and undeserving of Your grace and mercy shown to me through Jesus Christ, Your Son, who comes not in the likeness of Aaron and the Mosaic priesthood, but in the likeness of Melchizedek, king of righteousness and peace, Your perfect priest. Thank You that Jesus my Savior is the guarantor of a better covenant who saves me to the uttermost! Thank You for the bread and the wine which provide spiritual grace and divine blessing, pointing us to our great High Priest and bringing to our hearts and minds the benefits of His pierced body and shed blood. Indeed, blessed are You, God Most High, who through Christ, have delivered us from our enemies, sin, death, hell, and Satan. Amen.

The Promise and the Fulfillment of a Son and the Supper

And God said to Abraham, "As for Sarai your wife, you shall not call her name Sarai, but Sarah shall be her name. I will bless her, and moreover, I will give you a son by her. I will bless her, and she shall become nations; kings of peoples shall come from her."
(Genesis 17:15 – 16)

Principle: The Lord is a covenant-keeping God. That means that when He makes a promise to provide for His people, He will ever and always deliver on that promise. An early example of God's faithfulness in Scripture is the promise He made to Abraham to provide for him a true son and heir. Abraham had every reason to doubt God's promise based upon the outward appearance of things. He was quite old and his wife Sarah was well beyond the age for bearing children. They had been married for decades and there had never been a child. Perhaps we can understand somewhat how Abraham and Sarah took matters into their own hands and used Hagar to conceive a child.

But God was faithful to fulfill His promise to give Abraham and Sarah a son. The Lord's promise was fulfilled with the birth of Isaac, precisely as the Lord had declared. This faithful consistency — this lovingkindness to provide for His people — is displayed even more beautifully in the promise God made to provide a son, the Son — His Son — to redeem the world. In the prophecy of Isaiah 7:14 we read: *Therefore the Lord himself will give you a sign. Behold the virgin shall conceive and bear a son, and shall call his name Immanuel.*

This promise was fulfilled for God's people when in the course of time and according to the Lord's predetermined plan, the Lord Jesus Christ was born to a young virgin named Mary in Bethlehem some 2,000 years ago. Jesus was the greatest Son of the promise, because in Him, every promise to the adopted children of God was confirmed and sealed. And we celebrate that even the name given to him by the prophet some 600 to 700 years before His birth was fulfilled. For this promised Son who came and dwelt among us was indeed really and truly *God with us*!

And so as we gather around the Lord's Table we celebrate that the Lord's promise to His people — to us who believe by faith — was fulfilled in the incarnation and birth of Jesus Christ. And through His life, death, resurrection, and ascension we continue to enjoy His presence. For by the work of God's Holy Spirit, the Son remains Immanuel, the God who is with us. May the Spirit of Christ remind us at the Supper today that Jesus is ever with us, *even unto the end of the age*.

Prayer: Heavenly Father, we thank You that you fulfilled Your promise to Abraham and Sarah, giving them the son of promise, Isaac. We thank You that Isaac was part of Your redemptive plan through the descendants of Abraham to one day bring Your own Son of promise Jesus Christ into this world. Isaac was truly a symbol of Your greater promised Son, through Whom all the nations would be blessed – even as You promised to Your servant Abraham. We thank You that the Lord Jesus came at the proper time and identified with us, that He lived a sinless life, and that He suffered and He died in our place, bearing our sins away upon the cross on Calvary. We praise You and thank You for Your faithfulness and for keeping Your covenant promise of redemption. We also praise Jesus Your Son for taking the form of a servant and enduring so very, very much in order to save us from our sins and our sins' consequences. In Jesus' name we pray. Amen.

The Beloved Son's Offering, the Substitute, and the Supper

After these things God tested Abraham and said to him, "Abraham!" And he said, "Here am I." He said, "Take your son, your only son Isaac, whom you love, and go to the land of Moriah, and offer him there as a burnt offering on one of the mountains of which I shall tell you."
(Genesis 22:1 – 2)

Principle: Abraham's obedient willingness to offer his cherished son as a sacrifice to Yahweh is one of the most important events in God's unfolding redemptive plan. While some Bible teachers choose to emphasize Abraham's faith and obedience revealed in the details of the story, others point out the event's parallels with God the Father's willingness to offer His one and only Son to be our substitute, to make atonement for our sins. In fact, the Hebrew used in verse 2, rendered *your only son..., whom you love*, echoes the language used to describe God's own Son.

And yet, while these are crucial elements in understanding this important historical event, perhaps the most significant is the truth that just before the death of Isaac could take place, the Lord God provided a substitute for the sacrifice — *a ram, caught in a thicket by his horns* (Genesis 22:13). What a test this whole turn of events was for His servant, Abraham! After all, this was the patriarch's son, his *only son, whom he loved*, a description later used to describe God's relationship with His only Son, Jesus. What a joyous relief it must have been for this devoted father to see Isaac, the son of God's promise, spared from death by his own father's hands.

Ultimately, because of sin, all of us deserve to be put into the position that Abraham was asked to place Isaac into, dying to pay the penalty rightly due to God. However, as with Isaac, God in His great lovingkindness and mercy, reveals Himself to us as *The Lord will provide*, and places His Son, His only Son upon the cross to die in our place. It is God's gracious and glorious exchange of Christ for us. As the Scripture declares, *All we like sheep have gone astray; we have turned — every one — to his own way; and the Lord has laid on him the iniquity of us all* (Isaiah 53:6). Redemptively speaking, Christ is foreshadowed, or represented, in both Isaac and in the substitutionary ram! This substitution God has made for us through His one and only Son is recounted every time we celebrate the Lord's Supper. When we are able to see this great eternal truth through the eyes of faith as we come to the Lord's Table, our experience of the Sacrament is so much more than a familiar ritual or repetitive religious rite.

Prayer: Faithful Lord and Provider, thank You that You have provided a substitute for me – someone to bear the stains and penalties for my awful sins – Jesus Christ, Your one and only precious Son, whom You chose to hang in my place. Thank You, Lord Jesus Christ, spotless Lamb of God, my "ram caught in a thicket," that You were willing and committed to suffer and die so that I might live!

Thank You, Father, Son, and Holy Spirit, for reminding me, each time You call me to Your Table, of these astounding and transforming truths. Show me with each Communion celebration a glimpse of the Your glory in Christ, and work within me a deeper understanding of the price Jesus paid and the separation borne while hanging upon that cross. Amen.

The Passover and the Supper I

And you shall eat it in haste. It is the Lord's Passover. For I will pass through the land of Egypt that night, and I will strike all the firstborn in the land of Egypt, both man and beast; and on all the gods of Egypt I will execute judgments. I am the Lord. The blood shall be a sign for you, on the houses where you are. And when I see the blood, I will pass over you, and no plague will befall you to destroy you, when I strike the land of Egypt. This day shall be for you a memorial day, and you shall keep it as a feast to the Lord; throughout your generations, as a statute forever, you shall keep it as a feast.
(Exodus 12:11 – 14)

Principle: The Lord instituted the feast of Passover as a perpetual reminder for the people. Year after year, the Passover visibly displayed God's covenantal faithfulness and His mighty deliverance of Israel from slavery in Egypt. Yahweh proved Himself true and trustworthy in fulfilling His great promises to the sons of Abraham, and He proved Himself to be utterly and eternally committed to His chosen people. Through the provision of the blood of the Passover lambs, God provided for the deliverance of the Hebrews, while bringing terrible judgment upon all of the firstborns among the Egyptians.

The tribes of Israel celebrated the Passover with a specific menu — items such as unleavened bread, roasted lamb, a cup of blessing. By the first century era and the years of Jesus' teaching ministry, the Passover featuring these items was a long-established visual testimony of God's faithfulness to His people. The bread, the lamb, and the wine of the cup of blessing all acted as visual and tactile symbols of the Lord as Redeemer.

It is indeed fitting that Jesus Christ, whose shed blood delivers us from certain death and judgment, instituted the Lord's Supper during His celebration of the Passover with His disciples on the night He was betrayed and turned over to death. Just as the Hebrews were commanded to keep the Passover feast in perpetual reminder and thanksgiving for their mighty deliverance from slavery in Egypt, so also we today who believe in Christ are instructed to keep the Lord's Supper feast perpetually, celebrating our deliverance from bondage to sin and death through the shed blood of our Passover Lamb, Jesus.

Prayer: Lord Jesus Christ, I thank You that You are my Passover Lamb, whose shed blood covers all of my sin and stays the hand of judgment which I rightly deserve to receive from the Father. Precious Savior, I thank You that You instituted this new Passover feast – Your Supper – in order to remind me again and again of Your faithfulness to the promises of the Covenant of Redemption and of Your great love set upon me.

Father, Son, and Holy Spirit, help me I pray to walk in a manner worthy of this great deliverance from slavery to sin and death which You have provided for me. Work within me also an abiding love and appreciation for the delights and edifications You work in me through the celebration of Communion with You. Help me to long for this worshipful meal and the fullness of its blessings to me as Your Gospel Feast. In Jesus' name, Amen.

The Passover and the Supper II

Unleavened bread shall be eaten for seven days; no leavened bread shall be seen with you in all your territory. You shall tell your son on that day, 'It is because of what the Lord did for me when I cam out of Egypt.' And it shall be to you a sign on your hand and as a memorial between your eyes, that the law of the Lord may be in your mouth. For with a strong hand the Lord has brought you out of Egypt. You shall therefore keep this statute at its appointed time from year to year.
(Exodus 13:7 – 20)

Principle: People often wonder how churches today choose the visible form of bread for use in their Lord's Supper celebrations. While practices vary from denomination to denomination, and even from congregation to congregation, many churches choose unleavened bread for observing Communion. The practice in Judaism right up to the present day and extending back to the original institution of Passover by God during the Exodus features unleavened bread. We are told in Moses' account of the first Passover that the Lord instructed unleavened bread be used not only for the Passover evening, but for the seven days associated with Passover known as the Feast of Unleavened Bread. This unleavened bread reminded the people that they departed from Egypt in great haste. Unleavened bread also came to be associated with purity, or a symbol for lack of sinfulness.

As Jesus instituted the Lord's Supper during the Passover Feast with His disciples, He told them that the unleavened bread at the Table which He had blessed and broken represented His own body, *which is given for you* (Luke 22:19). It is fitting that unleavened Passover bread was used by Christ to visibly remind His disciples of the work He was about to accomplish, in taking upon His shoulders — His body — the sins which rightly belonged to us, while hanging upon that cruel cross. Many believers also note that the unleavened bread borrowed from the Jewish Passover which many churches use for Communion, also has numerous piercings and stripes. As such, it further makes an effective visual statement reminding us of the scourging Jesus received and also of the nails that pierced His sinless hands and feet. As we celebrate the Supper, whatever form of bread is used, let us recall that the bread serves to bring to our minds and hearts the sinless body of Christ, which became sin in our place, that we might become in Him the righteousness of God.

Prayer: Heavenly Father, Lord of all and Deliverer of Your chosen people, thank You for the perfect sinlessness of Jesus Christ Your Son, whom You willingly sent to suffer and horribly die upon the cross of Calvary. Thank You for His body, represented by the bread in Communion, which bore my awful transgressions upon the tree! Thank You that the foreshadows of the Passover were perfectly and eternally fulfilled in Your one and only Son. Help me now, O God, by the working of Your Spirit, to behold and to partake of the benefits of the body of Christ as I receive the bread provided at Your Table. In Jesus' sinless name I pray, Amen.

Manna from Heaven and the Supper

Then the Lord said to Moses, "Behold, I am about to rain bread from heaven for you, and the people shall go out and gather a day's portion every day, that I may test them, whether they will walk in my law or not. Now the house of Israel called its name manna. It was like coriander seed, white, and the taste of it was like wafers made with honey. Moses said, "This is what the Lord has commanded: 'Let an omer of it be kept throughout your generations, so that they may see the bread with which I fed you in the wilderness, when I brought you out of the land of Egypt.' "
(Exodus 16:4, 31 – 32)

Principle: The visible bread used for celebrating the Lord's Supper may vary in many different ways, from one church to another just down the same street, yet the meaning symbolized by the bread remains consistent. Just as the manna from heaven symbolized God's provision for His chosen people during the time of the Exodus, so now the bread used in the Lord's Supper symbolizes for us the true heavenly bread — *the living bread that came down from heaven* (John 6:51a) — that is, Jesus Christ, the bread of life. Just as the omer of manna served to remind the people of their deliverance from bondage in Egypt and the provision for their hunger that the Lord had made, so now the bread of Communion serves to regularly remind us of our deliverance from slavery to sin and the provision of God for our spiritual hunger, through the flesh of Jesus, the Son of Man.

The Bible also reveals that the manna rained down from heaven through God's lovingkindness not simply for one day, or six days out of seven for one week. And it did not stop after a full year's worth of weeks. In fact God provided such miraculous food for some forty years — the entire time from the forty-fifth day of the first year out of Egypt until the day when the people of God camped at the border of the Promised Land!

Now, just as God's provision of miraculous manna bread was always provided to His people as they walked the journey of faith between their freedom from slavery in Egypt to the day they entered into the land of His promise, so also the Lord gives us the true living manna of Jesus Christ, His Son, not just once at the moment of our salvation, but always — daily, constantly, as we also walk along our wilderness way of faith from salvation to His glorious Promised Land. Jesus promised us that, *If anyone eats of this bread, he will live forever. And the bread that I will give for the life of the world is my flesh* (John 6:51b). To eat of Jesus' bread is to believe in His name and to walk by faith in Jesus, by God's Word, and through the Holy Spirit.

This is symbolized and spiritually and truly communicated to us when we receive the bread and the cup of the Lord's Supper.

Prayer: Gracious heavenly Father, thank you for the visible signs You give to me and to all of Your people, which proclaim Your faithfulness in providing for deliverance from the chains and curse of sin, remind us of the willing work of Jesus Your Son in offering His body upon the cross, and declare Your eternal provision of grace for us as we come as Your invited guests to the Supper. Thank you for raining down upon us by Your Holy Spirit the living bread we daily need, which is Jesus Christ, Your Son and our Lord. May we come often to Your bountiful Table, as those whose spirits need refreshing and whose faith-hunger needs to be satisfied through the heavenly bread of Christ.

The Covenant Meal and the Supper

And Moses took the blood and threw it on the people and said, "Behold the blood of the covenant that the Lord has made with you in accordance with all these words." Then Moses and Aaron, Nadab, and Abihu, and seventy of the elders of Israel went up, and they saw the God of Israel. There was under his feet as it were a pavement of sapphire stone, like the very heaven for clearness. And he did not lay his hand on the chief men of the people of Israel; they beheld God, and ate and drank.
(Exodus 24:8 – 11)

Principle: Through the shed blood which sealed the covenant between the Lord and the Hebrews at Mt. Sinai, the leaders and seventy elders of Israel were admitted to table fellowship with the God of Israel. They and the people had been sprinkled with the blood of the sacrifice and they had accepted the Lord's covenant. The fellowship that had been forbidden just hours before — upon pain of death — was now an amazing reality by means of the covenant sealed in sacrificial blood. The fear and dread of the people at the foot of Mt. Sinai at even the sound of God's voice was replaced with confidence to enter into immediate fellowship with the one eternal God — Yahweh, the living God of Israel. The Lord had transformed the people's very real fear of certain death into a new and living hope, based upon close fellowship with their creator and deliverer.

The Lord's Supper is also a covenant meal. We, who were formerly cut off from fellowship with God and covered with sin, are instead covered by the shed blood of Christ, sealed into the covenant, and admitted into intimate communion with the great King of glory! Through Jesus by faith we have access to the heavenly Father's family dining table. Whereas we once were under a sentence of death for sin, we now hold a certificate of adoption as the Lord's own sons and daughters! As the author of Hebrews 12:17 – 24 declares:

> *For you have not come to what may be touched, a blazing fire and darkness and gloom and a tempest and the sound of a trumpet and a voice whose words made the hearers beg that no further messages be spoken to them. For they could not endure the order that was given, "If even a beast touches the mountain, it shall be stoned." Indeed, so terrifying was the sight that Moses said, "I tremble with fear." But you have come to Mount Zion and to the city of the living God, the heavenly Jerusalem, and to innumerable angels in festal gathering, and to the assembly of the firstborn who are enrolled in heaven, and to God, the judge of all, and to the spirits of the righteous made perfect, and to Jesus, the mediator of a*

new covenant, and to the sprinkled blood that speaks a better word than the blood of Abel.

Table fellowship with God through the Spirit of Christ during the Gospel Feast is a precious privilege that we dare not ever take for granted. We are as welcome in the Father's presence, through His Son, as is Jesus Himself, for when the Father looks at us, He sees the covering of the blood of Christ. This is one family meal we dare not miss or dismiss.

Prayer: God of Moses, God of Israel, God of the Covenant, and my God and Sovereign, I thank You for the shed blood of Jesus, which seals to me by faith the benefits of the Covenant of Redemption and all of your wonderful promises to Your adopted children. Thank You for inviting and admitting me and all those You love to Your heavenly dining table. To think that I can enjoy an even fuller privilege of communion with You than those who ate and drank the covenant meal at Sinai! Through Christ You invite me to dine with You, not once, or twice, or even three times – but always and forever, and represent this to me through the visible elements of the bread and wine of the Supper. Father, I know that in myself I am unworthy of appearing before Your presence and taking a seat at Your excellent table. Thank You that I am counted worthy, though, entirely worthy, through the perfect one-time sacrifice of Jesus, Your Son. In whose name I pray, Amen.

Jesus, Our Atonement and the Supper

Then he shall kill the goat of the sin offering that is for the people and bring its blood inside the veil and do with its blood as he did with the blood of the bull, sprinkling it over the mercy seat and in front of the mercy seat. Thus he shall make atonement for the Holy Place, because of the uncleanness of the people of Israel and because of their transgressions, all their sins… . No one may be in the tent of meeting from the time he enters to make atonement in the Holy Place until he comes out and has made atonement for himself and for his house and for all the assembly of Israel.
(Leviticus 16:15, 17)

Principle: The Day of Atonement was arguably the single most important day on the Jewish calendar. If anything should have gone wrong during the careful observance of all the sacrifices and rituals required, the people of Israel, rather than enjoying both cleansing and removal of sanctions for their sin, would have remained in their sins, bearing their own guilt and shame for another year. And of course, with each passing day following the Day of Atonement, their sins began to accumulate during the new year.

Through Jesus Christ, the Day of Atonement has indeed been completely fulfilled for all who believe in Him alone for salvation. Through Jesus, our uncleanness has been purged away. Through Jesus, our justly deserved penalties and sanctions from God have been borne away — carried upon His shoulders. And this one-time atonement of Christ was eternally sufficient, as the author of Hebrews makes plain, *Nor was it to offer himself repeatedly, as the high priest enters the holy places every year with blood not his own, for then he would have had to suffer repeatedly since the foundation of the world. But as it is, he has appeared once for all at the end of the ages to put away sin by the sacrifice of himself* (Hebrews 9:25 – 26).

Atonement is an interesting word. It turns out this word did not exist in the English language, let alone the concept it describes. In order to create this word and to describe this annual Jewish service, the three words "at," "one," and "ment" were brought together. This term then describes this important Jewish festival and the greater work of Jesus on our behalf. Indeed through the Son's atoning death we who believe in Him are made to be *at one* with God our Lord. The separation of sin is removed and we enjoy renewed fellowship with Yahweh. This is wonderfully depicted for us and made vividly tangible to our senses during the celebration of the Lord's Supper.

Prayer: Heavenly Father, I thank You that the sacrifices and rituals of the Day of Atonement and of the other rites of the Mosaic Covenant were really shadows and signs, pointing the way to Jesus Christ, the one-time perfect sin offering for me and for all those who believe. Thank You that Jesus is our Passover and our Atonement and that His blood is the blood sprinkled upon the heavenly mercy seat. Thank You that Jesus' blood grants me and all believers access into the true Holy Place, for which the Tabernacle and the Temple of Israel were merely patterns and visible representations.

Thank You, Lord Jesus Christ, that You have atoned for all of my sins once and for all when You suffered and died upon the cross at Calvary. And thank You that as I join my brothers and sisters around Your table for the Supper, together we remember and we celebrate Your completed offering until Your glorious return.

Jesus, Our Scapegoat and the Supper

And when he has made an end of atoning for the Holy Place and the tent of meeting and the altar, he shall present the live goat. And Aaron shall lay both his hands on the head of the live goat, and confess over it all the iniquities of the people of Israel, and all their transgressions, all their sins. And he shall put them on the head of the goat and send it away into the wilderness by the hand of a man who is in readiness. The goat shall bear all their iniquities on itself to a remote area, and he shall let the goat go free in the wilderness.
(Leviticus 16:20 – 22)

Principle: As part of the ceremony for the Day of Atonement, God instructed Moses to have Aaron *take from the congregation of the people of Israel two male goats for a sin offering, and one ram for a burnt offering.* The interesting aspect of God's directions concerning these two goats is that only one of them was to be sacrificed to Yahweh. The Lord told Moses that Aaron *shall take the two goats and set them before the Lord at the entrance of the tent of meeting. And Aaron shall cast lots over the two goats, one lot for the Lord and the other lot for Azazel.*

The goat upon which the lot fell for the Lord was to be sacrificed as a sin offering, much as other animals were offered as part of the Hebrew worship of Yahweh. However, the other goat, upon which the lot fell for Azazel, was to be kept alive and later that day set free in the wilderness. Before the goat was released by a man specially prepared for the task, the High Priest laid both his hands upon the head of the goat and confessed all of the sins of the people of Israel over it. In this way, the goat was a true scapegoat, bearing all the iniquities, transgressions, and sins of God's people and removing them from the boundaries of the camp.

In the fullest sense, Jesus Christ the Son of God is the great Scapegoat, in the sense that He bore all of the sins of those who believe in Him during the hours of His agony and death upon the cross. It is as though we laid our hands upon Him and confessed our sins, and as though He bore our sins away into the remotest of places. Yet Jesus is also the other goat — the goat of the sin offering — who died in our place. The symbolic and typological pictures portrayed for us in the two goats on the Day of Atonement are brought together in the one Person and work of Jesus Christ.

It is to this Lord Jesus that we come, as we seek Him at the Table. We come to the Suffering Servant, the Son of Man, who both bore the uncleanness of our sins and paid the penalty for our sins simultaneously upon the cross. Just as we see the rites and the reminders of Passover fulfilled in Christ, may we also see the many aspects of the Day of Atonement rituals and sacrifices once for all time achieved in Jesus' obedient and loving work for you and for me. And may we see as we are gathered around the glorious Table, first and foremost the completed and accepted atonement accomplished for us in the Son.

Prayer: Holy and loving heavenly Father, I know that You are perfectly holy and cannot tolerate sinfulness among Your people. Thank You that You provided for the truly faithful in Israel so long ago a means for the removal of sin's stain and a means to pay the ransom or penalty due to You for their sins. Now today, Father, I kneel before You as one, who like the people of old, have been marked out as You chosen seed and yet continue to fall into sin. I again today plead the atoning blood of Jesus Your Son for cleansing me from sin, and I also glorify Christ for bearing my sins away, just as the scapegoat bore them away for Your people so long ago. And yet I know Father that Jesus accomplished this once and for all and that the full Day of Atonement occurred one time when Your Son died upon that cross.

Loving Father, Son, and Holy Spirit, I thank You that Your love for me perfectly met the demands of Your holiness in dealing with my sin through Jesus. Great indeed are You and greatly to be praised! Help me as I come into Your presence in Communion with other men, women, and children for whom You have atoned. Open my eyes that I may thankfully see Your resolution of my uncleanness and my condemnation through the body and blood of Jesus Christ, which is represented for me in these simple elements of bread and wine. I give You all the glory, and honor, and praise for taking my sins away that terrible, yet glorious day outside the walls of Jerusalem on Mount Calvary! In Jesus, my atonement's name I pray, Amen.

Refuge in Christ and the Lord's Supper

Now therefore, O kings, be wise; be warned, O rulers of the earth. Serve the Lord with fear, and rejoice with trembling. Kiss the Son, lest he be angry, and you perish in the way, for his wrath is quickly kindled. Blessed are all who take refuge in him. (Psalm 2:10 – 13)

Principle: When we read Psalm 2, it is natural for us to apply its revealed truths to those who are divinely called to positions of authority over our city, our state, or our nation. Indeed, the psalmist does address kings and rulers in verses 1, 2, and 10. However, we must also take note that the psalm's instruction applies equally to each and every human being. Psalm 2 begins with a direct address to groups of persons — *nations*, and *peoples*. Admittedly, the inspired aim of the psalmist is to confront political nation-states and their ungodly rulers. Yet there is ever present in the text a consideration of each person from which these political organizations are composed. The very last line of Psalm 2 is very revealing in this regard, as it states: *Blessed are all who take refuge in him.*

Psalm 2 addresses that sinful inclination in every one of us, whether king or pauper — whether president or powerless, to rebel against the authority and ultimate rule of the King of kings and Lord of lords, Jesus Christ, the Son of the living God. The antidote, the psalm plainly declares, to our rebellious condition is to come before Jesus the Son, submit ourselves to His divine authority, and find in Him our one and only eternal refuge. In order for us to ever have the desire to turn from rebellion to obedience, the Holy Spirit of God must transform our rebellious hearts into hearts truly prepared to yield to the King of all. This is the free gift of God according to His electing love. The Father and the Son pour out the Holy Spirit upon all whose names are written in the Lamb's book of life. As the Spirit indwells the children of God, we are able to *kiss the Son.*

It is helpful for us to see in the Lord's Supper a living, Spirit-birthed symbol of the refuge we have found in Jesus. We gather around the King's Table, not as a rebellious *people plotting in vain,* but rather as God's own redeemed covenant people — *the people of his pasture and the sheep of his hand* — as Psalm 95 declares. We enter into the presence of our King and Savior *rejoicing with trembling.* And through the gift of faith and the Holy Spirit, we indeed have kissed the royal Son.

Prayer: Our gracious and loving heavenly Father, please help us now to truly find our refuge in You. And as we seek by faith to make You the fortress, shield, and shelter of our lives, may we also bring blessing and conviction to the civil affairs of which we are a part in this city, state, and nation. Like Joseph in Egypt, Daniel in Babylon, and Paul in Rome, may we testy of Your strength – Your power to deliver, and may we ever and always point others to Your Son, the Lord Jesus Christ, Your anointed servant and Savior. As we come to the Supper may we show our covenantal devotion and loyalty to King Jesus, Your kingly heir. And may we do so as citizens of Your kingdom, seeking to build that kingdom while subjecting the kingdoms and political systems of this world unto King Jesus. And it is in Jesus' name we pray. Amen.

Jesus the Good Shepherd and the Supper

You prepare a table before me in the presence of my enemies; you anoint my head with oil; my cup overflows. Surely goodness and mercy shall follow me all the days of my life, and I shall dwell in the house of the Lord forever.
(Psalm 23:5 – 6)

Principle: Within the most recognized among all of King David's psalms, the fourth and fifth verses of Psalm 23, we have recorded these marvelous words of confidence and hope in the abundant and faithful provision of the Lord for His covenant children. David declares that God's sustaining grace and blessings are generously bestowed upon His beloved sheep, even as we find ourselves under the spiteful gaze of our most fearful and ravenous enemies. Beyond the Lord's incredible sustaining goodness, as believers we enjoy the particular privilege of God's anointing to kingly authority as vice-regents upon the earth. The inspired psalmist adds that God's covenant faithfulness remains with us throughout the heights and the depths, for the totality of the days of our lives. Beyond all of these priceless gifts, David declares from the confident faith of his heart the certain hope we also share of eternal life in the everlasting presence of God our Lord.

As we consider Jesus' institution of the Lord's Supper on the eve of His sacrificial death, we recall that all of the blessings and comforts King David mentions in Psalm 23 derive from Christ's work on our behalf. He perfectly kept the covenant requirements that we couldn't keep and He sealed the covenant of grace and redemption in His own blood. Of course, the Lord Jesus also identified Himself as the Good Shepherd, even as he said in John 10:14, *I am the good shepherd. I know my own and my own know me*. Thanks to God's gift of saving faith, we now recognize Christ as our Good Shepherd. As Jesus describes it, *The sheep hear his voice, and he calls his own sheep by name and leads them out* (John 10:3b). This is the beautiful relationship we now enjoy because Jesus gave His life for His sheep.

When we gather together around the Table that Jesus has prepared, let us come as those whose table fellowship declares the Gospel to a watching and often hostile world. And let us also come as adopted sons and daughters of God who have been anointed as God's vice-regents by the power of the Holy Spirit, who are renewed and refreshed by His overflowing cup of blessing, that are daily sustained by His abiding presence, and that ever live and walk expectantly together as those *who will always be with the Lord* (1 Thessalonians 4:17).

Prayer: Our gracious and loving heavenly Father, please help us now to truly find our refuge in You. And as we seek by faith to make You the fortress, shield, and shelter of our lives, may we also bring blessing and conviction to the civil affairs of which we are a part in this city, state, and nation. Like Joseph in Egypt, Daniel in Babylon, and Paul in Rome, may we testy of Your strength – Your power to deliver, and may we ever and always point others to Your Son, the Lord Jesus Christ, Your anointed servant and Savior. As we come to the Supper may we show our covenantal devotion and loyalty to King Jesus, Your kingly heir. And may we do so as citizens of Your kingdom, seeking to build that kingdom while subjecting the kingdoms and political systems of this world unto King Jesus. And it is in Jesus' name we pray. Amen.

Taste and See the Lord's Goodness in the Supper!

Oh, taste and see that the Lord is good! Blessed is the man who takes refuge in him! Oh, fear the Lord, you his saints, for those who fear him have no lack! The young lions suffer want and hunger; but those who seek the Lord lack no good thing.
(Psalm 34:8 – 10)

Principle: Psalm 34 is an exuberant declaration of God's goodness and His delight in delivering those who cry out to Him. Verses 8 through 10 in this marvelous psalm exhort us to draw near to the Lord and experience His impregnable protection and abundant provision. The psalmist likens Yahweh's faithfulness and care for His saints to the most lavish and satisfying of food. This metaphor is heightened in the contrast between verse 9, in which the saints of God who fear him *have no lack*, and the young lions of verse 10, who *suffer want and hunger*. The point is underlined yet again at the end of the same verse as King David declares, *those who seek the Lord lack no good thing.*

How desperately we need to hear this declaration of God's goodness in providing and protecting His redeemed children. On the one hand, we are so prone to depend upon our own abilities and resources to provide for and safeguard ourselves and our families. And the other hand, we often envy the vitality and resources of the young and the wealthy. Yet the psalmist reminds us that it is only when we seek and we take refuge in the Lord that our deepest needs and spiritual hunger will be satisfied once and for all.

Scripture repeatedly testifies that it is the true food by which we are to live, and that the Word made flesh, Jesus Christ, is the living bread that came down from heaven. Ultimately Jesus is the bread of life for which we desperately hunger. We can only be satisfied in Him. This is precisely why the Lord's Supper so effectively reminds us of Christ. As we eat the bread and drink from the cup, our dependence upon the Savior for His eternal, spiritual food is brought to mind just as surely as our body's need of food and drink.

Jesus invited His disciples to take and eat the bread, and to drink from the cup in remembrance of Him. He calls us to do the very same today as His 21st century disciples. And each time, in doing as He has instructed, we remember, we proclaim, and through His amazing grace, we continually *taste and see that the Lord is good!*

Prayer: Heavenly Father, by Your Spirit please work in me this day, as I draw near to the table of Your kingdom feast. Remind me that I do not live by bread alone, but by every Word that proceeds from You. Likewise, that in Jesus I live and move and have my very being. May I this day indeed taste anew Your goodness, grace, and mercy given to me on account of Jesus! And it is in His good name that I pray. Amen.

God Is With Us

Therefore, the Lord himself will give you a sign. Behold, the virgin will conceive and bear a son, and you shall call his name Immanuel.
(Isaiah 7:14)

Principle: More than seven hundred years prior to the birth of the Lord Jesus Christ, His coming as the Messiah of God was prophesied by Isaiah. The circumstances of this birth were to be divinely miraculous. The very Son of God, the radiance of His glory and the exact imprint of His nature, would one day come to dwell among His people in human flesh. That would have been astounding enough. Yet Jesus' incarnation was a miracle of prophetic fulfillment — the prophecy that a virgin would conceive and bear Him.

This is precisely how God brought about the sending of Jesus His Son into the world in which we live. When the angel Gabriel appears to a young woman, named Mary, she asks the heavenly messenger, *How can this be, since I am a virgin?* The angel replied, *The Holy Spirit will come upon you, and the power of the Most High will overshadow you; therefore the child to be born will be called holy — the Son of God* (Luke 1:26 – 38).

When we focus upon these miraculous events during the Christmas season, or at any time of the year, we are reminded that the Lord Jesus Christ was sent into the world by means of the working of His Holy Spirit, in and through the human vessel of Mary. While we do not give unusual place to Mary as Catholics do, we nevertheless accord her the same honor as does the angel Gabriel, when he refers to her as *favored one*.

The particular and providential means that God chose to bring about Jesus' birth serve to identify Him with us — the created human beings He came to save. He is like us in every respect, yet without sin. And of course, He is set apart in the sense of His eternal divinity. Yet, Jesus the Son of God is also the Son of Man. He is, as Isaiah names Him, "Immanuel," the God Who is with us.

Christ's identification with us — His willingness to take the form of a servant and to deliver us from sin, death, and hell — is the key to His substitutionary, atoning work as our Passover Lamb. This is underlined for us multiple times in the words of institution and the shared elements of the bread and the cup when we celebrate Communion. Partaking with other believers in the Lord's Supper reminds us that we profess faith in the God who sent His one and only Son to be our Immanuel, that through Jesus and by His Spirit — God indeed was, and remains, with His saved people. And so as we remember and rejoice in Christ through the Supper, we remember that ever and always He is with us.

The Lord's Supper as Kingdom Celebration

For to us a child is born, to us a son is given; and the government shall be upon his shoulder, and his name shall be called Wonderful Counselor, Mighty God, Everlasting Father, Prince of Peace. Of the increase of his government and of peace there will be no end, on the throne of David and over his kingdom,
to establish it and to uphold it with justice
and with righteousness from this time forth and forevermore.
The zeal of the LORD of hosts will do this.
(Isaiah 9:6 – 7)

Principle: So often during the Christmas celebrations we recite this truly wonderful promise from the inspired hand of Isaiah. Its sublime yet lofty titles for the promised Son captivate our attention and give rise to a certain quiet reverence and awe. Indeed in these royal and divine titles we see the very image of Christ, who is fully the Wonderful Counselor, Mighty God, Everlasting Father, and Prince of Peace.

And yet this glorious passage begins with another highly significant truth about God's own Son. Expressed in the phrase, *and the government shall be upon his shoulder*, is the declaration that this Suffering Servant Son of God, is also the King of all. Now in order for someone to hold the title of king, he must in fact have a kingdom to rule. This is even much more so the case when someone bears the title King of kings and Lord of lords!

And what of this Christ kingdom? The prophet reveals to us, *of the increase of his government and of peace there will be no end... from this time forth and forevermore*. The emphatic declaration here is one of a kingdom that begins with the birth of this miraculous Son and then expands continually into eternity! Isaiah doesn't declare a kingdom that starts and stops, not even one that advances and retreats, but rather a kingdom that continuously increases forevermore. King Jesus' authority and the kingdom over which He reigns is ever-growing, ever-advancing, and ever-increasing. And this is so according to Scripture even during those times when our eyes look about us and we doubt and we worry over its present state.

And so as we come to the Table of the Lord with these truths in mind, let us come with joyful hearts — joyful not only for the birth of Christ, but also for the kingly reign of Christ and for His glorious kingdom upon this earth. After all, we gather around the Table of the King of kings, and we do so as His redeemed and adopted vice-regents, designated to sit with Him upon His throne, and appointed to reign with Him in light!

Prayer: Dear God and Father, we acknowledge with grateful hearts that Your Son Jesus is truly God, one with You. You have made it so clear through Isaiah in the revelation of some of Jesus' titles – *Wonderful Counselor, Mighty God, Everlasting Father, Prince of Peace*. We give glory and honor to You and to the Son, who is declared by You to be King – the King – ruling over a kingdom which is ever-increasing and certain to prevail. Your Word tells us that not even the gates of hell can prevail against it. What amazing reassurance this gives us. And what a privilege You have given us that we are invited to dine at Your kingly table. May we never take your invitation or this wonderful blessing for granted. May we in fact long more and more as time passes by to join in table fellowship with King Jesus and with our fellow redeemed citizens of Your prevailing kingdom. In Jesus' name. Amen.

He Is Risen, He Is Risen Indeed!

Now after the Sabbath, toward the dawn of the first day of the week, Mary Magdalene and the other Mary went to see the tomb. And behold, there was a great earthquake, for an angel of the Lord descended from heaven and came and rolled back the stone and sat on it. His appearance was like lightning, and his clothing white as snow. And for fear of him the guards trembled and became like dead men. But the angel said to the women, "Do not be afraid, for I know that you seek Jesus who was crucified. He is not here, for he has risen, as he said. Come, see the place where he lay. Then go quickly and tell his disciples that he has risen from the dead, and behold, he is going before you to Galilee; there you will see him. See, I have told you." So they departed quickly from the tomb with fear and great joy, and ran to tell his disciples. And behold, Jesus met them and said, "Greetings!" And they came up and took hold of his feet and worshiped him. Then Jesus said to them, "Do not be afraid; go and tell my brothers to go to Galilee, and there they will see me."
(Matthew 28:1 – 10)

Principle: Every day we celebrate the glorious resurrection of the Lord Jesus Christ! Our joy in Christ's victory is not limited to one Sabbath per year. The event described here in Matthew 28, and in the other Gospels, is the defining event of all of redemptive history, for early on that first day of the week just outside the walls of Jerusalem, sin, death, hell, and the devil were defeated by the victory of Jesus! The Lord's one-time substitutionary sacrifice was accepted by God the Father and proved in His Son's rising from the dead.

As we celebrate this amazing event, we glory not only in the fact that Jesus conquered sin and death, but also in the fact that we are united together with Him by the Holy Spirit in faith. We also are more than conquerors through Him who loved us so very much! In Christ, we walk in newness of life and one day will also live eternally in resurrection glory just as the Lord Jesus does at this very moment.

In our coming to the Lord's Supper, let us ask the Lord's Spirit to remind us of the blessed hope we profess in Jesus. Our blessed hope is that just as He rose from the dead and now lives forevermore in a glorified state — so one day we will also, as those found in Him by faith. The token of this promise that Jesus has given us is this fellowship meal called the Lord's Supper, or Communion. Symbolized in our present and real spiritual fellowship with the Lord Jesus is our ultimate, one day coming, future fuller fellowship with Him and all the glorified saints in life at the celebration of the great marriage supper of the Lamb!

Let us glory in the completed work of the Lord Jesus Christ in offering Himself once for all, for everyone who trusts in Him by faith. Let us raise our voices in praise and thanksgiving. And let us revel in the revelation of His resurrection and in His present fellowship with us by His Spirit. Let us also rejoice in our future expectation of His eternal immediate presence with us, represented in the Sacrament of the Lord's Supper.

Christ Is Risen! Christ Is Risen Indeed!

Kingdom Commission

And Jesus came and said to them, "All authority in heaven and on earth has been given to me. Go therefore and make disciples of all nations, baptizing them in the name of the Father and of the Son and of the Holy Spirit, teaching them to observe all that I have commanded you. And behold, I am with you always, to the end of the age."

(Matthew 28:18 – 20)

Principle: There are several interesting connections between the Great Commission, which the Lord Jesus Christ gave to us as His Church, and His institution of the Supper. Ever since the earliest days of the church, the distinguishing mark of someone who had been made a disciple of Jesus was his admission to the Lord's Table. In the ancient church, those who had not professed Christ and been baptized and received into visible membership were actually sent away during the worship service at the time just prior to the congregational celebration of Communion. Indeed, one of the most anticipated events in the life of a new believer in those days was his or her first opportunity to receive the Sacrament. As each new disciple was made, in fulfillment of Christ's Great Commission, the occasion was marked by the Lord's Supper.

Communion also operates, as a means of God's grace, in building up believers in their faith and practice, thus serving as a helper in the process of discipling. The importance of this was not lost on the early churches, as they typically broke bread together on a weekly basis in commemoration of the Lord's Last Supper with His disciples. The elders of the church saw it as part of their responsibility in carrying out the Great Commission to see to it that their flocks were fully nourished on the richness of God's grace provided by the preaching of the Word, prayer, and the celebration around the Lord's Table. In doing this, the pastors and other elders were simply doing as Christ directed, *teaching them to observe all that I have commanded you.* The Lord specifically directed the disciples to eat of the bread and drink of the cup in remembrance of Him. And of course the Apostle Paul was told by the Lord Jesus that whenever the Lord's Supper was celebrated, the believers *proclaimed the Lord's death until He comes* (1 Corinthians 11:26).

Finally, the Lord's Supper also communicates to us the reality of the kingdom age in which we now live as believers in Christ. For, just as the Lord Jesus promised the disciples in Matthew 28:20, *I am with you always, to the end of the age*, so it is with the Lord's Supper. For each and every time believers celebrate the Supper, the Lord

Jesus is truly present — not physically — but spiritually, through the powerful and gracious operation of His Holy Spirit. Christ's presence with us is continual in this way while He builds His kingdom here on the earth, right up until the day of His return and the end of this age. Yet, His presence with us on that will not end. Instead it will become all the more intense and immediate, as we celebrate the marriage supper of the Lamb and abide with Him forevermore!

The King, the Kingdom, and the Supper

And he said to them, "This is my blood of the covenant, which is poured out for many. Truly, I say to you, I will not drink again of the fruit of the vine until that day when I drink it new in the kingdom of God."
(Mark 14:24 – 25)

And when the hour came, he reclined at the table, and the apostles with him. And he said to them, "I have earnestly desired to eat this Passover with you before I suffer. For I tell you I will not eat it until it is fulfilled in the kingdom of God."
(Luke 22:14 – 16)

Principle: It is important for us to realize that Jesus preached and taught the kingdom of God as both present *and* future. From the very beginning of Jesus' ministry, He declared the kingdom's nearness, as in Mark 1:15: *The time is fulfilled, and the kingdom of God is at hand; repent and believe the gospel.* We understand that Jesus inaugurated His Father's kingdom during His lifetime and that the kingdom has been growing and developing ever since.

But there is also a future focus in Jesus' kingdom proclamations, such as His words to the disciples during His last Passover meal with them on the night He was betrayed. Based upon our Lord's statements to the disciples during that Last Supper, there is a "not-yet-ness" aspect of the kingdom of God that awaits its final consummation (or fulfillment) when Jesus returns in glory.

As we gather around the Lord's Table and remember the inauguration of the kingdom in Jesus' incarnation, life, suffering, death, and resurrection, we also anticipate the second coming of Christ, when the kingdom will be fully realized. At that time, Jesus our King and Savior will drink of the fruit of the vine with us *new in the kingdom of God.* Everyone who has been redeemed by the blood of Christ through the gift of faith will be invited to sit at the marriage supper of the Lamb. May our Communion celebration be for us a foretaste of that perpetual, worshipful feast unto God and to the Lamb. May our Lord's Supper observances always be visual proclamations of the kingdom of God and of the Gospel of Jesus Christ.

Prayer: Heavenly Father, we thank You that the struggles and trials of this present world – the constant battle between Your disciples and the enemies of Your kingdom – will one day cease. We thank You that there is a certain day of absolute victory and triumph when the Lord Jesus will return and the new heavens and new earth will be established forevermore. Dear Lord, until that bright and glorious day arrives, help us by Your Spirit to keep the Gospel feast that You have appointed, the Lord's Supper. And cause us to celebrate this kingdom feast as those who eagerly await the return of King Jesus, that we may celebrate His absolute victory with Him in the wonders of the Marriage Supper of the Lamb. In Jesus' name. Amen.

Strength with His Arm

And his mercy is for those who fear him from generation to generation. He has shown strength with his arm; he has scattered the proud in the thoughts of their hearts; he has brought down the mighty from their thrones and exalted those of humble estate; he has filled the hungry with good things, and the rich he has sent away empty. He has helped his servant Israel, in remembrance of his mercy, as he spoke to our fathers, to Abraham and to his offspring forever.
(Luke 1:50 – 55)

Principle: Our primary focus during our annual Christmastime is certainly and properly God's gift of His Son, our Savior. The Lord Jesus embodies the wondrousness of God's abundant provision, emphasized in the texts we usually choose for worship and for reflection. The text above is from a portion known as the Magnificat, Mary's exaltation of the God of our salvation and His marvelous means of bringing it to fruition.

This is a wonderful portion of the Gospel of Luke for us to use as we prepare to approach the Lord's Table. Notice how Mary is inspired to rejoice in the Lord's grace toward His people. While she begins her praise concerning what God has brought about specifically for her, she quickly is carried along by the Spirit's work to declare the praises of God's mercy and His provision for all God's elect — from generation to generation — to Abraham and to his offspring forever.

Through the child, promised and fulfilled, the mighty of the world have indeed been brought low, while those of humble estate have by faith been exalted. Those of the people of God hungry to be filled with the Word of God and with His righteousness have been given all the good things of Christ Jesus through the Holy Spirit. All of this brought about by the strength of His arm — that One who did not consider *equality with the Father a thing to be grasped, but made Himself nothing, taking the form of a servant* (Philippians 2:6 – 7). The divine servant, the Lord Jesus Christ, indeed helped the servants of God, accomplishing their deliverance when He came into this world, lived a perfect life, suffered and died, and then rose again — so that we who believe have everlasting life!

The portions of bread and fruit of the vine we receive during Communion are rather small. In purely physical terms they can do little to satisfy our hunger for nourishment and for good things. Yet, they serve to symbolically represent, and by the powerful working of the Holy Spirit, they do indeed provide immense, eternal, good things of God, for the nourishment of our souls, abounding to our growth in grace. Our daily food must be the Word of the living God, and like Jesus, to do the will of the One who sent Him and through Him saved us. As we come to the Lord's Supper, let us rejoice in the God of our salvation, through Jesus Christ, the Word made flesh — the One who is both Son of God and Son of Man!

The Gracious, Forgiving Father and the Supper

I will arise and go to my father, and I will say to him, "Father, I have sinned against heaven and before you. I am no longer worthy to be called your son. Treat me as one of your hired servants. And he arose and came to his father. But while he was still a long way off, his father saw him and felt compassion, and ran and embraced him and kissed him. And the son said to him, 'Father, I have sinned against heaven and before you. I am no longer worthy to be called your son.' But the father said to his servants, 'Bring quickly the best robe, and put it on him, and put a ring on his hand, and shoes on his feet. And bring the fattened calf and kill it, and let us eat and celebrate. For this my son was dead, and is alive again;
he was lost, and is found.' And they began to celebrate.
(Luke 15:18 – 24)

Principle: Jesus told the Parable of the Prodigal Son as an illustration for principles of His kingdom. This portion of the parable teaches us of the abundant grace, forgiveness, and compassion God our Father showers upon His wayward children when they are redeemed by faith in the Lord. The prodigal son's regret and repentance described in such poignant language by Jesus reminds us of our own Spirit-birthed conviction and turning to God in Christ. In many ways like this wayward child, we come before God painfully aware that we *have sinned against heaven and before Him*, and are unworthy in every respect.

But as we turn to our Father in true faith through Jesus, we find that He has already come and embraced us in His eternal love and compassion. Through the imputation, or crediting of Christ's righteousness to us, when God looks upon us He sees His one and only beloved Son — for we are adopted in Jesus. All of those markers of identity in God's family are sealed into us by His Spirit, much as the robe, the ring, and shoes are given to the returning son in the parable.

But the father's joy over his son's return did not end with his loving embrace, or with the bestowal of the outward signs of his 'readoption' into the family. The Father's joy was so abundant and exuberant that he wanted to share that joy with his family, his friends, and all the village. And so he ordered a great celebration — a feast with the finest of food and music and dancing. As he later tells his older son in the story, *It was fitting to celebrate and be glad, for this your brother was dead, and is alive; he was lost, and is found.*

Let us gather around the Lord's Table as those who are celebrating a great feast — a joyous event for each and all of us as those who were once dead in trespasses and sins, who have been made alive together in Jesus Christ; as those who once were lost — strangers and aliens from God, who have been found and declared to be sons and daughters of our heavenly Father.

Recognizing Jesus in the Supper

So they drew near to the village to which they were going. He acted as if he were going farther, but they urged him strongly, saying, "Stay with us, for it is toward evening and the day is now far spent." So he went in to stay with them. When he was at table with them, he took the bread and blessed and broke it and gave it to them. And their eyes were opened, and they recognized him. And he vanished from their sight. They said to each other, "Did not our hearts burn within us while he talked to us on the road, while he opened to us the Scriptures?
(Luke 24:28 – 32)

Principle: On the day of Jesus' resurrection there were two followers of Christ traveling down a road from Jerusalem to the village of Emmaus. As they engaged in a lively conversation about the things they had seen and heard in Jerusalem during the previous seven days, another man came alongside them and joined in their discussion. When these two disciples of Jesus expressed their amazement that some of the disciples and some of the women had found Jesus' tomb empty, the stranger said to them, *O foolish ones, and slow of heart to believe all that the prophets have spoken! Was it not necessary that the Christ should suffer these things and enter into his glory?* (Luke 24:25 – 26). And he continued with them, interpreting for them all that was written in the Scriptures concerning the Messiah.

All this time the two men had no idea who this fellow traveler was, for they were kept from recognizing him. It was only at the moment when they sat down to break bread with him that their eyes were opened and they realized that the one who had shared the road with them was in fact the risen Christ!

When we gather together for worship each Lord's Day, we have the revealed Word of God — the Scriptures — opened to us by faithful preaching. The Holy Spirit makes this effective, applying the Word to our hearts. When this is joined with the celebration of the Lord's bread and cup around the Communion table, we are enabled to receive a heightened recognition of the risen, resurrected, and reigning Lord Jesus. As we come to the Lord's Supper, in joyful praise to God for the resurrection of Jesus, let us ask our Father to open our eyes anew — to sharpen our spiritual vision — in order that we may recognize the spiritual presence of our risen Savior and King at table with us!

Prayer: Dear Lord our Redeemer, please reveal Yourself to us as we celebrate the Supper. Open our eyes to see You more fully through the working of the Holy Spirit. As the bread of Communion is blessed and broken may we come to understand Your special presence among Your people gathered for worship and the Sacrament. As You do this within us, may we long to behold You fully, face to face, as You have promised we will indeed be able to do when You return and we celebrate the Marriage Supper of the Lamb. In Your holy name we pray. Amen.

Jesus, the Resurrection and the Life and the Supper

Jesus said to her, "I am the resurrection and the life. Whoever believes in me, though he die, yet shall he live, and everyone who lives and believes in me shall never die. Do you believe this?"
(John 11:25 – 26)

Principle: Jesus reveals Himself to the grieving Martha as the resurrection and the life. And it is to this same Jesus that we also come by faith, acknowledging Him as truly and uniquely the resurrection and the life. It is the divine self-revelation of Christ our Savior that whoever believes in Him, *though he die, yet shall he live.* And so we understand and we cling by faith to the blessed hope contained in this promise — that Jesus will return in glory and that all those who have died in Him will rise in resurrection splendor. Jesus also declares to Martha that, *everyone who lives and believes in me shall never die.* And we understand that this refers to the newness of life we receive when the Holy Spirit comes and dwells within us, regenerating us, and exchanging our hearts of stone for hearts of flesh. Jesus asks a simple question — *Do you believe this?* And indeed, the faith we have received through the Spirit rises up within us to exclaim joyfully and confidently in answer — "Yes indeed!"

We understand that the promised resurrection and the newness of life we presently enjoy are completely dependent upon and entirely connected with Jesus' atoning work in our place on the cross of Calvary. In the Lord's Supper, Jesus' one-time sacrificial service on our behalf is represented by the bread and cup, which remind us of His sin-bearing body and sin-cleansing blood. Jesus says that our faith and believing* dependence upon Him — our spiritual intimacy with Him must be such that He describes it as though we were *eating* and *drinking* Him! Christ teaches in John 6:54 that, *Whoever feeds on my flesh and drinks my blood has eternal life, and I will raise him up on the last day.*

Now in saying this Jesus did not teach that when we partake of the Lord's Supper we actually eat and drink the flesh and blood of Christ. Rather, He declares that we must receive Him so fully through the indwelling Holy Spirit, and that our belief must be so inwardly settled, that eating and drinking is an appropriate metaphor or illustration of taking in and being sustained in this new relationship. Jesus does teach us, however, that the bread and the cup in the supper *represent* His body and blood, the benefits of which we have received by faith. And so as we celebrate the Supper, we are reminded through the bread and the cup of the newness of life and the promised resurrection purchased for us by Jesus' suffering body and poured-out blood so long ago. Let us come to the Lord's Table as those who indeed believe that Jesus is the resurrection and the life. And let us come as those who know that *whoever believes in Christ, though he die, yet shall he live, and everyone who lives and believes in Him shall never die.*

*Jesus speaks of "belief" three times in this passage.

Oneness in Jesus Displayed in the Supper

I do not ask for these only, but also for those who will believe in me through their word, that they may all be one, just as you, Father, are in me, and I in you, that they also may be in us, so that the world may believe that you have sent me. The glory that you have given me I have given to them, that they may be one even as we are one, I in them and you in me, that they may become perfectly one, so that the world may know that you sent me and loved them even as you loved me.
(John 17:20 – 23)

Principle: In the church I currently pastor, for our regular services of worship we use a small token of fellowship in Christ that comes from the Caribbean. It is a cup for the Lord's Supper, made by hand in the island nation of Haiti, where our brothers and sisters in Christ also gather to pray and praise, hear the Word of God proclaimed, and celebrate the Sacrament of the Lord's Supper. Isn't it interesting that we are so prone to think of ourselves when we come to Communion, or perhaps of our brothers and sisters in our local church. And yet in Christ there is a worldwide communion of all believers and congregations of which we are also a part!

This hand-made Communion cup from Haiti serves to visually remind our congregation of our oneness in the Holy Spirit, our shared faith in Christ Jesus, and our union together in the body with our Haitian covenant family. Among the churches ministered to by Jesus through our missionary partners, there are added daily many Haitians to the body of Christ, the Church. And as these believers gather together to worship the risen Lord, they lift up powerful prayers of intercession for us. What a beautiful, fragrant picture of unity in the Spirit, much as Jesus asked the Father for in John 17.

Every celebration of the Lord's Supper visually declares to us the Gospel of Jesus Christ and the oneness we enjoy in Him through the presence of His Holy Spirit. Our testimony to the reality of the saving work of Jesus Christ is in part made manifest through our unity in Him. Jesus prayed that we may become perfectly one, so that the world may know that God sent Jesus His Son and loved us even as the Father loved the Son. While we receive Communion, let's remember our shared oneness in Christ with each other in our fellowship in Christ's local body, and also remember our oneness in Jesus through the Spirit with our Haitian brothers and sisters, and with believers the world over.

Prayer: Heavenly Father, help us to see in the Supper our oneness with You and our oneness with one another as Your covenant family in Jesus Christ our Savior. Lead us by Your Spirit to put aside all malice and bitterness toward one another that there may be no divisions among us as we share together in the bread and the cup. May our oneness around the Communion table fulfill Jesus' High Priestly Prayer that we would be one even as You and the Son are one. We make this prayer in the blessed name of Jesus. Amen.

The Father's Cup and the Lord's Supper

So Jesus said to Peter, "Put your sword into its sheath; shall I not drink the cup that the Father has given me?"
(John 18:11)

Principle: There is an intimate and unbreakable connection between the cup, which the Father gave the Son to drink, and the cup, which we bless and receive during the Lord's Supper. For Jesus our Savior, the Father's cup was most bitter and terrible, for its contents were utterly saturated with our vile and wicked sins, mixed to the uttermost with the holy and fierce wrath of God. It is no wonder then that the holy and sinless Son of God recoiled and was *very sorrowful, even to death.*

We can sense Jesus' deep suffering, along with His unswerving and faithful commitment to His Father in the pleading prayer He uttered three times that terrible night in Gethsemane: *My Father, if it be possible, let this cup pass from me; nevertheless, not as I will, but as you will* (Matthew 26:39*ff*). And Jesus did indeed obediently drink the Father's bitter cup to the very last drop as His blood was poured out to satisfy the righteous judgment of God the Father toward our sins. Jesus consumed every moment of the eternity in Hell which had been reserved for our just punishment from God.

On the very same night that Jesus received the Father's cup of judgment, the Son offered to His disciples and all who would come after them in faith an entirely different cup. At the end of the Passover meal, our Lord raised the cup of blessing and declared, *This cup that is poured out for you is the new covenant in my blood* (Luke 22:20). While Jesus Christ drank to the very bottom the awful cup of the Father's wrath and our sin, He filled to overflowing the cup of God's marvelous grace for us to drink. The cup we drink is, according to Jesus Himself, the new covenant in His precious blood. This is the Covenant of Redemption applied by God to You and to me and all who believe through Jesus the Son. And now we both celebrate and remember, as the Apostle Paul exhorts the believers in Corinth, to *Do this, as often as you drink it, in remembrance of me.*

With each celebration of the Lord's Supper, the cup that we bless serves to remind us of the Father's bitter, bitter cup of condemnation which the Son humbly drank in our place. Jesus received our sins and the Father's just wrath, while we by faith receive the forgiveness and gracious covenant blessings of God in Christ! The bread and the cup we receive in the Supper are vivid pictures of what Jesus endured for our eternal sakes. Let us indeed receive this means of God's grace by the powerful working in us of His most Holy Spirit through the Gospel Feast!

Prayer: Dear Lord Jesus, thank You for drinking the terrible cup of the Father's great and just wrath for our sin, so that we would not have to drink it ourselves. We praise you that in place of the cup of God's wrath You have given to us the cup of the new covenant in Your blood – the cup in fact of God the Father's great and eternal blessings for all who believe in Your name. May we now see the reality of this wonderful exchange of cups as we celebration the Gospel Feast during our Sabbath day worship. And in all these things we give You the honor, the praise, and the glory. Amen.

He Will Return

He said to them, "It is not for you to know times or seasons that the Father has fixed by his own authority. But you will receive power when the Holy Spirit has come upon you, and you will be my witnesses in Jerusalem and in all Judea and Samaria, and to the end of the earth." And when he had said these things, as they were looking on, he was lifted up, and a cloud took him out of their sight. And while they were gazing into heaven as he went, behold, two men stood by them in white robes, and said, "Men of Galilee, why do you stand looking into heaven? This Jesus, who was taken up from you into heaven, will come in the same way as you saw him go into heaven."
(Acts 1:7 – 11)

Principle: There are two things powerfully declared to those who watched Jesus ascend into heaven and declared by revelation of God's Word to all those who believe in Christ. The first of these two truths is that with the ascension of Christ, the Holy Spirit was given a broader mission and poured out on all who come to faith in Jesus, transforming them and empowering them for kingdom work.

The second of these truths so precious to believers is that just as Jesus ascended into heaven and was received by the heavenly court with great honor and glory — seated beside His Father in power and authority — so also will our Savior one day return in the same way at the consummation of the new heaven and new earth. At that glorious second appearing of Christ, we will join Him in triumphal procession as He assumes the fullness of His reign upon the earth and we enjoy His presence forevermore in resurrected glory.

It is also these two truths that expand our appreciation of the Lord's Supper. The Spirit of Christ is the One who empowers our remembrance of Jesus' atoning death and His glorious resurrection. The Holy Spirit's presence with us ever reminds us of Jesus' ascension into heaven, while the Father makes all His enemies a footstool for His feet. And as we often observe when we gather around the Table, Christ is coming again one day and on that day, we who believe will be like Him, for we will be able to see Him fully, as those redeemed and resurrected to everlasting life.

The Sacrament of Communion is a time in which the Holy Spirit reminds us of Christ's completed work, His ongoing presence and empowerment with us today, and the encouragement and hope of Jesus' glorious return. The Spirit, poured out on Pentecost after Jesus' ascension, sustains us in Christ, and at the Lord's Supper feeds us upon the marvelous grace of God.

Prayer: Heavenly Father, although we were not standing on the mount with the Apostles watching Jesus ascend into heaven, we do thank You and praise You that at Jesus' glorious return we will see Him coming in the clouds and with great power and majesty. Every time we celebrate the Lord's Supper, Your servant the Apostle Paul reminds us that we proclaim the Lord's death until He comes. Please build up within us a joyful anticipation of the fulfillment of the blessed hope—which is the return of Jesus Christ in triumph. And it is in Jesus' name that we ask this. Amen.

Repent and Believe

Now when they heard this they were cut to the heart, and said to Peter and the rest of the apostles, "Brothers, what shall we do?" And Peter said to them, "Repent and be baptized every one of you in the name of Jesus Christ for the forgiveness of your sins, and you will receive the gift of the Holy Spirit. For the promise is for you and for your children and for all who are far off, everyone whom the Lord our God calls to himself." And with many other words he bore witness and continued to exhort them, saying, "Save yourselves from this crooked generation." So those who received his word were baptized, and there were added that day about three thousand souls.
(Acts 2:37 – 41)

Principle: Peter's great, Spirit-anointed sermon to the crowds gathered in Jerusalem on the day of Pentecost represents the very heart of the Gospel offer of salvation through faith in Jesus Christ. God mightily used the powerful truths of His Good News in bringing 3,000 people from all over the known world to faith in Jesus His Son on that very day. And the harvest of souls at Pentecost was just the beginning of the mighty, kingdom-building process the Lord continues even today through His preachers, teachers, missionaries, evangelists, and every believer who shares his or her faith.

The Apostle Peter, empowered by the Holy Spirit, declared on that day so long ago the absolute necessity of repentance, of receiving the covenant sign of baptism, of looking in faith to Jesus Christ for forgiveness of sins, and of receiving the indwelling power of the Spirit of Christ. These are the essentials of the faith we profess today as well. They are the basis for every evangelistic opportunity and every mission project.

But Peter also told the gathered crowd that the promises of God to redeem His chosen people through Jesus Christ were not only for them. The promises were also for their children *and for all who are far off, everyone whom the Lord our God calls to himself.* And so from the Apostle we learn that the Good News of Jesus Christ is declared in a multi-generational context. Its promises are also unbounded by the passage of time. Until the Lord Jesus Christ returns in glory, each and every generation will hear the Gospel and many in each generation will come to saving faith as the Lord exercises His calling upon them.

As we come to the Lord's Supper, let us bear in mind and heart the central message of the Gospel of Jesus Christ, which calls us to repentance, to membership in the visible body of Christ, to faithful dependence upon Jesus, and to appropriating, by faith, the sanctification and ongoing enabling of God's Holy Spirit, which now dwells within us. Let us also consider that the feast we celebrate in honor of Christ, connects us to those who have walked by faith before us in years long gone by, and also connects us to those generations who are yet to come — generations who will by faith call upon the same Lord Jesus and celebrate their communion with Him and with us, by means of this Lord's Supper.

The Lord's Day and the Lord's Supper

On the first day of the week, when we were gathered together to break bread, Paul talked with them, intending to depart on the next day, and he prolonged his speech until midnight.
(Acts 20:7)

Principle: When the Apostle Paul arrived in Troas, on the coast of what is now called Turkey, he met with the gathered believers and his traveling companions on the first day of the week — Sunday — for the breaking of bread and for the preaching of the Gospel. The expression *to break bread* is used throughout the New Testament to indicate the early congregations' fellowship or agape meals, which included the Sacrament of the Lord's Supper. These celebrations on the first day of the week were connected with preaching and teaching of the Word of God, as well as with other activities of worship. This is the worship-fellowship celebration we also have described in Acts 2:42:

And they devoted themselves to the apostles' teaching and fellowship, to the breaking of bread and the prayers.

While most churches today no longer share in a full fellowship meal featuring the Lord's Supper as a conclusion to Lord's Day worship, the divinely ordained pattern is preserved wherever and whenever the proclamation of the Word is audibly and visually declared through preaching and through the Sacrament of Communion. When we are joined together on the Christian Sabbath for morning worship, our celebration of God's gift of salvation through Jesus is heightened when we conclude our service of worship celebration as He has instructed — united around His table as one redeemed covenant family — doing this in remembrance of Him. Today many Christians might object to a weekly observance because partaking of the Supper frequently means that our services of worship might run longer than usual. And yet this seemed to be no problem for the church of believers in Troas! May the Holy Spirit do His work in us, creating such a longing in our hearts for the special presence of Christ in worship and for the means of grace God has provided in the Lord's Supper such that we might be less enslaved to time and more enraptured by Christ.

Prayer: O gracious and loving heavenly Father, by Your Holy Spirit, please bless our gathering together for the Lord's Supper. May our breaking of bread and drinking from the cup truly by faith display the wonderful work of Jesus Christ, Your Son and our Savior. Help us to find such joy and wonder in Christ through this Sacrament that we are never tempted to neglect participating, or simply coming to Your table as an empty religious ritual. May we always find our Communion celebration to in fact be a place of spiritual nourishment by Your grace. Through Your Word and by the Spirit of Christ draw us with eagerness to this Gospel Feast. And may Your Spirit work such love for You within us, that we pay no attention to the length of our worship this beautiful Sabbath day, that it in fact my seem for us to be a blessed foretaste of eternal glorified worship of You, the Son, and the Spirit. In Jesus' name. Amen.

Lord's Supper Meditation

But the free gift is not like the trespass. For if many died through one man's trespass, much more have the grace of God and the free gift by the grace of that one man Jesus Christ abounded for many. And the free gift is not like the result of that one man's sin. For the judgment following one trespass brought condemnation, but the free gift following many trespasses brought justification. For if, because of one man's trespass, death reigned through that one man, much more will those who receive the abundance of grace and the free gift of righteousness reign in life through the one man Jesus Christ.
(Romans 5:15 – 17)

Principle: As we sit under this portion of the Word of God, let's ask the Spirit of the living God to work its amazing message deeply into our hearts and our minds. In our churches' regular Sabbath morning congregational worship, we exalt the *Second Adam*, the Lord Jesus Christ, in both the Word preached and also the Word made visible through the Lord's Supper.

The Apostle Paul tells us that although the original sin of Adam brought the curse of death and eternal condemnation, the perfect obedience, righteousness, and atoning death of the Lord Jesus Christ brought the gift of justification and eternal life by means of faith by grace for many.

Our celebration of Communion underlines for us this central work of redemption accomplished by Christ Jesus. The context of the Supper originally was the night on which the Lord Jesus was betrayed into the hands of sinners, and it led the next day to Calvary and His atoning work, assuming the sins of God's elect as He died upon the cross.

Our Lord instituted the sacramental meal within the setting of the Passover celebration, for He Himself became our Passover Lamb. In His perfect, one-time sacrifice, the Son of God purchased our redemption from God's wrath and curse, clothing us in this great *transfer* in His own perfect righteousness. For those who believe in Jesus alone for salvation, the original sin curse passed down through Adam, as well as our own individual sinful guilt, is taken away. This is the great beauty displayed visually in the Lord Supper and brought to our hearts and minds by His Spirit and according to His grace. Thanks be to God Most High for the gift of the Second Adam, our Lord and Savior Jesus Christ!

Prayer: Our gracious and loving heavenly Father, thank you for removing the great wall of separation which divided us from You loving presence. Thank You for reconciling us to You through Jesus Christ, Your Son. We pray that You will remind us powerfully through the words of institution and through the elements we share of the life, death, and resurrection of Jesus Christ and its immediate and eternal effects in transforming our lives by Your Spirit. Bless this meal and this fellowship around the table, we pray, in Jesus' mighty name. Amen.

Hope that Does Not Disappoint

And not only the creation, but we ourselves, who have the firstfruits of the Spirit, groan inwardly as we wait eagerly for adoption as sons, the redemption of our bodies. For in this hope we were saved. Now hope that is seen is not hope. For who hopes for what he sees? But if we hope for what we do not see, we wait for it with patience.

(Romans 8:23 – 25)

Principle: In this section of Romans chapter 8, the Apostle Paul reveals to us the nature of the hope we profess as believers in the Lord Jesus Christ. The great hope of the redeemed body of Christ is for the full realization of the new heaven and the new earth, inhabited by the adopted sons and daughters of God in full radiant, resurrection glory — expressed and enjoyed eternally in the presence of our Triune God.

Paul writes of this hope in a more certain way than we typically use the term today. Perhaps an expression like *certain hope* would better describe his faith-birthed and Spirit-given expectation. While we do not yet see, any more than the Apostle Paul did in his day, the full realization of the reign of the kingdom of God, nevertheless we live and work under the bright and glorious hope purchased and trail blazed by the Son of God and now under constant preparation for those of us who are heirs with Christ.

As the Apostle writes, we already enjoy the first fruits — the initial indications and proof of the gloriousness to come — through the indwelling Holy Spirit and the evidences shown forth in our redemption, transformation, and ongoing sanctification. While our bodies have not yet been renewed after the likeness of the resurrected Son, we yet have the certainty that it will one day come to pass, for we have already received the Spirit-birthed transformation of our souls and our minds.

The Lord's Supper visually displays for us the work of the Lord Jesus Christ and the hope that we profess through Him. The Spirit of God uses the elements of the Supper, the words of institution, and the participation of the covenant people of God to work in us encouragement concerning the great hope. Throughout the Word of God, from Daniel 7 to Revelation 22, the return of the Lord Jesus Christ and the fullness of His reign is associated with the fulfillment of all the hopes of the

Covenant of Redemption for the elect children of God. And so, as we celebrate and as we remember the completed work of Christ on our behalf, we are also drawn by the Spirit to consider the hope of the Lord Jesus' glorious return.

May we always draw near to the Lord's Table as those who rejoice in the hope which does not disappoint. May the Spirit remind us vividly of Christ's work of redemption for us, His ongoing work of sanctification in us, and His pending return to fully restore all the creation, freed of the curse of sin, and inhabited by the resurrected saints in light! To God be all the glory, for His past, present, and future works in the creation and among His people!

Remembrance, Presence, and Anticipation through the Supper

For I received from the Lord what I also delivered to you,
that the Lord Jesus on the night when he was betrayed took bread,
and when he had given thanks, he broke it, and said,
"This is my body which is for you. Do this in remembrance of me."
In the same way also he took the cup, after supper, saying,
"This cup is the new covenant in my blood. Do this, as often as you drink it, in remembrance of me." For as often as you eat this bread and drink the cup,
you proclaim the lord's death until he comes.
(1 Corinthians 11:23 – 26)

Principle: The Apostle Paul provides an account for us of Jesus' words at the institution of the Supper which agrees with the Gospel writers' accounts and also provides some additional information. The words Paul received from the Lord Jesus and passed on to the Corinthians emphasize three concepts which are important for our own observances of Communion today.

The first principle is that of representation or symbolic correspondence between the elements and the person and work of Jesus. As in the Gospel accounts, the bread serves to represent Jesus' body, *which is for you*. Likewise, the cup represents Jesus' poured out blood, *the new covenant*. These simple elements are used by the Spirit to convey to us the benefits and blessings of Jesus' sin-bearing yet sinless body and His atoning blood.

The second principle brought to light on the Supper in 1 Corinthians 11 is that of remembrance. This concept is emphasized in this passage by its inclusion within both statements concerning the elements. Both the bread and the cup include the words, *Do this... in remembrance of me*. And so Jesus intends that we be reminded of His completed work, suffering and dying in our place, whenever we gather together to receive the Lord's Supper.

Finally, the third principle, which appears only in this passage and not in the Gospel record, is the concept of anticipation. Our celebration of Communion brings together for us the past, the present, and the future. The Lord's Supper is indeed a remembrance or memorial, bringing to mind and heart the completed work of Christ. And it serves to celebrate Jesus' accepted work and present reign at the Father's right hand, through which we presently - by the Holy Spirit - have fellowship with

Him. Yet it also includes a future aspect. For as we celebrate the Lord's Supper, we have hopeful anticipation of our Savior's return in glory.

May the Lord Jesus Christ, through the powerful operation of His Spirit within and among us, vividly display in our hearts and our minds these three aspects of His sacrificial love. No wonder that some congregations throughout the history of the Church have also referred to the Lord's Supper as a *Love Feast!*

The Body of Christ: Diverse and Unified

But grace was given to each one of us according to the measure of Christ's gift. Therefore it says, "When he ascended on high he led a host of captives, and he gave gifts to men." . . . And he gave the apostles, the prophets, the evangelists, the shepherds and teachers, to equip the saints for the work of ministry, for building up the body of Christ, until we all attain to the unity of the faith and of the knowledge of the Son of God, to mature manhood, to the measure of the stature of the fullness of Christ, so that we may no longer be children, tossed to and fro by the waves and carried about by every wind of doctrine, by human cunning, by craftiness in deceitful schemes. Rather, speaking the truth in love, we are to grow up in every way into him who is the head, into Christ, from whom the whole body, joined and held together by every joint with which it is equipped, when each part is working properly, makes the body grow so that it builds itself up in love.
(Ephesians 4:7 – 8, 11 – 16)

Principle: The Lord Jesus Christ designed the Church to display both amazing diversity and marvelous unity at the very same time. This great truth of God's kingdom is described for us here in Paul's letter to the believers of the Ephesian congregation in chapter 4. Paul is given the Spirit-inspired vision of the Lord Jesus Christ's ascension into heaven and the implications of that for those who believe in Him.

Paul writes that like the mightiest of conquerors the resurrected Lord Jesus led in triumph *a host of captives*, while simultaneously giving great gifts to His kingdom people. The Apostle reveals that among these gifts are those called to be *apostles, prophets, evangelists, shepherds and teachers*. And Jesus gave these people, with their special equipping and kingdom tasks to perform, as gifts for the building up of the people of God, the Church.

This diversity of gifts and callings, represented by the list Paul gives us in this passage, is carefully designed and granted to His Church in order that all of us who believe may *attain to the unity of the faith and of the knowledge of the Son of God,* to Christian maturity, and to the measure of the fullness of Christ. As we are equipped by those so-called, we will grow up into Christ, into a whole body joined together, growing so that we are built up in the love of God.

Just as Christ works among His people in the Church, utilizing diversity to achieve unity, so also the Lord's Supper displays for us both the diversity and the unity of the body of Christ as the redeemed family of God. Though there are as many giftings and callings in our local congregation as there are brothers and sisters present, at the same time we are unified as one body in Christ. We all share in the same Spirit, and in *one Lord, one faith, one baptism, one hope, one God and Father of all, who is in all and through all* (Ephesians 4:5 – 6). As participants around His table, we are one in the Lord Jesus Christ, all saved through His marvelous grace!

The Mind of Christ

Have this mind among yourselves, which is yours in Christ Jesus, who, though he was in the form of God, did not count equality with God a thing to be grasped, but made himself nothing, taking the form of a servant, being born in the likeness of men. And being found in human form, he humbled himself by becoming obedient to the point of death, even death on a cross. Therefore God has highly exalted him and bestowed on him the name that is above every name, so that at the name of Jesus every knee should bow, in heaven and on earth and under the earth, and every tongue confess that Jesus Christ is Lord, to the glory of God the Father.
(Philippians 2:5 – 10)

Principle: The Christmas season is a wonderful time to remind our children and our grandchildren (and for some of you, great-grandchildren) just what God gave us when He sent His Son Jesus some two thousand years ago into a world desperately in need of a Savior. For many centuries God had promised His people through patriarchs, kings, and prophets that He would send them a Deliverer — a Messiah. And then one night in the Judean countryside in the little town of Bethlehem the promised Savior was born, Jesus Christ the Lord.

The Apostle Paul, while writing to the church in Philippi, understood so very personally how much Jesus had done so that he could have eternal life. He knew how Jesus had come, identified with us, suffered, died, then rose again and ascended into heaven. But the Spirit of God also gave Paul the insight to understand the sacrifice Jesus made BEFORE his sacrifice on the cross. Paul reveals in Philippians 2 that Jesus' sacrifice of love for us began well before He was arrested, tried, and put to death in Calvary. Christ's sacrifice began in the heavenly realm, in the gloriousness of God's throne chamber, when Jesus agreed with His Father that He would lay aside His exalted status, and as Paul writes, *made himself nothing, taking the form of a servant, being born in the likeness of men.*

"What wondrous love is this, O my soul, O my soul," as the American folk hymn of 1835 goes, "that caused the Lord of bliss to bear the dreadful curse for my soul, for my soul!" And indeed the greatest gift of love ever given, the most perfect act of selflessness and humility, was this humbling of Himself that Christ willingly endured so that we would become children of God and co-heirs with Him in glory. Jesus' humbling pathway began in the glories of God the Father's presence, led to His incarnation and humble birth to a poor couple in a small town, continued to His itinerant preaching ministry, reached its fullness in His betrayal, afflictions, and cruel death. And yet with His triumphant resurrection to His humility was added anew His glorious exaltation. As Paul writes, *Therefore God has highly exalted him and bestowed on him the name that is above every name, so that at the name of Jesus every knee should bow, in heaven and on earth and under the earth, and every tongue confess that Jesus Christ is Lord, to the glory of God the Father.*

As we gather with our families and friends during the Christmas season, may we do so not only in celebration of the first coming of Jesus Christ as a small babe crying in a manger. May we also celebrate what that birth meant and continues to mean today. And may we remember what Jesus came to do and actually accomplished — offering Himself as a perfect and living sacrifice in our place, so that we by faith receive the free gift of eternal life through Him. May our worship in song, in prayer, in Word, and in the Sacrament, guide us in celebrating this greatest of all gifts!

Jesus' Purifying Blood, Servanthood, and the Supper

For if the sprinkling of defiled persons with the blood of goats and bulls and with the ashes of a heifer sanctifies for the purification of the flesh, how much more will the blood of Christ, who through the eternal Spirit offered himself without blemish to God, purify our conscience from dead works to serve the living God.
(Hebrews 9:13 – 14)

Principle: The author of the letter to the Hebrews was moved by God to demonstrate that all the shadows, types, and principles displayed in the Old Testament sacrificial system were fulfilled once and for all eternity in the one-time sacrifice of Jesus Christ. Indeed, the shed of blood of Jesus, so powerfully represented in the cup at the Lord's Table through the working of the Holy Spirit, is the means by which our consciences have been purified from dead works — as Hebrews so powerfully declares. And our purification was accomplished so that we may fulfill our calling – *to serve the living God.*

We understand by faith that Jesus' atoning death and His precious spilt blood have removed the guilt and weight of our sins. Christ bore all our defiling transgressions and disobedience upon His sinless shoulders the hours He hung on that cross as our substitute. What we often may not fully understand or may simply forget, however, is the second transforming truth declared in this passage about what the blood of Christ accomplished. In purifying us as God's elect children through His shed blood, Jesus *also called and consecrated us in kingdom service to God our Father.*

As we come to celebrate the Lord's Supper, we are powerfully reminded of Jesus' completed, cleansing work on our behalf. We are reminded of the restored fellowship with God that His shed blood purchased for us. We experience assurance of Christ's constant intercession for us today. And we are also reminded and encouraged by the joyous promise of the hope of our resurrection by faith in Him. Yet we must also partake of the Supper as those called to serve the living God. As those redeemed and regenerated in Jesus, we have received the call to serve. We are first and foremost servants of Christ. But we are also servants to one another for the edification of all the saints in the body. And it is only with the help of the Holy Spirit that we will fulfill this essential call of God upon our lives — *to have this mind among ourselves, which is ours in Christ Jesus... taking the form of a servant* (Philippians 2:5, 7b).

Prayer: Lord Jesus Christ, You came and You lived a sinless life and yet died a sinner's death in order to serve us as our eternal Savior. We offer You all our worship, our praise, and our adoration, for You are the promised Messiah, the Son of the blessed living God. We thank You that through the Spirit's work in us we have been cleansed from the deadness of our former way of living and have been called by You to kingdom service. As we come now to the Supper, Holy Spirit help us to die more fully to ourselves and to live more fully – more abundantly unto Christ our Redeemer and King. In Jesus' name we pray. Amen.

The Heavenly Assembly and the Supper

But you have come to Mount Zion and to the city of the living God, the heavenly Jerusalem, and to the innumerable angels in festal gathering, and to the assembly of the firstborn who are enrolled in heaven, and to God, the judge of all, and to the spirits of the righteous made perfect, and to Jesus, the mediator of a new covenant, and to the sprinkled blood that speaks a better word than the blood of Abel. (Hebrews 12:22 – 24)

Principle: The author of Hebrews assures us in this passage that as believers in Jesus we have for all intents and purposes really and truly joined ourselves by living faith to the *assembly of the firstborn who are enrolled in heaven.* Our faith in Christ assures us direct access — even to God Himself, *the judge of all.* The soaring, lofty language used in this passage serves to emphasize not only the grandeur and glory of the heavenly realms but our own participation in them as heirs of the new covenant in Jesus. We are not mere spectators you see, but are full participants in the praise and worship of God. The text begins, *But you have come*..., revealing that here is some sense in which this is an ever-present reality for us. It is not only something that sustains our hope for the future, for in worship we enjoy its foretaste in the here and the now.

And what are we to make of the comparison of Abel's blood with Christ's? Remember that the author of Hebrews declares in the previous chapter (11) that, *By faith Abel offered to God a more acceptable sacrifice than Cain, through which he was commended as righteous, God commending him by accepting his gifts. And through his faith, though he died, he still speaks.* This reference to Genesis 4:10, in which God tells Cain, *the voice of your brother's blood is crying to me from the ground*, is used by the inspired writer of Hebrews to emphasize the power and testimony of faith, in this case sealed by martyrdom.

And yet Hebrews declares that while the shed blood of Abel testified to faith and righteousness, the blood of Jesus speaks of the *fulfillment* of faith and righteousness. Abel's blood testifies to the way of faith, but Jesus' blood is the *source and seal* of all true faith. And it is only by the sprinkled blood of Jesus Christ that the faithful are granted the joy and privilege of participation in the heavenly assembly.

John Calvin viewed each celebration of the Lord's Supper as a gathering of God's people upon the earth, who are in effect brought by the Holy Spirit into *the festal gathering and to the assembly of the firstborn enrolled in heaven.* We celebrate together at Communion a prefigurement of the marriage supper of the Lamb, and we are admitted to our places around our Father's Table by the sprinkled blood of Jesus Christ *the mediator of a new covenant*. Our participation in the Sacrament is spiritually linked with the celebration of Communion in Christ enjoyed by *the spirits of the righteous made perfect*, as they gather around God's throne.

Prayer: Lord Jesus Christ, we honor and adore You, we praise and worship You as we come to the bread and the cup of our Communion celebration. We thank You that as we gather around Your Table we are spiritually communing with the righteous who have been made perfect worshiping You in the heavenly places. We praise You that Your have purchased our salvation and adopted us into the Father's family, which is composed of redeemed men, women, and children from every tribe and nation and language and people. We give You praise and honor that this meal is but a small foretaste of the fellowship we will enjoy with You and with all the saints in the heights of glory. May Your name forever be exalted and praised. In Your saving name we pray. Amen.

The Diversity of the Kingdom and the Supper

And they sang a new song, saying,
"Worthy are you to take the scroll
and to open its seals,
for you were slain, and by your blood
you ransomed people for God
from every tribe and language and people and nation,
and you have made them a kingdom
and priests to our God
and they shall reign on the earth."
(Revelation 5:9 – 10)

Principle: When we hear the word *diversity* used today we often associate it with modern cultural attempts to approve of all manner of ideas, lifestyles, religions, and worldviews, without reference to the guiding, defining truth of the Word of God. And yet the term *diversity* is an appropriate one to use in describing what we find in Revelation chapter 5, as the Apostle John reveals the vision he received of the redeemed saints — those whom Jesus has made into a kingdom and priests to God.

The kingdom of Jesus Christ is composed of people *from every tribe and language and people and nation.* The shed blood of God's own Son, the true Passover Lamb, has been applied by God's electing grace through the working of the Holy Spirit, by faith, to ransom a particular people for His own glory. The redeemed people of God's kingdom are composed of the most diverse array of cultures, languages, nationalities, and even periods of time imaginable.

And yet, this diverse array of men, women, and children from every corner of the earth share in one common and binding identity. We are blood-bought covenant children of the living God. We share a common calling as priests to God. And we are all endowed with a magnificent purpose, to reign upon the earth.

It is most appropriate as we gather around the King's Table to ask the Spirit of Christ to remind us of the diversity and immensity of God's ransomed people. Also, that the Holy Spirit will give us a broader sense that we are united by faith around the Table with those who share our identity in Jesus. We dine in the King's presence with them, whatever their language, culture, or nationality. And may we ever be reminded of the shed blood of Jesus Christ, who alone is worthy, and the great work He accomplished on our behalf. For as a result of His glorious mercy and love, displayed in His suffering and death on the cross, we who believe by faith are united in a common calling and purpose — as priests and servants of the King!

Prayer: Dear Lord Jesus Christ, we honor You. We adore You. We lift our hearts in praise and thanksgiving before You. Your covenantal kingdom amazes us in so many, many ways. We thank You for purchasing us and all who believe by the blood of the Lamb. We thank You for calling us to be both a kingdom and a royal priesthood. We thank You for tasking us and privileging us to reign upon the earth. We glory in You, King Jesus, our slain and risen Lamb, because You have ransomed us for the Father and for Your glory. Help us now, we pray, to approach this Gospel Feast of the kingdom in awe of You and what You have done for us. Cause us to look upon believers in every place as our family according to God's amazing grace. And by the Spirit encourage us to go forth and fulfill our kingdom calling as priests and vice-regents, bearing the name of Jesus and carrying the banner of our eternal God. In Jesus' name we pray. Amen.

Firstfruits for God

Then I looked, and behold, on Mount Zion stood the Lamb, and with him 144,000 who had his name and his Father's name written on their foreheads. And I heard a voice from heaven like the roar of many waters and like the sound of loud thunder. The voice I heard was like the sound of harpists playing on their harps, and they were singing a new song before the throne and before the four living creatures and before the elders. No one could learn that song except the 144,000 who had been redeemed from the earth. It is these who have not defiled themselves with women, for they are virgins. It is these who follow the Lamb wherever he goes. These have been redeemed from mankind as firstfruits for God and the Lamb, and in their mouth no lie was found, for they are blameless.
(Revelation 14:1 – 5)

Principle: In Revelation 14:1 – 5 we are given yet another glimpse into a heavenly victory celebration. And the way this celebration unfolds reminds us of the various victory songs that precede it in the Holy Scriptures. The episode that immediately comes to mind includes the victory songs of Moses and Miriam in Exodus 15:1 – 21. The people of God were so overcome with rejoicing for the deliverance God had given them from the oppression and hardship of slavery in Egypt, and they were so amazed at the way that the Lord defeated the mighty chariots of Pharaoh using the Red Sea, that they composed hymns of praise and danced before the Lord.

John sees in this Revelation celebration a group of *144,000 who had [the Lamb's] name and His Father's name written on their foreheads*, and we later learn that these *follow the Lamb wherever He goes* and that *they have been redeemed from mankind.* These redeemed believers are engaged in joyful heavenly worship using a new song that only they could learn. And all the descriptive language John uses about them indicates that they are righteous and they are pure.

Jesus gave this vision to John so that he and the believers in the seven churches in Asia would be encouraged. Our Savior wanted them and He wants us to understand the great blessings we have in the Lamb now and will enjoy alongside these 144,000 one day in the presence of God and the heavenly host. How do we arrive at this application? From the passage, in which Jesus reveals to John that these 144,000 *have been redeemed from mankind as firstfruits for God and the Lamb.* This means that just as the Old Testament celebration of the Feast of Firstfruits represented the expectation of a full harvest to follow, so also this redemptive celebration of God's firstfruits represents the expectation of countless more redeemed men and women to follow.

You and I, if we are believers in Jesus Christ as Lord and Savior, now follow the Lamb in this life and already enjoy the label 'blameless,' for Jesus bore away our sins and gave to us by the Holy Spirit the declaration of His blamelessness. And for this we have every reason to celebrate as well — both in this life and the life that we will enjoy with the Lamb through all eternity. Like the Hebrews of old and these 144,000 of Revelation, we have been delivered from hard bondage — from captivity to sin and the dominion of Satan, into the glorious, eternal kingdom of holiness and grace with God the Father and our risen Lord Jesus as our Head. Just as John's vision uses visual imagery and symbols to declare this great truth, so also does our celebration of the Lord's Supper, as the bread and the cup declare our redemption and justification through our Lamb, Jesus Christ.

Until He Comes

Then I looked, and behold, a white cloud, and seated on the cloud one like a son of man, with a golden crown on his head, and a sharp sickle in his hand. And another angel came out of the temple, calling with a loud voice to him who sat on the cloud, "Put in your sickle, and reap, for the hour to reap has come, for the harvest of the earth is fully ripe." So he who sat on the cloud swung his sickle across the earth, and the earth was reaped.
(Revelation 14:14 – 16)

Principle: This passage describes John's vision of the second coming of the Lord Jesus and the final in gathering of the redeemed saints. While the 144,000 earlier in the chapter are described as *the firstfruits for God and for the Lamb*, this later group represents the final peak harvest of the saints in Jesus at His triumphal return. In 1 Thessalonians 4:16 – 18, the Apostle Paul writes of this same glorious event: *For the Lord himself will descend from heaven with a cry of command, with the voice of an archangel, and with the sound of the trumpet of God. And the dead in Christ will rise first. Then we who are alive, who are left, will be caught up together with them in the clouds to meet the Lord in the air, and so we will always be with the Lord. Therefore encourage one another with these words.*

The Bible tells us always to be ready for the Lord Jesus' return. Like faithful stewards, given authority over our master's holdings while he is away on a far away business trip, we who serve the Lord Jesus are to always be alert, laboring faithfully, and joyfully anticipating the return of Christ at any moment. When that moment finally arrives, we will see our risen Lord in all His glory and beauty, arrayed just as Daniel saw Him in his vision — just as John also sees Him here, *seated on a cloud like a son of man, with a golden crown on his head*. This is also the fulfillment of the proclamation of the two men who appeared next to the Apostles as Jesus ascended into heaven. The Apostles saw Jesus received by a cloud as He rose out of their sight. At that moment the two men declared to the Apostles that Jesus *will come again in the same way just as you saw him go into heaven.*

What amazing things will happen the moment of Jesus' triumphant return! All those who have died in the Lord will be raised imperishable — in glorified resurrection bodies like the body of the risen Christ. We who are alive when our Lord returns will also be changed in an instant. And all of us together will accompany Christ in His kingly procession. The new heaven and new earth will be unveiled and those who have rejected Jesus as Lord and Savior will be cast into hell and eternal torment. Yet for those who are in Jesus the second coming of Christ ushers in an eternity of joyfulness, peacefulness, and perfect blessedness in the presence of God and the Lamb.

Each and every time we celebrate the Lord's Supper, the Scriptures tell us that we *proclaim the Lord's death until He comes*. And so as we are reminded by the Holy Spirit of what Jesus did when He died for us upon that cross so long ago, we are also mindful of the blessed hope we share together in the Lord's victorious return. May the Holy Spirit renew your joyfulness and expectation of the return of Jesus as you engage with this Revelation passage and as you share together as covenant brothers and sisters in the Sacrament of the Lord's Supper.

King of Kings

They will make war on the Lamb, and the Lamb will conquer them, for he is Lord of lords and King of kings, and those with him are called and chosen and faithful. (Revelation 17:14)

Principle: Despite all of the rebellion against the Lord which is highlighted throughout the book of Revelation, the ultimate theme of Jesus' message to the seven churches and to believers of every generation is contained in this triumphant verse. One of the angels who poured out a bowl of God's wrath provides John with clear encouragement as to where all of the rebellion of humanity and the judgment of God is heading. The final outcome is the complete and absolute victory of the Lord Jesus Christ over all His and our enemies. The angel's declaration is of Jesus the Lamb as Lord of lords and King of kings, the possessor of all authority in heaven and on earth (Matthew 28:18).

This declaration is also encouraging in the way that it describes those who have been saved by faith in Jesus. Believers here are declared to be called and chosen and faithful. It is interesting to note these three terms and even the order in which they occur. We recognize the first two from another famous passage of Scripture: *For many are called, but few are chosen* (Matthew 22:14). Those who are identified with the Lamb in this revelation are not only those who have heard the call of Christ to trust in Him. They are also those few who have been chosen in Jesus from before the foundation of the world, have been given the gift of faith by the Holy Spirit, and have truly believed. The passage also says that those who are called and chosen are also faithful. I take this to mean that as Paul also wrote, *he who began a good work in you will bring it to completion at the day of Jesus Christ* (Philippians 1:6). That is, that although believers are not perfectly faithful in this life, often falling far short of God's beautiful glory and holiness, nevertheless, they are sanctified day by day and are ultimately made perfect at Jesus' return or at their believing deaths. Indeed, although not perfect in this life, all who believe are as the term implies, filled with faith.

If you are a believer in Jesus today, trusting in Him fully and completely as your Lord and Savior — the only source of eternal salvation and blessing, then these declarations from Revelation 17:14 about those who follow Jesus also apply today to you. And just as we celebrate the wonder of Christ's redeeming work in our lives through the declaration of His revealed Word, so also we celebrate His regenerating and sanctifying work in our lives as we gather around the Lord's Table. Just as the bread and the cup visually proclaim the Lord's death until He returns, so also Communion serves to remind us of His call that we be faithful, and at the same time provides His grace to help us to fulfill more fully that call. May you find much blessing and encouragement in God's Word today — written, preached, and visually proclaimed.

Prayer: Dear Lord Jesus, we praise You that although we often fall short of Your perfection in this life, one day You will complete the good work that You have begun in us. We also praise You that although it often seems as though the powers of darkness are gaining the upper hand in this present world, in the end You will utterly conquer them as the Lamb Who was slain and yet lives forevermore! We hail You as King of kings and Lord of lords—hallelujah! And as we come partake of the bread and the cup, may the certainty of Your ultimate and complete victory be firmly etched in our hearts and our minds. And may this assurance of Your glorious triumph spur us on in this present life. May we truly believe by faith the promise in Your Word that the gates of hell will not prevail against the testimony of Jesus Christ. We make this prayer in the mighty name of Jesus. Amen.

The Lamb's Wedding Supper and the Lord's Supper

Then I heard what seemed to be the voice of a great multitude, like the roar of many waters and like the sound of mighty peals of thunder, crying out, "Hallelujah! For the Lord our God the Almighty reigns. Let us rejoice and exult and give him the glory, for the marriage of the Lamb has come, and his Bride has made herself ready; it was granted her to clothe herself with fine linen, bright and pure" – for the fine linen is the righteous deeds of the saints. And the angel said to me, "Write this: Blessed are those who are invited to the marriage supper of the Lamb." And he said to me, "These are the true words of God."
(Revelation 19:6 – 9)

Principle: The Apostle Paul, writing in Ephesians 5:25 – 33, draws a direct correspondence between the relationship of a man and woman in the covenant of marriage and the relationship of Christ to His Church. Paul describes how *Christ loved the church and gave himself up for her, that he might sanctify her, having cleansed her by the washing of water with the word, so that he might present the church to himself in splendor, without spot or wrinkle or any such thing, that she might be holy and without blemish.*

We know that ever since His triumphal ascension and the pouring out of the Holy Spirit, Christ has been building His Church and sanctifying its members, all in preparation for His glorious return and the full consummation of His kingdom. The book of Revelation describes for us the great celebration that will take place at Christ's return with His resurrected saints. All who have been redeemed in Christ will be on that day completely sanctified and made ready, much as a bride, adorned in fine pure linen, is beautifully adorned on her wedding day. On that joyous day, all the sanctified and glorified saints composing Christ's Bride the Church will gather in fellowship with Christ the Lamb to celebrate the consummation of all things under the headship of the covenant King.

The Lord's Supper we frequently celebrate acts as a reminder and as a forward pointer for our future hope — the return of Jesus Christ and the great marriage supper of the Lamb. We have, with every Sabbath day participation in the Supper, the privilege of tasting a sweet and satisfying sample of the much fuller and greater Gospel Feast which is to come in the new heaven and new earth. As we partake together in this foretaste of the great feast of the Last Day, let us reflect upon the profound truth Scripture declares that Jesus Christ is our Head, and we as His assembled Church are also in His eyes the most beloved of brides!

Prayer: Heavenly Father, please make us ready as Christ's perfect Bride. Please continue Your sanctifying work in and through us by Your Spirit that we may be perfectly and spotlessly adorned for our Lord Jesus' great return. Even as brides today and their bridesmaids anticipate and prepare themselves for the wedding celebration, may we also eagerly await and earnestly prepare ourselves for the wedding of Christ and His Church and for the Marriage Supper of the Lamb. We thank and praise You that in Jesus You have invited us to this most blessed of celebrations. And we also thank You that even in this present life, You have ordained for us a regular Sabbath celebration of the Lord's Supper, which lifts our eyes from the trials of this life toward the new heavens and the new earth coming in the clouds with King Jesus. Adorn us, we pray, Lord Jesus, in Your righteousness and the beauty of Your grace. Amen.

Kingdom Dominion

Blessed and holy is the one who shares in the first resurrection! Over such the second death has no power, but they will be priests of God and of Christ, and they will reign with him for a thousand years.
(Revelation 20:6)

Principle: How truly blessed we really are if we have faith in Christ Jesus. This is what the Apostle John is saying when he says, *Blessed and holy is the one who shares in the first resurrection!* Through the free gift of faith in Jesus and His atoning death on the cross, we participate also in His resurrection. We share in the victory and the benefits which come as a result of Jesus' triumph over sin, hell, Satan, and death. Because of this, John can also joyfully declare that *the second death has no power* over us. This latter part means that through Christ we have been saved from the eternal condemnation death reserved for those who have not trusted in Him.

King Jesus also revealed to John in this vision of the saints that we are *priests of God and of Christ* and that we will reign with Christ. This is a familiar theme in Revelation for it is just as John unveiled in a previous vision from chapter 5: *Worthy are you to take the scroll and to open its seals, for you were slain, and by your blood you ransomed people for God from every tribe and language and people and nation, and you have made them a kingdom and priests to our God, and they shall reign on the earth.* Our ransom has been paid by the shed blood of Christ and we are now citizens of His kingdom and a royal priesthood of believers, following after Jesus, our Head.

Now these great realities of who we are as believers in Jesus Christ, purchased by His precious blood, are not only waiting for us in some future dispensation of God's redemptive ages. These are truly blessings we currently possess in Christ our Savior. The span of a thousand years' reign proclaimed in this chapter represents the dominion and authority of the true, invisible Church, both its members in this life, and its faithful members who have gone on to be with the Lord, in its mission and work between the first appearing of Christ and His future return in glory. We reign with King Jesus and share in His kingdom authority and in the building of His kingdom through the power of His Word and by His Holy Spirit. This is the dominion we possess and the calling we have as His kingdom priests and His kingdom agents.

As we come again to the King's table for our Communion celebration, let us do so with the revelation of God's decree that you and I have been saved through faith in Jesus Christ. We come to His Supper in order to be reminded of what He has done for us and to be reminded of who He has redeemed us to be — a kingdom and priests to our God — empowered by the Spirit to exercise kingdom dominion at Jesus' side, following and exercising authority as He leads, guides, and directs. The Lord's Supper is a kingdom feast. It is the remembrance of how Jesus purchased His kingdom and His people. It is the reminder of His kingdom in the present and the work He has for us to do today. And it is the refresher and rekindler of our hope in the return of King Jesus, when the kingdom with reach its fullness, and every knee will bow and every tongue confess Jesus as Lord.

You Are Invited

Then I saw a new heaven and a new earth, for the first heaven and the first earth had passed away, and the sea was no more. And I saw the holy city, new Jerusalem, coming down out of heaven from God, prepared as a bride adorned for her husband. And I heard a loud voice from the throne saying, "Behold, the dwelling place of God is with man. He will dwell with them, and they will be his people, and God himself will be with them as their God. He will wipe away every tear from their eyes, and death shall be no more, neither shall there be mourning, nor crying, nor pain anymore, for the former things have passed away."
(Revelation 21:1 – 4)

Principle: The Apostle John receives the glorious unveiling of the recreation of heaven and earth in the final two chapters of Revelation. Everything that has taken place in redemptive history from the fall of Genesis 3:1 – 19 and the Lord's promise to reverse the curse, through the great covenants of God, through the patriarchs, kings, and prophets, up to the appearing of Jesus Christ — then forward through the centuries of the growth of Christ's church — all of it culminates in the full consummation of the restoration of Eden, free of sin, pain, sorrow, and death.

How encouraging this incredible revelation from Jesus must have been to His servant and disciple John! And how encouraging these words must have been to the believers in those seven churches in Asia Minor so long ago. Surely this vision of the return of Christ and the glorification of His saints through eternity must have sustained and given hope to every generation of believers from the time of John to the modern era. And these verses remain just as powerful and glorious for us when we gather as God's people for worship in the 21st century.

Of all the blessings described in this portion of the Revelation, none is more full of promise and encouragement than this: *Behold, the dwelling place of God is with man. He will dwell with them, and they will be his people, and God himself will be with them as their God.* While it is certainly true in the here and now that God is with us, by means of His Holy Spirit, and that He is our God and we are His people, the lofty language and repetition of "with" indicates that God's presence will be fully living and radiating among us on the Last Day. This simply means that we will know God more fully than we do today and enjoy a much fuller measure of His presence than we do today. God and Christ His Son will truly live and walk alongside us through all eternity future. We will behold God our Father and Jesus our Savior face to face!

This most beautiful promise Jesus makes to us through John in Revelation 21 is actually symbolized for us each time we celebrate the Lord's Supper. Our Lord told His disciples, as He was about to enjoy His Last Supper with them in Luke 22:15 – 16: *I have earnestly desired to eat this Passover with you before I suffer. For I tell you I will not eat it until it is fulfilled in the kingdom of God.* Jesus on the same night later says to the disciples, *You are those who have stayed with me in my trials, and I assign to you, as my Father assigned to me, a kingdom, that you may eat and drink at my table in my kingdom and sit on thrones judging the twelve tribes of Israel.* So we see that celebrating the Lord's Supper as Christ directed us to do points us symbolically forward to the great marriage supper of the Lamb which we will celebrate when Jesus returns. And the celebration of that future feast at Jesus' return will mark the beginning of our enjoyment of the immediate presence of God the Father and Jesus the Son through all eternity future.

Appendix II

A PLEA FOR THE CREATION OF A NEW COMMUNICANTS MANUAL FOR THE REFORMED CHURCHES

The Author, in preparing for the Holy Supper, has, for many years been in the habit of conducting his private unwritten meditations, in a manner somewhat like the form adopted in these meditations. Recently it occurred, that a series of written Meditations on appropriate topics, might assist communicants who are unskilled in the art of private meditation.

(J. J. Janeway, D. D., Philadelphia, 1848)[225]

I have for some time in my capacity as a minister, and one who leads at the Lord's Table, collected the now quite antiquated little volumes which used to be found in ubiquity throughout the Christian West, known in those days as *communicant's manuals*. As I peruse these pocket-sized volumes, dating from 1700 to 1848, I am struck by the connection I sense with the former owners, or generations of owners, who combed their pages in the weeks prior to their anticipated Communion celebrations. Many of them are tattered and the owner's observations are penciled or penned inside. I imagine them in some waistcoat or vest pocket traveling along colonial-era roadways in the American colonies.

These manuals were printed in large numbers, and although the Anglican Church theologians and ministers were prolific in their contributions, I also have discovered plenty of Presbyterian examples as well. Many of the manuals authored by Reformed ministers functioned as teaching aids, as well as devotional guides for preparation. Some of these, it must be admitted, were far more catechetical than devotional!

---

[225] J. J. Janeway, *The Communicant's Manual or a Series of Meditations Designed to Assist Communicants in Making Preparation for the Lord's Supper* (Philadelphia: Presbyterian Board of Publication, 1848), p. 9.

One example from a Presbyterian minister was published in 1812 in Philadelphia, authored by the Rev. James P. Wilson, D. D., pastor of the First Presbyterian Church in that influential American city. Titled as *Sacramental Selections or the Nature and Design of The Lord's Supper: With the Preparatory Self-examination and Subsequent Walk of Communicants*, his work featured a compilation of some of the best then-known treatments of aspects of the Supper. Included in his volume are topics such as:

- Of the Nature and uses of this Ordinance of the Lord's Supper
- Of the Obligations to partake, and Answers to the usual excuses for neglecting the Ordinance
- Of the Self-examination, which ought to precede participation
- Of the dispositions and meditations suitable to that solemn occasion
- Of the subsequent Life and Deportment of the worthy Communicant
- Of frequent Communicating proved from the Scripture and Ancient Fathers.[226]

Perhaps the notion of returning to these devotional and catechetical tools is anachronistic. Yet I believe that if a new one were written, in modern language with current culture and context fully taken into account, it would be of great benefit as part of a larger effort to revitalize the use of the Lord's Supper as gospel proclamation in the 21st century. And then of course, we now have even more means to distribute such a work, from the traditional printed pocket volume to the Internet, cds, and of course products such as electronic readers. All of these tools should be put to work in proclaiming the Lord's Supper as a key means of God's grace and calling believers to come and rejoice at the Gospel Feast.

What would such a 21st century communicant's manual contain? Surely it must offer both practical teaching on the nature and the importance of the Lord's Supper, much as the ones our Reformed forebears included, and also a series of devotions, based upon Scripture and including aids for prayer and further study. Discipling materials for communicates, both new and experienced, should prepare both the mind and the heart to faithfully and joyfully partake in the Sacrament. A 21st century communicant's manual must include sound biblical teaching regarding the

---

[226] James P. Wilson, *Sacramental Selections or the Nature and Design of The Lord's Supper: With the Preparatory Self-examination and Subsequent Walk of Communicants* (Philadelphia: W. W. Woodward, 1812), "Contents."

Lord's Table as a means of God's grace. It must also explain the Sacrament in its spiritual aspects as remembrance, thanksgiving (*Eucharist*), Godward and manward covenantal relationship (*Communion*), and as proclamation of the Lord's death until he returns (*Gospel Feast*).

The devotional component of the manual ought to be based upon Scripture verses, rather than pious Christian anecdotes. These have a place in Christian literature or as illustrations in sermons or devotions. However, they should not be the foundation upon which the Communion devotions are built. The living Word of God as contained in the Old and New Testaments is the surest and only power basis for preparing believers in Jesus Christ to come to his holy Supper.

Through the texts of Scripture, the twenty-first century people of God may be shown the richness and the profoundness of God's progressive revelation. They can be given views throughout the Bible of working out of God's covenant of redemption and the ever-increasing prophetic revelations of the glory and sufferings of the promised Messiah, Jesus Christ. Only in the matchless Word of God may we glimpse the beauty, the power, the holiness, the lovingkindness, and the grace of God the Father, God the Son, and God the Holy Spirit.

And it is also by use of the Scriptures that blood-bought sons and daughters of God in Christ may be both convicted of struggles in sin and yet at the same be encouraged to draw near to the Lord to find the help, the forgiveness, and the grace they so desperately, daily need. The living Word, applied to the believer by the Spirit of Christ, will do more to bring repentance, as well as a longing to come to the Lord's Supper and to eat and drink deeply, than any other sort of human exhortation.

Will such manuals or handbooks, or whatever we choose to call them, when published, be received and used by our congregations? The answer to that question remains to be seen. The Protestant Church has for so long neglected teaching and training, even preaching on the Lord's Supper, that it will take a great effort in our generation to bring about genuine change. Nevertheless it is our charge from the Lord to feed his sheep and pastor his flock. We have been entrusted with the means of grace, including the Lord's Supper, which indeed besides preaching, is God's means for *proclaiming the Lord's death until he comes*. May the churches of Jesus Christ in this 21st century rediscover and make use of the Supper as the Lord's Gospel Feast, for the sake of his redeemed covenant people and for displaying God's good news for those who as yet do not know him.

With this need for new materials to help Christians rediscover the Lord's Supper in mind, a new devotional manual is being published in conjunction with this volume, entitled, *Gospel Feasting: 104 Lord's Supper Devotions from the Old and New Testaments*. *Gospel Feasting* provides short preparations from the Word of God for those coming to Communion in churches celebrating the Sacrament on a weekly, monthly, or less frequent basis. A Sunday school or small group study guide and workbook is also planned for publication later this year.

BIBLIOGRAPHY

Adamson, Robert M. *The Christian Doctrine of the Lord's Supper*. Edinburgh: T & T Clark, 1905.

Aquilina, Mike. *The Mass of the Early Christians*. Huntington, IN: Our Sunday Visitor Publishing Division, 2007.

Aquinas, Thomas. *The Blessed Sacrament and the Mass*. Translated and Edited by Rev. F. O'Neill. Fort Collins, CO: Roman Catholic Books, 1955.

Armstrong, John H. "Do This in Remembrance of Me." In *Understanding Four Views on the Lord's Supper*. Grand Rapids: Zondervan, 2007.

Baillie, D. M. *The Theology of the Sacraments*. London: Faber and Faber, 1957.

Barker, William S. *The Westminster Standards: An Original Facsimile*. Forward by William S. Barker. Audobon, NJ: Old Paths Publications, 1997 from an original 1648 ed..

Barnett, Maurice. "Arrangement for the Lord's Supper (1)." In *The Gospel Anchor*. June 1986. pages 297 – 299.

Bartels, Ernest. *Take Eat, Take Drink: The Lord's Supper Through the Centuries*. St. Louis: Concordia Publishing, 2004.

Beattie, Francis R. *The Presbyterian Standards*. Greenville, SC: The Southern Presbyterian Press, 1997.

Benedict, Philip. *Christ's Churches Purely Reformed: A Social History of Calvinism*. New Haven: Yale University Press, 2002.

Berkhof, L. *Systematic Theology*. Grand Rapids: Wm. B. Eerdmans Publishing Co., reprint Dec. 1979.

Bercot, David W. *A Dictionary of Early Christian Beliefs*. Peabody, MA: Hendrickson Publishers, Inc., 1998.

Berkouwer, G. C. *The Sacraments*. Grand Rapids: William B. Eerdmans, 1969.

Beveridge, William. *The Theological Works of William Beveridge, D. D.* Volume VI. Sermons CXXIX – CXLVI. Oxford: John Henry Parker, 1845.

Blass, F. and A. Debrunner, *A Greek Grammar of the New Testament and Other Early Christian Literature*. Robert W. Funk trans., ed. Chicago: University of Chicago Press, 1961, 5th ed. 1973.

Bradshaw, Paul. *Eucharistic Origins*. London: SPCK Publishing, 2004.

Bray, Gerald, ed. *1 – 2 Corinthians*. Ancient Commentary on Scripture, New Testament, vol. VII. Downers Grove, IL: InterVaristy Press, 1999.

Burki, Bruno. "The Celebration of the Eucharist in *Common Order* (1994) and in Continental Reformed liturgies." In *To Glorify God: Essays on Modern Reformed Liturgy*. Edited by Bryan D. Spinks and Iain R. Torrance. Grand Rapids: William B. Eerdmans, 1999.

Calvin, John. *Institutes of the Christian Religion*. Vol. 2. Translated by Ford Lewis Battles. Edited by John T. McNeill. Philadelphia: The Westminster Press, 1960.

__________. *The First Epistle of Paul to the Corinthians*. Translated by John W. Fraser. Edited by David W. Torrance and Thomas F. Torrance. Grand Rapids: Wm. B. Eerdmans Publishing Company, 1960, reprint 1968.

__________. *Treatises on the Sacraments*. Translated by Henry Beveridge. Grand Rapids: Reformation Heritage Books, 2002.

Carson, D. A. *Worship: Adoration and Action*. Grand Rapids: Baker Book House, 1993.

Chrysostom, John. "Homily XXVII (1 Cor. XI. 17.)," in *Homilies on First and Second Corinthians, The Nicene and Post-Nicene Fathers*, vol. XII. Edited by Philip Schaff. Grand Rapids: Wm. B. Eerdmans Publishing Company, reprint July 1969.

Collins, Mary D. "Eucharistic Proclamation of God's Presence." *Worship*, vol. 41, no. 9 (1967): 531 – 541.

Coutsoumpos, Panayotis. *Paul and the Lord's Supper: A Socio-Historical Investigation*. Studies in Biblical Literature, vol. 84. New York: Peter Lang Publishing, 2005.

Cullman, Oscar. *Early Christian Worship*. London: SCM Press, 1953, reprint 1956.

Cullman, Oscar, F. J. Leenhardt. *Essays on the Lord's Supper*. Translated by J. G. Davies. Richmond, VA: John Knox Press, 1958.

Cyprian of Carthage. *The Letters of St. Cyprian of Carthage*, Vol. 3. G. W. Clarke, editor. Mahwah, NJ: Paulist Press, 1986.

Dabney, Robert Lewis. *Lectures in Systematic Theology*. Grand Rapids, Baker Book House, reprint 1985.

Davies, J. G. *The Early Christian Church: A History of Its First Five Centuries*. Grand Rapids: Baker Book House 1965, reprint 1980.

Dennison, Jr., James T. *Reformed Confessions of the 16th and 17th Centuries in English Translation: Volume 1, 1523 – 1552*. Grand Rapids: Reformation Heritage Books, 2008.

__________________. *Reformed Confessions of the 16th and 17th Centuries in English Translation: Volume 2, 1552 – 1566*. Grand Rapids: Reformation Heritage Books, 2010.

Dunn, James D. G. *The Theology of Paul the Apostle*. Grand Rapids: William B. Eerdmans, 1998.

Elert, Werner. *Eucharist and Church Fellowship in the First Four Centuries*. Translated from the German by N. E. Nagel. Saint Louis: Concordia Publishing House, 1966.

Engberg-Pedersen, T. "Proclaiming the Lord's Death: 1 Corinthians 11:17 – 34 and the Forms of Paul's Theological Argument." In *Pauline Theology. Vol II: 1 and 2 Corinthians.* Minneapolis: Fortress Press, 1993.

_________________. "Proclaiming the Lord's Death: 1 Corinthians 11:17 – 34 and the Forms of Paul's Theological Argument." In *Society of Biblical Literature Seminar Papers*, no. 30, 1991. (This article contains material not included in the above referenced 1993 volume.)

Fee, Gordon D. *The First Epistle to the Corinthians*. (The New International Commentary on the New Testament.) Grand Rapids: William B. Eerdmans, 1987.

Ferguson, Everett. *Encyclopedia of Early Christianity* New York: Garland Publishing, 1997, 1999 printing.

Fernandez, Erasto. *Eucharist As Proclamation*. Albatross Books, 1987.

Flavel, John. "An Exposition of the Assembly's Catechism." In *The Works of John Flavel*, vol. VI. Edinburgh: Banner of Truth Trust, 1820, reprint 1997.

Forde, Gerhard O. *The Preached God: Proclamation in Word and Sacrament*. Edited by Mark C. Mattes and Steven D. Paulson. Grand Rapids: William B. Eerdmans, 2007.

Garlatti, Guillermo J. "La eucaristia como memoria y proclamacion de la muerte del Senor (Aspectos de la celebracion de la cena del Senor segun San Pablo)." In *Revista Bíblica* 47 no. 1-2 1985.

Gaventa, Beverly Roberts. " 'You Proclaim the Lord's Death': 1 Corinthians 11:26 and Paul's Understanding of Worship." In *Review and Expositor 80*, 1983.

Goppelt, Leonhard. *Apostolic and Post-Apostolic Times*. Translated by Robert A. Guelich. Grand Rapids: Baker Book House, 1977, 2nd ed. 1980.

Gore, R. J. Jr. *Covenantal Worship: Reconsidering the Puritan Regulative Principle.* Phillipsburg, NJ: P & R Publishing, 2002.

Greeley, Dolores. *The Church as 'Body of Christ' According to the Teaching of Saint John Chrysostom.* Dissertation. Notre Dame, IN: Unpublished.

Grosheide, F. W. *Commentary on the First Epistle to the Corinthians. The New International Commentary on the New Testament.* Grand Rapids: Wm. B. Eerdmans Publishing Company, 1953, ninth printing, 1979.

Hall, Stuart G. *Doctrine and Practice in the Early Church.* Grand Rapids: William B Eerdmans Publishing Company, 1992.

Hamilton, James M. "The Lord's Supper in Paul: An Identity-Forming Proclamation of the Gospel." In *The Lord's Supper: Remembering and Proclaiming Christ Until He Comes.* Edited by Thomas R. Schreiner and Matthew R. Crawford. Nashville: B & H Publishing, 2010.

Hawthorne, Gerald F. "The Lord's Supper." In *The Biblical Foundations of Christian Worship.* Edited by Robert E. Webber. Nashville: Star Song Publishing, 1993.

Hay, David. *Pauline Theology, Volume II: 1 & 2 Corinthians.* Philadelphia: Fortress Press, 1993.

Henry, Matthew. *The Communicant's Companion.* New York, NY: Crocker & Brewster, 1828.

Hicks, John Mark. *Come to the Table: Revisioning the Lord's Supper.* Abilene, TX: Leafwood Publishers, 2002.

Higgins, A. J. B. *The Lord's Supper in the New Testament.* London: SCM Press LTD, 1952, reprint 1956.

Hodge, A. A. *The Confession of Faith.* Edinburgh: The Banner of Truth Trust, reprint 1978.

Hodge, Charles. *Commentary on the First Epistle to the Corinthians.* Grand Rapids: Wm. B. Eermans Publishing Company, 1950.

Hofius, Otfried. "The Lord's Supper and the Lord's Supper Tradition: Reflections on 1 Corinthians 11:23b – 25." In *One Loaf, One Cup: Ecumenical Studies of 1 Cor 11 and Other Eucharistic Texts.* (The Cambridge Conference on the Eucharist, August 1988.) Macon, GA: Mercer University Press, 1993.

Hook, Norman. *The Eucharist in the New Testament.* London: The Epworth Press, 1964.

Horell, David G. *The Social Ethos of the Corinthian Correspondence: Interests and Ideology from 1 Corinthians to 1 Clement.* Edinburgh: T & T Clark, 1996.

Hughes, Philip Edgcumbe. *Theology of the English Reformers*. Grand Rapids: William B. Eerdmans Publishing Company, 1965.

Hurtado, Larry W. *Lord Jesus Christ: Devotion to Jesus in Earliest Christianity.* Grand Rapids: William B. Eerdmans Publishing Company, 2003.

Janeway, J. J. *The Communicant's Manual or a Series of Meditations Designed to Assist Communicants in Making Preparation for the Lord's Supper.* Philadelphia: Presbyterian Board of Publication, 1848.

Jeremias, Joachim. *The Eucharistic Words of Jesus*. Philadelphia: Fortress Press, 1977, 2nd ed. 1981.

Johnson, William Stacy and John H. Leith, editors. *Reformed Reader: A Sourcebook in Christian Theology*. Volume 1, 1519 – 1799. Louisville, KY: Westminster/John Knox Press, 1993.

Keddie, Gordon J. *The Lord's Supper Is a Celebration of Grace: What the Bible Teaches About Communion*. Darlington, UK: Evangelical Press, 2000.

Kelder, Peter. "Until He Comes: Six themes for the Lord's Supper." In *Reformed Worship: Resources for Planning and Leading Worship*, March 1990.

Knoch, Otto. " 'Do This in Memory of Me!' (Luke 22:20; 1 Corinthians 11:24ff.): The Celebration of the Eucharist in the Primitive Christian Communities." In *One Loaf, One Cup: Ecumenical Studies of 1 Cor 11 and Other Eucharistic Texts.* (The Cambridge Conference on the Eucharist, August 1988.) Macon, GA: Mercer University Press, 1993.

Koenig, John. *Feast of the World's Redemption: Eucharistic Origins and Christian Mission.* Harrisburg, PA: Trinity Press International, 2000.

Krugler, Arnold F. "The Words of Institution: Proclamation or Prayer?" *Concordia Journal* (March 1976): 53 – 60.

LaVerdiere, Eugene. *The Eucharist in the New Testament and the Early Church.* Collegeville, MN: Liturgical Press, 1996.

Leithart, Peter J. *Blessed Are the Hungry: Meditations on the Lord's Supper.* Moscow, ID: Canon Press, 2000.

Mackenzie, Ross. "Reformed Theology and Roman Catholic Doctrine of the Eucharist as Sacrifice." In Journal of Ecumenical Studies, 15 no 3 Sum 1978, pages 429 – 438.

Maclean, Malcolm. *The Lord's Supper*. Ross-shire, Scotland: Christian Focus Publications, 2009.

Macy, Gary. *Treasures from the Storeroom: Medieval Religion and the Eucharist.* Collegeville, MN: The Liturgical Press, 1999.

Marrow, Stanley. "Eucharist in Scripture." In *The Biblical Foundations of Christian Worship*. Edited by Robert E. Webber. Nashville: Star Song Publishing, 1993.

Marshall, I. Howard. *Last Supper and Lord's Supper*. Grand Rapids: William B. Eerdmans, 1981, reprint 1982.

Martin, James Perry. "Belonging to History: A Communion Meditation on 1 Corinthians 11:23 – 26." In *Interpretation*, April 1963.

Mathison, Keith A. *Given for You: Reclaiming Calvin's Doctrine on the Lord's Supper*. Phillipsburg, NJ: P & R Publishing, 2002.

McKechnie, Paul. *The First Christian Centuries: Perspectives on the Early Church.* Downers Grove, IL: InterVarsity Press, 2001.

Nevin, John W. *The Mystical Presence. A Vindication of the Reformed or Calvinistic Doctrine of the Holy Eucharist.* Philadelphia: S. R. Fisher & Co., 1867.

Old, Hughes Oliphant. *Holy Communion in the Piety of the Reformed Church.* Powder Springs, GA: Tolle Lege Press, 2013.

Paquier, Richard. *Dynamics of Worship: Foundations and Uses of Liturgy.* Philadelphia: Fortress Press, 1967.

Patzia , Arthur G. *The Emergence of the Church: Context, Growth, Leadership & Worship*. Downers Grove, IL: InterVarsity Press, 2001.

Payne, Jon D. *John Owen on the Lord's Supper*. Edinburgh: Banner of Truth Trust, 2004.

Pfitzner, Victor C. "Proclaiming the Name : Cultic Narrative and Eucharistic Proclamation in First Corinthians". *Lutheran Theological Journal* 25 no. 1 (May 1991): 15 – 25.

Plummer, A. "Lord's Supper." In *A Dictionary of the Bible*, vol. III. Edited by James Hastings. Edinburgh: T & T Clark, 1900, 11th impression, 1950.

Redpath, Alan. *The Royal Route to Heaven: Studies in First Corinthians.* Westwood, NJ: Fleming H. Revell Company, 1960.

Reymond, Robert L. *A New Systematic Theology of the Christian Faith*. Nashville: Thomas Nelson, 1998.

_______________. *Paul Missionary Theologian*. Ross-shire, UK: Christian Focus Publications, 2000.

Ridley, Nicholas. *A Brief Declaration of the Lord's Supper*. Edited and biographical sketch by H. C. G. Moule. London, UK: Seeley and Co., Limited, 1895 (reprint of 1556 and 1688 editions).

Rordorf, Willy, et al. *The Eucharist of the Early Christians*. Translated by Matthew J. O'Connell. Collegeville, MN: The Liturgical Press, 1978.

Schaff, Philip. *The Creeds of Christendom*; *Volume III, The Evangelical Protestant Creeds*. Grand Rapids: Baker Book House, 1998 reprint.

Schmemann, Alexander. *The Eucharist: Sacrament of the Kingdom*. New York: St. Vladimir's Seminary Press, 1987.

Schmidt, Dan. *Taken By Communion: How the Lord's Supper Nourishes the Soul*. Grand Rapids: Baker Books, 2003.

Senn, Frank C. *Christian Liturgy: Catholic and Evangelical*. Minneapolis: Fortress Press, 1997.

Shultz, Joseph R. *The Soul of the Symbols: A Theological Study of Holy Communion*. Grand Rapids: William B. Eerdmans, 1966.

Spurgeon, C. H. *Till He Come: Communion Meditations and Addresses by C. H. Spurgeon*. London: Passmore & Alabaster, 1896.

Sullivan, T. R. ed. *Sermons on Christian Communion*. Boston: Wm. Crosby and H. P. Nichols, 1848.

Taylor, Vincent. *The Atonement in New Testament Teaching*. London: The Epworth Press, 1940; reprint 1954.

Thiselton, Anthony C. *The First Epistle to the Corinthians*. (The New International Greek Testament Commentary.) Grand Rapids: William B. Eerdmans, 2000.

Ursinus, Zacharias. *The Commentary of Zarcharias Ursinus on the Heidelberg Catechism*. Translated by G. W. Williard. Phillipsburg, NJ: Presbyterian and Reformed Publishing Company, 1852, undated reprint.

Van Cangh, J. M. "Le Texte Primitif De La Cène." In *The Corinthian Correspondence*. Edited by R. Bieringer. Leuven, Belgium: Leuven University Press, 1996.

Vander Zee, Leonard J. *Christ, Baptism and the Lord's Supper*. Downers Grove, IL: InterVarsity Press, 2004.

Vines, Richard. "The Passover: Its Significance, and the Analogy Between it and Christ our Passover." In *The Puritans on the Lord's Supper*, edited by Don Kistler. Morgan, PA: Soli Deo Gloria, 1997.

Volf, Miroslav. "Proclaiming the Lord's Death." In *Christian Century* 116, no 7, March 3, 1999.

Wallace, Daniel B. *Greek Grammar Beyond the Basics: An Exegetical Syntax of the New Testament*. Grand Rapids: Zondervan Publishing House, 1996.

Wallace, Ronald S. *Calvin's Doctrine of the Word and Sacrament*. Grand Rapids: Wm. B. Eerdmans, 1953, 2nd ed. 1957.

Wandel, Lee Palmer. *The Eucharist in the Reformation: Incarnation and Liturgy*. New York: Cambridge University Press, 2006.

Warren, F. E. *The Liturgy and Ritual of the Anti-Nicene Church*. New York: E. & J. B. Young and Co., 1897.

Watson, Thomas. "The Mystery of the Lord's Supper." In *The Puritans on the Lord's Supper*. Edited by Don Kistler. Morgan, PA: Soli Deo Gloria, 1997.

Weil, Louis. "Proclamation of Faith in the Eucharist." In *Time and Community*. Edited by J. Neil Alexander. Washington, DC: The Pastoral Press, 1990.

Wickstead, Edward. *The New Weeks Preparation for a Worthy Receiving of the Lord's Supper, as Recommended and Appointed by the Church of England*. London: Thomas Wilson and Sons York, 1740.

Wiles, Maurice and Mark Santer. *Documents in Early Christian Thought*. Cambridge: Cambridge University Press, 1975, 12th edition 2005.

Willison, John. *A Sacramental Catechism*. 1720, reprinted, Morgan, PA: Soli Deo Gloria Publications, 2000.

Wilson, James P. *Sacramental Selections or the Nature and Design of The Lord's Supper: With the Preparatory Self-examination and Subsequent Walk of Communicants*. Philadelphia: W. W. Woodward, 1812.

Wright, N. T. *Jesus and the Victory of God*. Minneapolis: Fortress Press, 1996.

INDEX OF SCRIPTURE VERSES

OLD TESTAMENT

Genesis 2:9 143 – 144
Genesis 3 143
Genesis 3:1 – 19 227
Genesis 3:8 – 9 145 – 146
Genesis 3:22 143
Genesis 12:1 – 3 147 – 148
Genesis 14:17 – 20 149 – 150
Genesis 17:15 – 16 151 – 152
Genesis 22:1 – 2 153 – 154
Genesis 22:13 153

Exodus 12:11 – 14 155 – 156
Exodus 13:6 – 10 13
Exodus 13:7 – 20 157 – 158
Exodus 13:8 12
Exodus 15:1 – 21 217
Exodus 16:4, 31 – 32 159 – 160
Exodus 24:8 – 11 161 – 162

Leviticus 16:15 – 17 163 – 164
Leviticus 16:20 – 22 165 – 166

Psalm 2:10 – 13 167 – 168
Psalm 23:5 – 6 169 – 170
Psalm 34:8 – 10 171 – 172

Isaiah 7:14 151, 173 – 174
Isaiah 9:6 – 7 175 – 176

NEW TESTAMENT

Matthew 28:1 – 10 177 – 178
Matthew 28:18 221
Matthew 28:18 – 20 128, 179 – 180

Mark 1:15 181
Mark 14:15 12
Mark 14:22 76
Mark 14:22 – 25 73
Mark 14:24 – 25 181 – 182

Luke 1:26 – 38 173
Luke 1:50 – 55 183 – 184
Luke 15:18 – 24 185 – 186
Luke 22:14 – 16 181 – 182
Luke 22:15 13
Luke 22:15 – 16 228
Luke 22:18 12
Luke 22:19 64, 73, 76 – 77, 157
Luke 24:28 – 32 187 – 188

John 6:51a 159
John 6:51b 159
John 11:25 – 26 189 – 190
John 17:20 – 23 191 – 192
John 18:11 193 – 194

Acts 1:7 – 11 195 – 196
Acts 2:37 – 41 197 – 198
Acts 2:41, 42 73
Acts 2:42 199
Acts 2:42 – 46 105
Acts 2:42, 46 134
Acts 2:42 – 47 iii
Acts 4:2 9, 13
Acts 13:5 9, 13
Acts 13:38 9
Acts 15:36 9
Acts 16:17 9
Acts 16:21 9 – 10
Acts 17:3 10
Acts 17:13 10
Acts 17:23 10
Acts 20:7 96, 199 – 200
Acts 26:23 10

Romans 5:15 – 17 201 – 202
Romans 6:7 – 9 138
Romans 8:23 – 25 203 – 204
Romans 10:10 91
Romans 10:17 133

1 Corinthians 1:10 – 17 5
1 Corinthians 2:1 9
1 Corinthians 2:1 – 5 128

1 Corinthians 9:14 9
1 Corinthians 10:16, 17 107
1 Corinthians 10:21 11
1 Corinthians 11:17 – 34 6, 8n, 14n, 13, 26, 30 – 31, 32, 39, 84, 114, 134
1 Corinthians 11:23 – 25 57, 85
1 Corinthians 11:23 – 26 1, 6n, 11, 14, 25 – 26, 57, 67, 74, 87 – 88, 99, 112, 127, 205 – 206
1 Corinthians 11:25 – 26 139
1 Corinthians 11:26 iv, 2 – 9, 11 – 13,15 – 18, 23n, 35, 36, 43 – 44, 55, 64 – 66, 74, 78 – 79, 83, 86, 88 – 90, 92 – 95, 97, 101, 105, 107 – 108, 115 – 116, 118, 120 – 121, 123, 125, 128 – 129
1 Corinthians 15:22 – 28 138

Ephesians 4:5 – 6 208
Ephesians 4:7 – 8, 11 – 16 207 – 208
Ephesians 5:25 – 33 223

Philippians 1:6 221
Philippians 1:17 9
Philippians 1:17, 18 13
Philippians 1:18 9
Philippians 2:5 – 10 209 – 210

Colossians 1:18 9
Colossians 1:28 9

1 Thessalonians 4:13 – 18 138
1 Thessalonians 4:16 – 18 219
1 Thessalonians 4:17 169

Hebrews 7 149
Hebrews 9:13 – 14 211 – 212
Hebrews 10:1 64
Hebrews 12:17 – 24 161
Hebrews 12:22 – 24 213 – 214

Revelation 5:9 – 10 215 – 216
Revelation 14:1 – 5 217 – 218
Revelation 14:14 – 16 219 – 220
Revelation 17:14 221 – 222
Revelation 19:6 – 9 223 – 224
Revelation 20:6 225 – 226
Revelation 21:1 – 4 227 – 228

GENERAL INDEX

Abbot LanFranc 63

Adamson, Robert M. 89n, 98n, 99n

Agape Meals (feast) 26 – 27, 29 – 30, 33, 40, 53, 200

Ambrose of Milan 57 – 58, 61, 64

Answers to Solomon Edwards 99

Aquilina, Mike 41n, 45n

Aquinas, Thomas 63 – 66, 115

Armstrong, John H. 120, 121n

Augustine of Hippo 58, 61, 110, 115

Baillie, D. M. 1n, 109 – 110, 112

Barker, William S. 88n

Barnett, Maurice 8

Bartels, Ernest 48n, 58n, 59, 60, 61, 62n, 66n

Beattie, Francis R. 106

Benedict, Philip 74n

Bercot, David W. 39n, 45n, 49n

Berengar of Tours 62 – 63, 65

Berengar's Oath of 1059 54, 63

Berkhof, L. 107 – 108

Berkouwer, G. C. 36, 108, 109n

Beveridge, William 69n, 96 – 97

Beza, Theodore 80, 81n

Blass, F. and A. Debrunner 23n

Bohemian Brethren 71

Bohemian Confession 73

Bradshaw, Paul 42n, 43n, 46n, 50n, 51n, 57n

Brefe Declaration of the Lordes Supper 75 – 76

Bruce, Robert 83

Calvin, John 63, 68, 69, 72, 74n, 77 – 80, 82, 87n, 99, 102 – 104, 116 – 117, 124, 126, 132n 139, 213

Carson, D. A. 114

Christ, Baptism and the Lord's Supper 119

Chrysostom, John 37, 54 – 56, 81

Clement of Alexandria 40, 45

Clement of Rome, 1st Epistle of 28, 39 – 40

Collins, Mary D. 3n, 64n

Come to the Table 117, 118n

Confession of the Glastonbury Congregation 76

Council of Nicea 51

Council of Trent 84 – 85

Coutsoumpos, Panayotis 11, 12n

Covenantal Worship 117

Cranmer, Thomas 74 – 76

Cullman, Oscar 112n

Cyprian of Carthage 38, 48 – 52

Dabney, Robert Lewis 105

Davies, J. G. 112n

De Sacramento 57 – 58

Dennison, Jr., James T. 73n, 76n, 80n, 81n

Dick, John 104

Didache 39 – 40, 42

Dunn, James D. G. 34n, 35

Dura-Europos 48

Dynamics of Worship 110 – 111

Edwards, Jonathan 97 – 100, 126

Elert, Werner 47 – 48

Emden Examination of Faith 76

Engberg-Pedersen, T. 7 – 8, 15

Essays on the Lord's Supper 111, 112n

Eucharistein 40

Eucharist as Proclamation 113 – 114

Fee, Gordon D. 19, 29

Ferguson, Everett 48n

Fernandez, Erasto 113 – 114

Firmilian, Bishop of Caesarea of Cappadocia 50 – 51

First Confession of Basel 73

First Scots Confession 82

Flavel, John 92

Forde, Gerhard O. 121

Garlatti, Guillermo J. 34n

Gaventa, Beverly Roberts 15n, 16, 36

Goppelt, Leonhard 23

Gore, R. J. Jr. 117

Gospel Feast iv, 4, 116, 120, 124, 126, 127 – 128, 133, 135, 136, 139, 141 – 142, 156, 162, 182, 194, 200, 222, 230 – 232

Greeley, Dolores 55 – 56

Gregory of Nyssa 56

Gregory the Great 59

Grosheide, F. W. 4n, 7, 20n, 22

Hall, Stuart G. 47

Hamilton, James M. 31, 122 – 123, 133n

Heidelberg Catechism 81 – 82, 125

Henry, Matthew 92 – 94, 140

Hicks, John Mark 117 – 118

Higgins, A. J. B. 27n, 31 – 32

Hodge, A. A. 105

Hodge, Charles 19 – 20

Hook, Norman 12n

Horell, David G. 27 – 28

Hughes, Philip Edgcumbe 71n, 75n

Hurtado, Larry W. 6n

Ignatius of Antioch 40 – 41, 45, 51

Institutes of the Christian Religion 77 – 78, 80

Irenaeus 40, 43 – 45

Janeway, J. J. 229

Jeremias, Joachim 17

John of Damascus 60

Johnson, William Stacy 72n

Καταγγέλλετε 4, 7 – 13, 15 – 19, 21, 25, 29, 35, 82

katangello 8

Keddie, Gordon J. 5

Kerygmatic 139

Knox, John 72, 82 – 83

Koenig, John 130 – 131

Lasco, John à 76

LaVerdiere, Eugene 44 – 45

Leithart, Peter J. 115 – 116

Leo X 69

Liber de Corpore Et Sanguine Domini 63

Lord's Supper: Remembering and Proclaiming Christ Until He Comes 31, 122 – 123

Luther, Martin 54, 66 – 67, 70 – 71, 72, 77, 85, 123

Mackenzie, Ross 83n, 84n, 85n

Maclean, Malcolm 17 – 18, 122

Macy, Gary 53n, 62n, 63n

Marshall, I. Howard 36 – 37

Martyr, Justin 40, 43

Mathison, Keith A. 116 – 117

Nevin, John W. 87, 102 – 104

Nicholas II 53, 62

Old, Hughes Oliphant 123, 132, 139

Origen of Alexandria 48 - 51

Owen, John 90 – 91, 99, 103 – 104

Paquier, Richard 110 – 111

Passover iv, 12 – 14, 20, 36, 89n, 90, 155 – 156, 157 – 158, 164, 165, 173, 181, 193, 201, 215, 228

Patzia , Arthur G. 24 – 25

Payne, Jon D. 90 – 91

Phillips, Richard D. 119

Pius V 85

Pliny the Younger 41 – 42

Plummer, A. 37n

Poullain, Vallérandus 76

Presbyterian Standards 106

Proclamation iv, 1 – 4, 7– 22, 24, 26, 29, 31 – 37, 39, 43, 45, 47, 50, 53, 57, 59, 63, 66, 70 – 74, 76 – 78, 80, 88, 90, 94, 96 – 97, 108, 112 – 116, 118 – 134, 136 – 139, 141, 231 – 232

Radbertus, Paschasius 60 – 62

Ratramnus of Corbie 60 – 62

Redpath, Alan 125

Resacrifice 2, 42, 45, 51 – 55, 57, 59, 63, 65 – 66, 78, 85, 123, 127

Reymond, Robert L. 2n, 23n, 33n

Ridley, Nicholas 75 – 76

Roman Mass 54, 61, 69 – 70, 77, 83, 89

Rordorf, Willy 40n, 43n, 44n, 48n, 49n, 50n

Schaff, Philip 54n, 62n, 71n, 81n, 83n

Schmemann, Alexander 111n

Schmidt, Dan 118 – 119

Scotus, John Duns 66

Senn, Frank C. 57, 58n, 63n, 66, 70, 82n

Sermons on Christian Communion 100, 101n, 102n

Shultz, Joseph R. 112 – 113

Soul of the Symbols 112 – 113

Spurgeon, C. H. 86, 106 – 107

Sullivan, T. R. 101 – 102

Taken by Communion 118 – 119

Taylor, Vincent 16 – 17

Theodore of Mopsuestia 56 – 57

Theology of the Sacraments 1n, 110n, 112n

Thiselton, Anthony C. 13 – 14, 16 – 17, 21n, 27n, 35

Transubstantiation 2, 41, 43, 45, 54, 56, 60 – 62, 75 – 76, 84 – 85, 92, 123

Understanding Four Views on the Lord's Supper 120 – 121

Ursinus, Zacharias 82

Van Cangh, J. M. 20

Vander Zee, Leonard J. 119

Vines, Richard 89

Wallace, Daniel B. 18, 23n

Wallace, Ronald S. 78, 79n, 80n

Wandel, Lee Palmer 83 – 84

Warren, F. E. 46n

Watson, Thomas 91 – 92

Weil, Louis 62n

Westminster Confession of Faith 88, 105 – 106, 125 – 126

Westminster Larger Catechism 125 – 126

What Is the Lord's Supper? 119

Wickstead, Edward 93n

Willison, John 94 – 95, 97

Wilson, James P. 230

Wisløff, Carl Fredrik 70

Wright, N. T. 14

Zwingli, Ulrich 63, 71 – 72, 123

Made in the USA
Charleston, SC
11 June 2015